AMERICA
ABANDONED

The Secret Velvet Coup
That Cost Us Our Democracy

Jill Cody, MPA

Writing Endeavors Press
7960 B Soquel Dr., St. 222
Aptos, CA 95003

www.americaabandoned.com

info@americaabandoned.com

Library of Congress Control Number: 2016914483
Writing Endeavors Press, Aptos, CA

Cody, Jill

America Abandoned ~ The Secret Velvet Coup That Cost Us Our Democracy/ Jill Cody

ISBN 978-0-9977962-0-9

Cover Design By Killer Covers
Interior Design by BookStarter

Printed in the United States of America

This book is dedicated to

my hero hubby, my mom and dad, Doc and Millie

and you.

ACKNOWLEDGMENTS

I am overwhelmed by the support and love I received from my husband, Jerry, throughout the three years of researching and writing this book. His love, advice, and stability I will admire for the rest of my life. Through this long process, he took care of the cooking, the house, our two dogs, and me without one word of complaint, ever. I love you to infinity and beyond.

Thank you to my Life Coach, Liz Ainsworth, who assisted me with storyboarding and mind-mapping, the product of which eventually came together into a book and for keeping me on task when I would falter.

My first editor and dear friend, Lisa Fishman, slogged thought the first rough draft and polished grammar and asked great questions to help me achieve clarity in a thought or concept and to the manuscript's literary editor, Autumn Conley, who took my completed manuscript and edited it into a professional document. Thank you both.

My research assistants, Lisa Nagamine and Pam Hudson, both worked enthusiastically behind the scenes on numerous publishing and administrative details so that I might stay focused on research and writing. Thank you both for sticking with me though the unexciting tasks of preparing a book for publication. Thank you to Deana Riddle for her professional interior design and to Killer Covers for their striking book cover graphics.

Thank you to Alena Chapman for coming up with the subtitle of this book after six months of talking with coaches and friends, she understood the purpose of the message and quickly suggested it one, warm summer evening over wine.

Many thanks go to Steve Harrison and the Bradley Communications Corp., Broomall, PA for his amazing commitment to upcoming authors, immense library of author information and trainings, and terrific and patient coaches: Geoffrey Berwind, Martha Bullen, Barb Early, Brian Edmonson, Raia King,Tamra Nashman, Virginia Sheppard and Gail Snyder and the company's valuable customer service-oriented staff who all provided expert input and encouragement.

I would be remiss if I did not acknowledge and extend my heartfelt appreciations to Thom Hartmann and his wife, Louise. After many years of listening to Thom's radio program and hearing him say, "tag you're it" and "despair is not an option," I got busy utilizing my knowledge and expertise. As he always says, "Democracy is not a spectator sport." Thom exemplifies Living in the Black constructive, creative and compelling energies.

Thank you to all the others whom I have learned new and astonishing information from every week during many years of listening to their fair, passionate and respectful opinions such as Ring of Fire's hosts (Robert F. Kennedy Jr., Mike Papantonio, Sam Seder, and Farron Cousins and from Randi Rhodes, Ed Schultz, and Welton Gaddy of Interfaith Alliance's State of Belief). No Living in the Red, destructive, disruptive and repelling energies found on any of their shows.

TABLE OF CONTENTS

The Beginning of Abandonment: My Story and Personal Insights

Abandonment: "To withdraw one's support or help from, especially in spite of duty, allegiance, or responsibility; desert."

The Free Dictionary

Abandonment is breathtakingly pervasive in America. Collectively, we have abandoned ourselves, our country, and even our planet.

In 1948, my parents were in their early twenties, facing the bright promise of unlimited opportunity. World War II had been over for a few years, and the country was infused with a new energy. San Francisco, where they met at a phone company, was undergoing a transformation, becoming a center of optimism, prosperity, and growth. Our country, after fighting foreign wars for so long, was ready to focus on its own future.

The time was alive with new possibilities, and there was a hope and belief that America could do anything if she put her collective mind to it. We had beaten Hitler and the Japanese. America was strong. The world was my parents' oyster when they met; nevertheless, even enveloped by all that unbridled optimism, my mother could not escape the irreparable damage that had already been caused by abandonment. Those scars simply ran too deep, and no amount of positivity, not even on a national scale, was able to completely heal her.

When my mother was a small child, her mother and grandmother emotionally and physically abandoned her repeatedly. Sadly, my mother's history was fraught with unimaginable, horrific things that no child or teenager should ever have to suffer. To compound the problem, there were no federal safety net programs in the country at the time, nothing that would have kept my mother from being victimized.

These grim events took a toll on her psyche and her sense of security, spawning a profound fear that would plague her for the rest of her life. As Cheryl Strayed, an award-winning memoirist, novelist, and essayist, said, "Fear, to a great extent, is born of a story we tell ourselves." Because my mother's childhood abandonment was so deeply imbedded in her soul, she could never *tell* herself an alternative story, a happily-ever-after tale that would free her to find true relief and happiness. My mother never spoke of her bitter childhood; in fact, I only know about the horror of it because my stepfather revealed all of this to me after her death.

My stepfather's relationship with her is parallel to the point I wish to make in this book. My mother was saved from total abandonment because he listened to her and loved her, thereby providing her security. Nevertheless, love alone was not enough. He also made an effort to understand her *real* needs by being sympathetic and realistic throughout their life together.

It is the same on a larger scale. Love of country and others is good, but it is not enough. We must also be realistic and sympathetic when it comes to the problems we face, in advancing our love of country by activating our individual duty and responsibility in addressing the great multitude of abandonment issues that have overtaken our society.

The genesis of this book occurred one autumn evening, while I was on vacation and reminiscing about what little I knew of my parents' childhoods. I pondered how their rearing affected me. I searched for a word to tie it all together, and I found a common thread: *Abandonment* emerged and fostered a deep resonance. As my life unfolded, abandonment was a common theme in one form or another, whether emotionally, physically or both.

As I began writing this book, I realized that *responsibility* is the converse of abandonment. Abandonment destroys; it demolishes everything it touches because people expect duty, allegiance, and responsibility from those close to them. When the responsible parties are not dependable, those they fail are left deeply hurt and may become cynical. Cynicism is really just a symptom of a deep heart wound, a gash in the heart of someone who feels abandoned.

My purpose in writing this book is to increase awareness of the breadth and depth of personal and societal abandonment and how pervasive they have become — and to offer practical suggestions on how to control the negative impact of abandonment on our lives. Only through awareness can change truly begin.

Can any good come from abandonment? Yes, it can, when we willingly abandon a thought or behavior that hurts us or others and opt for healthier choices. However, when we consider the meaning and serious side effects of abandonment by people and institutions we trust, it is wholly undesirable, dangerous, and something to be avoided. Truly, we should abandon abandonment as a society.

The only way to overcome abandonment and the vacuum it creates is to take real responsibility in all areas of our lives. Realizing the impact abandonment has had on our lives will ignite hope that it does not have to subconsciously control us. We need to live principled lives and truly own our thoughts and behaviors. If we fail to take responsibility for ourselves, our society, and even our planet, we will abandon our lives and futures to someone who will be delighted to exploit them...which they certainly will.

Indeed, they will want to exploit the frog sitting in the boiling pot.

INTRODUCTION

Are We all Frogs?

"Our problems are manmade; therefore, they can be solved by man and can be as big as [mankind] wants. No human problem of destiny is beyond human beings."

John F. Kennedy Jr.

Are we all frogs? Maybe we are. The analogy goes something like this: If we put a frog in a pot of hot water, it will jump out immediately. If, however, we put a frog in a pot of cold water and raise the temperature incrementally, little by little, the frog will never jump out, and we'll have a roiling pot of frog soup.

The purpose of this book, the first in the *America Abandoned* series, is to increase our awareness and understanding of abandonment as a real force in ourselves and in our society. Abandonment consists of withdrawing our support or help from someone or something that especially needs and deserves our duty, allegiance, or responsibility.

This book and series are meant to inspire hope. A powerful moment in our lives happens when we first realize we have lost something, especially something of great value. We are stunned. We feel empty inside. We feel betrayed. We want it back. When we realize our loss, we hope to remedy it, to get that thing back, and only then will we take immediate action to make that happen. Absence really does make the heart grow fonder, as the old cliché says; sometimes we have to lose something before we can understand its value.

When we realize its value, we will fight to get back what we have abandoned to those who are more manipulative and powerful. When we fight, we win. We really can recapture what we have lost if we push hard against those who have the authority to make the changes we seek. We must shame and shun those who have abandoned us and our country and vote accordingly.

Ultimately, the power is really in *our* hands, as part of *our* democracy; the very first sign of abandonment is buying into the false notion that we do not have that power to wield.

What you read herein may anger you. Use that anger as fuel for your fire, to make you stand up. We cannot allow our anger to cause us to make unwise choices; have you ever made a rational, good decision when you were consumed by anger? We have to channel our anger into action and use it to assist in that task. Thus, in each chapter of this book, I include Stand Up Activities that may be adopted for *deliberate* action rather than angry reaction.

"We are creatures full of energy," stated Wilfred Jarvis, an Australian behavioral scientist, in his "Four Quadrant Leadership Program," which I had the great pleasure of attending. Mr. Jarvis created a simple yet powerful Energies Dimension Model. In building his model, Jarvis used an accounting analogy: Being in the *black* is the desired state of our finances, while being in the *red* is an undesirable one. The "energies" referred to in his model are those we present to the world. In his model, Jarvis divides emotions, or energies, into two dimensions: constructive or destructive and compelling or repelling. He designates creative and constructive emotions as Living in the Black; when we are near them, we naturally desire to move toward people who radiate them. Destructive and disruptive emotions were labeled as Living in the Red; when we are near people who radiate negative energy, we are naturally repelled and want to get away. Interestingly, the phrase "seeing red" is typically equated with anger and rage.

As of the time of this writing, two presidential primary candidates exemplify these two emotion categories perfectly. Senator Bernie Sanders radiates constructive, compelling actions and ideas. In doing so, he creates hopefulness in his supporters that recapturing America from its abandonment is possible by promoting affordable higher education, addressing income inequality, and facing the challenge of the climate crisis. Donald Trump, a player in income inequality (not paying his vendors and avoiding paying taxes), radiates destructive, repelling ideas and actions. He literally wants to repel Muslims and Mexicans. He radiates destructive behaviors too numerous to list, but some include: using derisive names to label people, refusing to disavow white supremacists, and supporting the violent actions of those who attend his campaign rallies.

A cure for Living in the Red, being engulfed by negative energies such as helplessness, anger, apathy, frustration, disappointment, defeat, fear, and cynicism, is action. A great majority of us possess these emotions and are crippled by them. I recently heard someone say, "If you are not grieving, you are not paying attention to the urgent times in which we live." Whether we are proactive regarding something in ourselves or fighting to recapture something we no longer want to abandon, action works! Constructive and compelling action forces us to leap out of the pot before it boils. The necessity of acting in direct opposition to abandonment is my motive for writing this book. America is no longer the we-the-people country in which I was born. I have felt profound powerlessness in regard to the dark, perverse, and antagonistic change I have observed and experienced in our culture, but what can I influence? Where is my personal power?

Matt Taibbi, an author and political journalist, remarked at a Commonwealth Club meeting, "[If you are] writing about something outrageous and you don't write with outrage, it is deceptive, and you are lying to your readers." As you read this book, my friend, know that it was, in fact, penned with constructive outrage.

As Thom Hartmann, prolific author and radio host (and all-around genius), says, "Despair is not an option!" Despair can, however, be habit forming, a persistent state, one we begin to feed on day in and day out. It feeds on us as well, sucking the life and hope right out of us. This parasite of despair only has one cure: action. In the short term, writing about my epiphany on abandonment helped me take my power back, so I no longer feel like a victim of issues larger than myself. In the long run, I believe I can inspire others to take their own power back and to avoid abandoning it to those who benefit by stealing it away. Why have we abandoned so much? Because the opposite of abandonment is *responsibility,* something far too many of us have grown to fear. Frankly, we abandon critical issues because we do not want to be responsible for anything or for changing anything. This results in paralysis, in inaction, and inaction cannot be an option. Inaction leads to abandonment; in fact, it was the precursor to the abandonment America now suffers.

I want this book to be thought provoking, as before action comes thinking and self-reflection. I encourage you to delve more deeply into a subject or subjects that are motivating enough to move beyond the knowing-doing gap. Most of us know what we need to do but do not transform that knowledge into action. In *The Knowing-Doing Gap*, business management consultants Jeffrey Pfeiffer and Robert I. Sutton state that one common barrier is confusing talk with action. In other words, simply talking to others about an issue may be perceived as doing something. We simply discuss it, then move on, without taking any real action or implementing any real change. This is prevalent in today's society, with all the Tweeting and social media posts and press conferences and sound bytes, but we have donated more than enough time to useless griping, complaining, and whining. Now, it is time to act.

Another research observation Pfeiffer and Sutton made was that we learn better by doing than we do from just reading or listening. However, we all need a catalyst, a jumpstart to action, and a conversation or a book can play that role for us. Even a class of school children can show us how.

Recently, a California state assembly law (AB1369), referred to as "the dyslexia bill," passed by an unprecedented unanimous vote. How did this happen? Of course childhood dyslexia is an important, serious topic deserving of law, but so are many other very worthwhile issues that do not garner the same attention and unanimous vote. State Senator Bill Monning (D) told a class of school children, "I'm here to confirm your letter-writing makes a huge difference. The letters we receive from you get extra attention [because] they're handwritten and personal, not the result of mass emailing." If we can learn a lesson from those students, we, too, can be powerful agents in service of recapturing some of the issues illuminated in this book. Activism works against abandonment.

I expect that some who read this book will disagree with a point or maybe several. I am an idealist and a teacher. My purpose in life is to try to improve and inform the world around me. My hope is that this book will serve as a catalyst for positive, ethical, humane, and moral action in recapturing what we have lost, either personally or collectively, due to abandonment. Dr. Martin Luther King, Jr. once said, "Nothing in all the world is more dangerous than sincere ignorance and conscientious stupidity."

The teacher in me says you may disagree and debate all you like, as long as it is based on informed reasoning – not just some unquestioned ideology, anger, or other red (negative) energy. You do not have to believe me. Do your own research and evaluation of issues. Use your information literacy skills. Learn. Be curious. The idealist in me says you should, at the same time, be open to changing your mind if you find in your reasoning a better, more positive, less toxic way forward for yourself and others. Otherwise, you may just be demonstrating that "sincere ignorance and conscientious stupidity" Dr. King warned about. What we have to ask ourselves is this: Is what we know constructive or destructive? Responsibility is constructive; abandonment is destructive.

The destruction has truly been tragic for those born after 1980. How can they even know what they are missing, what the previous generation allowed to slip away, to fall into the hands of powerful and manipulative political, religious, industry and ideological forces (PRIIF)? They are not the ones who abandoned America, but they, in addition to the rest of us who realize what has happened, will be a powerful group if they (and we) can grab on to our duty, allegiance, and responsibility and work together to recapture what has been lost.

So what, exactly, has been lost? In my attempt to answer this question, at least in part, I found that compiling the following non-comprehensive list was quite disturbing. How can our young people not be cynical and feel powerless having been born into a country that:

- is facing catastrophic climate change

- was subjected to the largest Wall Street theft ever known, yet saw no criminal jailed

- is experiencing rampant inequality

- charges obscenely higher education tuition, student loan interest rates, and resulting burdensome debt

- privatizes public education, prisons, police, roads, water, and even attempting to privatize our national parks

- offers virtually no job opportunities after graduation that pay well enough to support an individual, let alone a family

- saw the burst of the .com bubble

- experienced the horror of 9/11

- allows corporations to break the rules (i.e. British Petroleum and its environmental and economic destruction of the Gulf Coast)

- takes no meaningful action on gun control

- was deceived into horrible and costly wars

- has witnessed one political party obstructing everything that might better lives, all while accepting publicly funded paychecks and pensions

- no longer protects citizens from the damaging excesses of capitalism

- exemplifies unbridled racism and fosters hate

- no longer has a trustworthy corporate media (infotainment and ratings are more important than journalism)

- has become a corporatocracy, abandoning 240 years of democracy

- has created smart televisions that log when and how long they are used, sets tracking cookies to identify when content or an email message is read, what websites are visited, and how content is utilized, and ignore do-not-track requests. There is also a microphone that monitors spoken words in the room in which it is located; those unaware may have personal, touchy conversations that are recorded and sent to a third party, because smart televisions can listen while not even being watched. How smart are we for even having them?

My sincere hope is that learning what is possible and seeing what once was will motivate our young people and us to realize that powerlessness is not an option and that we must vote and fight to recapture what the previous generation irresponsibly abandoned. It is heartening to see so many young people becoming active, leading change and voting in spite of their pessimism regarding the greatness of the United States and their distrust of the nation's leaders. Those between the ages of 18-30 understand the urgent social justice times in which they live with this being demonstrated by 80% of them voting for Bernie Sanders for president who is calling for a political movement to recapture what has been lost to corporations and billionaires that especially impact the Millennials.

Herein, I will raise difficult issues that will be hard to face, but face them we must. In my view, the only power we, the people, have left at this point is activism and voting. The issues are raised here to encourage you to think and really reflect upon, so you might decide to actively participate in changing them. When I began this project, I wholeheartedly believed it would demand even-handedness between the two major political parties. I must now apologize to my Republican friends in advance, for while researching many of these political issues, I discovered that the Republican Party is especially problematic. This is reflected in many of the chapters. It is not meant to offend; rather, it is meant to amend.

Although the material covered in each chapter is quite detailed and extensively researched, I know this book merely scratches the surface. Thus, I highly encourage you to delve more deeply on issues of interest. At the end of each chapter, I include an organization development evaluation tool, "Keep/Start/Stop." The purpose of this is to jumpstart action, since we now understand that we learn and affect change by actually doing, rather than just reading or talking about it. In addition, each chapter ends with a question borrowed from Dr. Stephen R. Covey, who was a personal acquaintance and mentor; I earned my licensure many years ago to facilitate his *Seven Habits of Highly Effective People* workshop, based on his bestselling book. One such question he poses is this: If you could do one thing marvelously well, what would that one thing be?

There are countless abandoned areas in our lives and our society. Future books in the America Abandoned series will cover many of these, including: the abandonment of freedom of thought, choice and of self; the abandonment of truth, science, and reason; abandonment by the media; abandonment of democracy; and the abandonment of the planet. Abandonment permeates so much of our lives that if we want to continue our so-called pursuit of happiness, that worthy gift promised to us all, as individuals and as a society, abandonment must be recognized for the destructive virus it is. Only then can we seek a cure and deal with it.

Together, we must change our *zeitgeist*, the spirit and mood of our period in history. We must recapture that which we have abandoned over time, little by little, like the proverbial frogs too foolish to jump out of the hot pot.

Yet, there are those who love the conditions and limelight that our current zeitgeist offers.

CHAPTER ONE

We, the People, Have Relinquished Our Rights to the Rich

"We've become now an oligarchy instead of a democracy. And I think that's been the worst damage to the basic moral and ethical standards of the American political system that I've ever seen in my life."

President Jimmy Carter

We, the people, have been abandoned and no longer matter, but there is good news: We can regain our authority as long as we collectively take a stand. We have been abandoned by most elected representatives, corporations whose products and services we purchase, the Supreme Court and a wide array of wealthy individuals, in addition to numerous political, religious, industry, and ideological forces (PRIIF).

"We, the people of the United States, in order to form a more perfect union, establish justice, insure domestic tranquility, provide for the common defense, promote the general Welfare, and secure the Blessings of Liberty to ourselves and our Posterity, do ordain and establish this Constitution of the United States of America."

Preamble to the Constitution of the United States

"We, the people," are the first three words of the preamble of the United States Constitution and the three most powerful words in our democracy. The framers intended that the people of our new country would be responsible for upholding, together, the foundations of the American Constitution. We can also learn from what the framers did *not* intend by what they did *not* say; the preamble does *not* begin with "We, the people of Landed Gentry" or "We, the men of the colonies" or "We, the founding fathers" or "We, the wealthy" or "We, the corporations." They used only three words and used them beautifully to say that *everyone* governed by the newly drafted document is responsible

1

for and required to keep it alive, even women and African-Americans who, at the time, were intentionally not included.

The deliberations of the Constitutional Convention were kept secret, and many waited outside Independence Hall to be the first to learn what those inside had voted for, a republic or a monarchy. When asked this question, Benjamin Franklin, without skipping a beat, answered, "A republic, if you can keep it."

Have we kept it? Technically, no. Do ordinary citizens still have the power to govern our democracy? Not right now, but we can and must again.

Why We Must Take a Stand!

"When the preferences of economic elites and the stands of organized interest groups are controlled, the preferences of the average American appear to have only a minuscule, near-zero, statistically non-significant impact upon public policy." These words were written in a scholarly article titled, "Testing Theories of American Politics: Elites, Interest Groups, and Average Citizens," completed in a partnership between Princeton and Northwestern Universities. It was an article that truly rocked its readers.

In addition, the report stated:

> Multivariate analysis indicates that economic elites and organized groups representing business interests have substantial independent impacts on U.S. government policy, while average citizens and mass-based interest groups have little or no independent influence.

The report authors, Martin Gilens and Benjamin I. Page, studied 1,771 bills passed by Congress. Notably, they completed their analysis before the Citizen's United Supreme Court decision. One may easily assume the situation has only worsened, since that decision opened corporate funding floodgates. We were shocked to learn that unless something we, the people, want directly aligns with what the disgustingly rich (d-rich) want, then our needs and wants are abandoned for the "economic elites and organized groups representing business interests." Chris Hedges, American journalist, author and activist, said at the 2016 Left Forum, "Democracy in the United States is a façade."

What does this all mean? Simple: Our country, the alleged United States of America, is technically no longer a democracy. It has been abandoned to an *oligarchy*, defined as a "government run by the few" and "a government in which a small group exercises control especially for corrupt and selfish purposes."

Psychopaths Like the Limelight

It may seem strange, if not positively weird, to begin a discussion regarding how we have been abandoned by first discussing psychopaths; however, understanding the traits of psychopathy may be foundational to several issues our country is facing, as well as some of the subjects discussed in this book.

There appears to be a difference between a *sociopath* and a *psychopath*. Sociopathy is more a result of a traumatic childhood, when there may have been severe physical and emotional abuse. Sociopaths tend to be volatile, live on the fringe of society, and are unable to hold a steady job. They may form an unhealthy attachment to a group or person, but they exhibit no regard for society and its rules. To most of us, sociopaths would appear to be very disturbed. To attempt to answer the age-old question regarding nature versus nurture, I suggest that in the sociopath's case, it is probably more a case of nurturing – or lack thereof.

To properly address the issues in this book, however, it is more important to understand how a psychopath behaves, to observe how these individuals function in society. In the presence of a sociopath, you may sense that something is just not right; on the other hand, in the presence of a psychopath, you may not even realize there is a problem. We have to spend time observing them, getting to know them better, and taking note of their actions and reactions. Erroneously, most of us think all psychopaths are mass murderers, the stuff outright nightmares and the caricatures that manifest in horror films. In reality, this may not be the case at all, and the tinge of normalcy almost makes them more dangerous.

A person with psychopathy is believed to have a genetic malfunction, and their thought processes and resulting behaviors are a result of a psychological defect, an underdeveloped part of the brain. For the psychopath, the answer to that age-old question is likely nature.

Psychopaths can be very charming. They may gain our trust, yet they are incapable of forming actual emotional attachments. Think of the example of the con artist in the definition of manipulation: "to control or take advantage of by artful, unfair, or insidious means; the conman would slyly manipulate the emotions of his marks in order to win their sympathy and trust." It is likely that a con artist's inability to form emotional attachments allows him or her to succeed and continue in his line of work. Psychopaths do not feel empathy for others; being devoid of emotions themselves makes it extremely easy for them to con the rest of us.

Psychopaths observe emotions but have an inability to feel them; instead, they learn how to mimic feelings so they appear normal. They can be so expert at manipulating others and copying emotions that they may even appear normal to their closest relatives and friends. One core, vital aspect of psychopathic individuals is their lack of moral restraint, as morals are irrelevant, the whole idea unfathomable to them.

Psychopaths and sociopaths do share some common attributes: the inability to feel remorse and guilt, disregard for the rights of others, a tendency toward violent behavior, and a blatant disregard for laws and social mores. Beyond these commonalities, they differentiate: Sociopaths are usually more noticeable in society, while psychopaths may not be noticeable at all, until we witness and understand how they behave.

In his book, *The Psychopath Test*, Jon Ronson, a Welsh journalist, author, and documentary filmmaker, interviewed several psychiatrists and psychologists. He learned that about 1 percent of the general population are psychopaths. That percentage does not sound troubling until we realize that psychopaths are attracted to the limelight, to possessing power and control. It follows, then, that a disproportionate number of psychopaths can be found in top-tier corporate management, in power positions at financial institutions and within state and federal politics. This is not to say all corporate CEOs and politicians are psychopaths, but we cannot eliminate the possibility that a great number of them do fall within that 1 percent of psychopathic humanity.

Upon learning of this higher percentage in top-tier positions of power, Jon Ronson pondered the fact that the ninety-nice percent of us are "having out lives pushed and pulled" by those who possess these abnormal behaviors under a façade of "engaging normalcy."

Dr. Robert Hare, who authored *Without Conscience: The Disturbing*

World of the Psychopaths Among Us and co-authored *Corporate Psychopathy*, related a study that demonstrated that the percentage of psychopathology in corporate professionals is four to five times greater than in the general population, and these rank very high on the twenty-point Hare Psychopathy Checklist that can be found on Wikipedia.

In his book, Jon Ronson listed all twenty items on Bob Hare's checklist, but here are a few that were not already mentioned but are very pertinent to the theme of abandonment:

- glibness/superficial charm

- grandiose sense of self-worth

- pathological lying

- conning/manipulation

- failure to accept responsibility for one's own actions

- criminal versatility

Jon Ronson also related an experience Dr. Hare had when he sent his findings to *Science* magazine, results that the editor refused to publish and promptly returned. About the rejection from that editor, Dr. Hare said, "He wrote me a letter. I'll never forget it. He wrote, 'Frankly, we found some of the brainwave patterns depicted in your paper very odd. Those EEGs couldn't have come from real people.'" They were, in fact, from very real people, those who may make decisions at the highest levels of our corporate, financial, and political institutions. In some cases, they may also be the wealthiest of the wealthy.

Who Abandoned Us – The Billionaire Party?

To understand how America has been abandoned, we must first understand exactly what one billion dollars is. Simply put, it is 1,000 million dollars. If we stacked one billion dollars, in one-dollar bills, into one pile it would be 67.9 miles high.

In 2015, Bill Gates once again topped the Forbes 400 list, at a whopping worth of seventy-nine billion dollars, his sixteenth appearance at the top of that list. Grasping the enormity of this amount of money is crucial; it is almost impossible to fathom that 79 billion dollars is 79,000 million dollars and that just one human being has removed that much money from our economy. His money, if put in one pile of one-dollar bills, would nearly be 5,333 miles high.

Vermont Senator, Bernie Sanders (I), stated:

> In my view, there are now three major political forces in this country: the Democratic Party, the Republican Party, and the Koch-led Billionaire Party. As a result of the disastrous Citizens United Supreme Court ruling, which regards corporations as people and allows the super-rich to spend as much as they want on elections, the Billionaire Party (aligned with the Republicans) is now the major political force in the country.

I have also heard Senator Sanders say that the millionaires and billionaires are the "only real citizens of our times." As Chris Hayes humorously explained in a segment that aired on January 21, 2015, after the State of the Union address, "The State of Billionaires is Strong." Comedian George Carlin, in his usual outrageous manner, said it best years ago in a three-minute bit about the American Dream that now may be seen on You Tube, including a transcript.

How does this new major political force, the Billionaire Party, see themselves and the rest of the country? Frankly, their perspective is ghastly. For example, Steve Swartzman, The Blackstone Group CEO, said in 2010 regarding a three percent tax increase that, "It's a war. It's like when Hitler invaded Poland in 1939." Most billionaires see themselves as Libertarians who want to due away with taxes altogether. It is a philosophical and political view that lay to the right of the Republican Tea Party. Wikipedia defines it as:

> Libertarianism is a political philosophy that upholds liberty as its principle objective. Libertarians seek to maximize autonomy and freedom of choice, emphasizing political freedom, voluntary association and the primacy of individual judgment.

These words may sound quite impressive strung together that way, but if we dig a little more deeply, we will discover that what these folks really desire is a selfish free-for-all. To them, liberty means they can do whatever they want whenever they want, without any constraints such as regulations or laws. It is the philosophy of a 13-year-old adolescent; they want their way and will throw a tantrum until they get it. Four excellent examples are as follows:

- Pete Peterson, an American investment banker, under the guise of a deficit/debt scare campaign, is focused like a laser beam on gutting Social Security. His future and that of his progeny is set for life, but he does not want anyone else in the country to enjoy that security. He will spend 1 billion dollars ($1,000 million) to convince everyone – even those who would benefit from this safety net program – that Social Security is dastardly. He will do so by manipulating our thinking into considering the issue a national debt crisis. He is bent on the destruction of the Social Security program, even though the Obama administration and Congress's sequestration on the budget have significantly cut the debt. It is a propaganda and bribery campaign, and, as Michael Hilzik wrote in The Los Angeles Times, "The shame of Washington...comes from the fact that almost every organization promoting the grand fiscal bargain in which those programs will be on the table has accepted, somewhere and somehow, money from Pete Peterson."

- Jeff Greene, who made billions betting against subprime mortgages – and, therefore, benefited greatly from others losing their homes – stated, in a Daily Mail article written by Joel Christie, "America's lifestyle expectations are far too high and need to be adjusted so we have less things and a smaller, better existence." Wait. "We"? This statement comes from a man who flew his wife, children, and two nannies on a private jet to Davos for the World Economic Forum for billionaires worldwide, in January 14 through 21, 2015. Greene also owns five, multimillion-dollar mansions, one of which is a $195,000,000 Beverly Hills estate that has been called "America's most expensive house." Do as I say, not as I do.

- Tom Perkins, a founder of the venture capital firm Klein Perkins Caufield & Byers, is the multibillionaire who spoke at the Commonwealth Club in San Francisco and had the unmitigated gall to proclaim, "[There is a] war on the 1 percent." He further compared the "persecution" of America's wealthiest to the treatment of the Jews in Nazi Germany. He actually said that! Unbelievably, many of the multibillionaires in this country see themselves as victims. Tom Perkins also owns the Maltese Falcon, known as the greatest sailboat of all time. That pricy vessel is just one showy example of what the d-rich do with some of their discretionary income. It cost $130 million, only a little over 10 percent of a billion dollars. Poor Tom only has eight billion, though, so he's a relatively impoverished billionaire, as billionaires go.

- I used the word "tantrum" in the above examples as a metaphor, but in Conrad Hilton's case, he had an honest-to-goodness one on a British Airlines flight on July 31, 2014. He refused to turn off his phone, refused to stay in his seat when the seatbelt sign was on, and berated the flight attendants with profanity when they tried to speak to him. In the correlating FBI report, it is reported that Hilton's behavior, his toddler-like tantrum, escalated to yelling at a flight attendant numerous times, saying: "I will fucking own anyone on this flight. They are fucking peasants," and, "I will fucking bury you." Conrad Hilton also complained to the flight attendants that they were not listening to him and that they were "taking the peasants' side." His behavior is a perfect example of inheritance baby behavior and what they and their families apparently think of we, the peasants. What decisions and power will Conrad Hilton wield when he grows up? That, my friends, is a frightening thought.

We know tantrum behavior in the d-rich is pervasive when a mere millionaire also plays the game. Dobo Swinney, Head Coach of the Clemson Tigers, makes about three million a year. In response, when asked if the NCAA players should be paid for their talent and hard work in games, he threatened to leave and do something else if that happened. Leave a three million-dollar job? Really? Sadly, it only gets worse, as he actually had the audacity to declare, "There's enough entitlement in the world as it is." I can only believe he never understood the irony of his statement.

In a discussion about the Billionaire Party, my father, Arthur Cody Ph.D., used the term "contemptuous power" to explain the mindset of this specific class of people. I asked him to comment further, and he offered:

> Contemptuous power...the most common use of power other than immediate advantage, the use that pleases because it is unnecessary. Those who have money have more than they can possibly use. There is not enough time in life to live in much less to enjoy the activities associated with an estate in the Bahamas, a penthouse in New York, on a private 400-foot yacht, and in a mansion in Colorado, nor enough time to enjoy possessions such as expensive paintings or cars or even to choose them. The list goes on, from

clothes to people. I am thinking of the huge houses the rich own, those that are too large to enjoy, much less inhabit, unless they entertain on an enormous scale, too enormous for them to even speak with everyone who is on that long guest list. Power to make real change in the world cannot be wielded by modern Napoleons. Actually, doing anything powerful is denied the powerful, except to cause misery. It is not hard to make people poorer or sicker or more deprived of the comforts and pleasures in life than they might otherwise be. This mischief appears everywhere. The Obamas, for instance, and HRC, as well as the Republicans generally say such things as, "If you work hard and obey the rules, then you ought to realize the American Dream." This sentiment will obviously have deleterious effects, if implemented by laws and attitudes, on the lives of most people who are in no position to "work hard," people who simply do well to have jobs. The rules they are supposed to live by have been made by the powerful, not the weak. It is a sentiment that implies—and is so taken— that those who are poor, sick, drunk, doped up, dense, physically inferior, and so on deserve their deprivations. It is an assumption that ordinary people deserve to lack the benefits society could give them without causing deprivation to anyone else. Student loans is one example. Free college is available in most European countries; no one there must give up comforts, much less essentials, so their kids can be educated and enter the world without the oppression of undischargeable debt. So, contemptuous power is power used to insult and make miserable without a correlative advantage; not without any advantage, however, as one thing the powerful do get is a kick out of it.

If the above is not shocking enough, even worse is to take a look at how the d-rich view the country and the rest of us.

In a May 2014 survey, "The 1% Are Different," sponsored by the Russell Sage Foundation one of the oldest American foundations established in 1907, devoted exclusively to research in the social sciences, ascertained the perspectives of the 1 percent (elite interests) and the 99 percent (public priorities). The study analyzed their respective responses to survey questions such as: "The government's top policy should be protecting the jobs of American workers." Only 29 percent of the elites agreed with this statement, while 81 percent of the public agreed. Just this one survey question speaks volumes about how and why the practice of outsourcing has decimated our manufacturing jobs.

It also proves that trickle-down economics is, as George HW Bush called it, voodoo economics. The voodoo factor was simple and obvious: In the U.S., jobs seemed to magically dematerialize and were sent overseas because the rich, who own the corporations, do not value middle-class, working Americans, nor do they possess any loyalty to the United States, particularly economic. They abandoned America for profit.

Another survey statement from the Russell Sage Foundation study was: "The federal government should spend whatever is necessary to ensure that all children have really good public schools they can go to." Only 35 percent of the elites agreed with this statement, but 87 percent of the public agreed. Now we understand why our public schools are being thrown to the wolves (charter schools) and that the well-off have little empathy toward middle-class and less fortunate children. *Their* children, most assuredly, attend private schools.

If you combine the wealth of Charles and David Koch – and since there is not a hair's breadth of difference in their political views, it is easy to think of them as one – together, they have $82 billion, or 82,000 million dollars. President Franklin Delano Roosevelt (FDR) called the amazingly wealthy people of his time "economic royalists," and he did not encounter as many of these monarchs as we do today; in fact, there are more billionaires on the planet today than ever before in history.

Even though FDR was technically a member of their class, he said of the economic royalists, "They hate me, and I welcome their hate." Why did they hate him and consider him a traitor to his class? Because President Roosevelt did not abandon the people and did not use government to benefit the wealthy class. The country had just experienced a devastating, life-altering, Republican-exacerbated economic disaster, now known as the Great Depression. Ideologically, the previous Hoover administration would not approve increasing federal intervention or spending to pull the country out of that Depression.

FDR, who inherited the economic disaster, knew he needed to use a portion of the government treasury to "promote the general welfare" of the people. Thousands of our country's facilities, those we still highly value today, were created during the post-Depression years, through the Work Projects Administration (WPA). Today, many require repair and maintenance, but we cannot seem to afford the upkeep because of the enormous defense budget and because so much has been withdrawn from general economic circulation by the d-rich and corporations, much of which is being stored offshore for tax evasion purposes.

It is shocking to know that the number of billionaires in the world has increased by 70 percent since 2009, the year President Obama took office. In just six years, billionaires totaled, worldwide, a staggering 1,826 people, with an astonishing and almost unthinkable combined wealth of $7.05 trillion, or $700,500,000,000,000. How much is a trillion dollars? If you stacked this amount of money in one pile, it would be 478,455 miles high. The moon is 238,900 miles away. These 1,826 people have so much money that we would need to pile *two* stacks of one-dollar bills to the moon. Imagine that.

In just one year, 2014, a Truth-Out BuzzFlash article stated that 14 individuals, without lifting a hand, increased their wealth by eighty-two billion dollars, $82,000 million, through investments. The ramifications are astounding and heartbreaking. That amount of money could have employed two million preschool teachers or emergency medical technicians, as well as addressed many other societal needs. An unimaginable sum of cash trickled up, not down, to those fourteen people over the course of twelve short months. Mysteriously, there is not enough money to fund local, state, and federal programs and commitments, like filling the potholes in our streets. Funny how that worked, or maybe not such funny voodoo at all. As we will learn later, it sadly worked precisely as planned.

Most of us are enamored by the constant influx of new technological gadgets, applications, and innovations developed and designed today. The computer and internet era has brought us some wondrous things, and as these miraculous inventions flooded our homes and our lives, we determined that techies are modern-day heroes, cool and daring and motivated by the intention of making our world a better, more efficient place, with far less paper to recycle. Are they really heroes or villains though?

Joel Kotkin, a demographic, social, and economic trends writer, pointed out in his article, "Today's Tech Oligarchs Are Worse than the Robber Barons," that "Tech oligarchs are something less attractive: a fearsome threat whose ambitions to control our future politics, media, and commerce seem without limits...and as their fortunes have ballooned, so has their hubris." He also related, "Their contempt for the less cognitively gifted [according to whom?], they are waging what *The Atlantic* recently called 'a war on stupid people.'"

It appears that even these newly rich have fallen prey to the thought virus that directly correlates money with brains when, in reality, it is a false equivalency. Albert Einstein is regarded as one of the most intelligent men the world has ever known, if not the most intelligent. Even Apple, Inc. once draped an enormous banner on the side of its corporate headquarters in his honor, but the wild-haired genius never became rich. Why? Because in the grand scheme of things, money does *not* equal brains, and the converse is true as well. Nevertheless, as Joel Kotkin so bravely explained, these hubris people think of themselves as better than the "scum of Wall Street" and are the "proper global rulers," and I'm sure every dictator throughout history has held him or herself in the same deluded high regard.

Wealth inequality has grown so striking in America that we have lost our democracy to an oligarchy. This is also a global problem. Only two years after the Russell Sage Foundation study, Oxfam International released a study, "An Economy for the 1%," stating that the wealth of 62 billionaires equaled the wealth of the lower half of the planet; even more discouraging, the economically elite hoard their $7.6 trillion in offshore accounts to avoid paying the taxes that could help the rest of the world. The d-rich do not *have* to avoid paying their taxes; they simply *want* to, yet another example of those tantrums we talked about. The power they possess is intoxicating, and they view government as merely a pawn, a means to enrich themselves. Edmond Burke, an eighteenth-century author, orator, and political theorist, once said, "The greater the power, the more dangerous the abuse." He could not have been more correct.

The Oxfam study also wisely states that this much-needed tax revenue "denies poor countries the resources they need to tackle poverty, put children in school, and prevent their citizens from dying from easily curable diseases." If the multibillionaires want to do something remarkable for mankind, to affect positive change, they merely have to pay the taxes that they owe. Unfortunately, no one believes the d-rich will ever do so willingly. Is there a word worse than selfish? At best, these monarchs rule their personal kingdoms and feed those kingdoms at the expense of the government and us taxpayers at best; at their worst, they intentionally steal our freedom and liberty, without so much as a shred of regret.

One multibillionaire in India built a 34-story, 800,000 square-foot home and named it *Antilia*, after a mythical island; in the fifteenth century, the isle was originally thought to be in the Atlantic Ocean but dropped off the maps as more vessels shipped the seas. The house cost a billion to build. Josh Boak, Associated Press, in an article titled, " $100 million for a home? Luxury buyers are reaching a new threshold," wrote that billionaires' new status collectibles are multimillion-dollar mansions, just more territory for their respective kingdoms. He related that Christi's international real estate analysis said:

> The poshest of luxury homes are acquiring the cachet of a masterwork by Picasso or Matisse. Rather than settle for the garages of antique cars or a museum's worth of paintings, billionaires are increasingly willing to pay $100 million for homes that can serve as showcases for their fortunes.

Antilia makes Mitt Romney's California house, the one equipped with an elevator for his cars, look positively quaint. Don Conn, CEO of Christi's real estate brokerage, said, "It tells you that there is a new class of collectible… [Houses are] trophies now." This extraordinary class of billionaires who scour the world for pretentious, flamboyant homes will continue, since the world is creating hundreds of new billionaires each year; at the same time, hundreds of thousands are thrown into poverty or losing economic ground, wondering how they will keep a roof over their heads. Hundreds of new billionaires may be beneficial for Christi's business, but the amount of wealth being redistributed upward to these few families is destroying the lives of everyone else, literally crumbling us at our very foundations while they build more and more mansions on their own in the exotic paradises of the world.

Dangerous Egos of Inheritance Babies

Interestingly, over half of today's billionaires inherited all or part of their staggering wealth by winning the lottery of birth. These are the inheritance babies, with the Walton family and the Koch brothers serving as our country's most notable examples. James Madison, one of our Founding Fathers and a principal author of the Constitution, stated that inequality is evil and that the government should thwart "an immoderate, and especially unmerited, accumulation of riches."

The family members who own the mega Walmart chain, the largest corporation in the United States are Christy Walton ($42 billion), Jim

Walton ($41 billion), Alice Walton ($40 billion) and S. Robson Walton ($39 billion) who have amassed a combined $162 billion or $162,000 million, or 162,000,000,000 dollars. Combined, their stack of money would be 10,864 miles high. All they did was have the good fortune to be born to Samuel Walton. On the face of it, this is an "unmerited accumulation of riches." Walmart has done everything it can to pay the lowest wages to its employees and train its staff on how to apply for government subsidies. They even held a food drive during the holidays for them, with the subtext being that their employees could not afford to buy food; this was blatantly offensive and shameless, to be sure.

The Waltons are the richest family in America, and they have accomplished that by being stingy with wages and benefits and by pushing as many of their corporate expenses as they can onto the taxpayers. The taxpayers, in turn, also buy their products, so it's a win-win situation for them, a nice strategy that lets them pocket our money twice. Even worse, this formula is a tried-and-true corporate organizational model. As the rich do, Walmart privatizes profits and subsidizes losses. This one family, the Waltons – and I'm not talking about that hardworking one that used to show up on primetime TV – has abandoned America in order to become the largest beneficiaries of government welfare. This does not even take into account the number of people forced to rely on government programs because every new Walmart that opens puts several small businesses out of business. One tenth of one percent (0.01 percent) owns as much wealth as 90 percent of the country, and the Walton family owns 42 percent of that. For all their smiley-face advertisements, they are putting frowns on a lot of faces come payday.

More frightening than the Waltons are the Koch brothers, Charles and David. The Kochs are the second-richest family in America, wannabe kings working to re-create America into their own vision. Naomi Klein explained that the Koch brothers' metanarrative is that *collectivism* is wrong for the country; this term refers to any group of people getting together for a purpose, and this can include unions coming to an agreement on regulations or a gathering in protest. The Koch brothers believe this must be stopped, by any and all means necessary. Even though their Libertarian viewpoint "upholds liberty as its principle objective," we, the people, apparently do not have the liberty to join together on our own behalf.

In his article, "The Kochs Are Ghostwriting America's Story," Michael Winship, contributor to Moyers & Company wrote:

In other words, Koch and his brother David, and the extraordinary machine they have built in cahoots with fellow billionaires and others, have spent hundreds and hundreds of millions to get their way – "the great wealth grab," in the words of Richard Eskow – all part of one long story told in pursuit of a specific end: to make the needs of the very, very few our nation's top priority and to thwart or destroy any group effort among the poor and middle class to do or say otherwise.

The retelling of America's story requires us to stand together so not to be destroyed.

The Koch brothers are the spitting image of FDR's aptly termed economic royalists. Their political network, the "Kochtapus," created and financed the Tea Party, a party that is now generating ideas of tyranny on a grand scale. The Tea Party so strongly believes in thwarting "unjust or oppressive governmental power; undue severity or harshness," such as shutting down the federal government of the United States of America in a temper tantrum, thereby creating severity and harshness by bleeding twenty-six billion dollars from the economy.

Like the Waltons and numerous other multibillionaires, Charles and David Koch inherited their money from dear old dad, Fred C. Koch. It is important to know who their father was, in order to understand how the brothers came to their ideology. Fred wrote in his book, *A Business Man Looks at Communism,* "The colored man looms in the Communist plan to take over America." The elder Koch also thought welfare was a secret plot to attract blacks and other minorities to vote for Communist causes, and attempt at "getting a vicious race war started." Fred C. Koch, initially unsuccessful in the United States, looked for business opportunities in Europe and made some of his fortune by building the third-biggest oil refinery in Nazi Germany, approved by Adolf Hitler himself.

Fred C. Koch was instrumental in the creation of the John Birch Society, an ultraconservative, far-right, extremist organization that is explained in "Bringing Back Birch" written by Don Terry, Southern Poverty Law Center. While it claims to identify with Christian principles, they openly oppose the Civil Rights Movement, wealth redistribution, economic intervention, and government, and they always do so in the name of the Constitution. Ironically, they refer to themselves as patriots, when they are anything but; I will never understand how those who possess and project into society extreme Living-in-the-Red energies such as fear, anger, hatred, disapproval, and cynicism toward their own country and their fellow Americans can identify themselves as patriotic. This is a perversion of patriotism and is, if anything, clear-cut hatriotism at its worst

The Koch brothers were spoiled, raised with a sense of false entitlement that infected everything they have thought, said, and done. They were allowed and encouraged to think they are superior, and this idea did not just come from their father but also from the nanny he chose to raise them. Jane Mayer, an American investigative journalist and staff writer for *The New Yorker* since 1995, wrote in her definitive book on the Koch family, *Dark Money*, that Fred Koch brought the nanny from Germany, and she was confirmed to be a Nazi.

Conveniently, the Koch brothers believe that wealth redistribution (down to the middle class or those less fortunate) is evil and label that redistribution (through taxes) as socialism; however, when wealth is redistributed upward, from the middle class to their pockets (through tax breaks and loopholes), they call it capitalism. They believe themselves to be Libertarians, fighting for freedom and liberty by deregulating everything that effects Koch Industries, and they want this country to become their own version of a Libertarian utopia; they pay no mind to the fact that there have been no successful Libertarian governments anywhere on the planet and that Libertarianism is the direct opposite of democracy. The Koch brothers truly believe they have earned and created all their wealth themselves, so they have the right to abuse people and the environment for their benefit. Their interpretation of freedom and liberty is that they should be allowed to use and abuse anything they want, even if it means buying presidencies or polluting the planet with fossil fuels.

According to the University of Massachusetts Amherst's Political Economy Research Institute, Koch Industries' toxic output is staggering, and an Environmental Protection Agency 2012 database listed Koch Industries as the single-biggest producer of toxic waste in the country. When they treat the planet, the environment, and its people as their personal septic tank and know they are richer than God, how can they not think of themselves as kings? The Koch family is an outright threat to our country and our democracy. They recently announced that they and their d-rich friends will spend nearly a billion dollars to buy the 2016 election at all levels – presidential, congressional, gubernatorial, state legislative, school board elections, etc. We must be smart and ignore their endless political campaign ads and maneuverings, which serve only as self-aggrandizement.

Furthermore, there are no truth-in-advertising laws for political ads so many, if not all, are not trustworthy.

Senator Bernie Sanders, referring to the Koch brothers, explained in a May, 2014 newsletter:

> While they are obviously putting huge sums of money into elections (much of it hidden from public scrutiny), political consultants and lobbyists, their influence goes far beyond political campaigns or congressional policy. Incredibly, and not widely known, is the reality that they have created or supported organizations active in almost every area of public life – the law, education, healthcare, economics, academia, the environment and climate change, state legislative initiatives, media and veterans' needs. In other words, they are spending billions not only to win elections and legislative victories today but to aggressively shape public consciousness to bring about the extreme right-wing society they wish to see.

How are they aggressively shaping public consciousness? The Koch brothers own a little-known, for-profit company called i360. Yes, that *is* its actual name. They refer to i360 as "the leading data and technology resource for the free market political advocacy community." That may sound nice and modern, even catchy, but it certainly does not explain what they really do.

This Koch-owned company links your voter information with your consumer data, which is purchased from credit bureaus and numerous other vendors you have done business with. They couple this information with social networks, along with any interactions you have had with affiliated campaigns and advocacy groups. They know more about you than your Auntie Em! In fact, the database is larger and more powerful than that of the Republican Party; i360 is basically the voter database and strategy company for the Billionaire Party, whether they will admit it or not.

Moreover, i360 drills into television-viewing information to help campaigns target ads skillfully, specifically, and cost effectively for GOP campaigns, not Democratic ones. The Democratic National Committee has nothing like it. Neither are there left-leaning, privately owned companies that undertake this type of stalking for political gain. Republican politicians could go to the Republican National Committee for voter information, but they prefer to pay more for i360 data because it offers superior profiles of their candidates' constituents. Michael Palmer, the former chief technology officer for Senator John McCain's 2008 presidential campaign, said i360 can build superior campaign strategies because they receive a steady stream of money (Koch money). The company is not governed by a political calendar, and they can plan for the long term. What long-term plan do they have, I wonder?

Find a favorite d-rich person at Forbes The World's Billionaires, while at the same time keep in mind that $1 billion is equal to $1,000 million. Everyone on that list has endless amounts of money to play with. The richest has 79,000 million dollars, and the least wealthy has nearly 5,000 million. Remember, too, that their wealth increases exponentially every second. For more fun, check out the greediest d-rich people of 2013, on the Too Much website, one of whom vapidly said, "[I just want] to live in a world full of candy."

As mentioned, over half of the d-rich are inheritance babies, but what of the other half? As Thom Hartmann explained in his article, "Time to Rein in the Robber Barons Again," most are byproducts of a 940 percent increase in CEO pay from 1978 to 2013, with an average annual salary of $15.5 million (15,500,000,000 dollars/year) plus, in many cases, enormous stock options. Workers' wages, on the other hand, only increased 10.3 percent. The CEO bonus loophole is just one outrage most of us are not aware.

A Communications Workers of America (CWA) "CEO Bonus Loophole" factsheet states:

> Under current law, the more corporations pay their executives, the less they pay in federal taxes. This is the result of a loophole that allows corporations to deduct unlimited amounts of executive compensation from their taxable income – as long as the pay is performance-based.

In 35 years, worker pay rose by only 10 percent, while CEO pay increased over 900 percent. Data collected in 2015 shows Bill Gates with $79.2 billion (Microsoft), Warren Buffett with $66.7 billion (Berkshire Hathaway), Larry Ellison with $49.3 billion (Oracle, and the purchaser of the entire Hawaiian Island of Lanai), and Mark Zuckerberg with $35.7 billion (Facebook). Talk about updating their status! Those four individuals own and control $230.9 billion. A *Bizarro* comic by Dan Piraro now comes to mind, an illustration of two men at the water cooler. One said to the other, "I was angry about income disparity, too, until the boss assured me that he actually does work 380 times harder than we do."

According to Oxfam, a British humanitarian group, the individuals mentioned above are a few examples of the 85 richest people on earth "who have the same amount of wealth as the bottom half of the population" of the entire planet. Think about that for a moment. A small movie theater can hold eighty-five people, and those few individuals own as much wealth as the lower half of the worldwide population.

Stand Up Activities

The perfect antidote to frustration, anger, helplessness, apathy, divisiveness, and fear is to get involved. Where there is no involvement, there is no commitment. It is my intention that these Stand Up Activities will help you recapture, reignite, and reengage your participation as one who knows it's time to take a stand!

Below, for your consideration, are several suggested Stand Up Activities. You may want to select a few that resonate with you and run with them. To present the activities, I have used a Keep/Start/Stop organization development tool. After reading this chapter, you may think of additional Stand Up Activities that are constructive and compelling. If you would like to share ideas, please do so at: www.facebook.com/americaabandoned.

KEEP:

1. Keep in consistent contact with your elected representatives (local, state, and federal). Let them know your position on the issues you care about, those that concern you most. In Congress, if enough citizens call and overload the switchboard, they call it "blowing up the phones." We must stand up. We must be willing to blow up the phones on a regular basis. Take heart! There is a real example of success when we collectively exercise our power. Telecom companies, Comcast and AT&T, lobbied the Federal Communications Commission (FCC) to be allowed to make the internet like cable service so they could charge more for faster

service. The result would have been if someone (or non-profit organization) could not afford to pay the higher fee then they would receive slower, less desirable internet speed. The telecom companies lost that argument. As Troy Wolverton, Bay Area News Group, explained, " But the ruling – which will most likely survive an expected appeal – is a big win for everyday citizens in another way. It shows the power that people can have when they get involved in government and the political process."

2. To make this as quick and easy as possible, put the office telephone numbers of your elected representatives in your phone. This will only require one entry, and you will then have it handy at the press of a button. If you do not know your senator's or representative's name or phone number, you may call 202-224-3221, and the Congressional switchboard will put you through to your elected official. To reach the president, dial the White House switchboard at 222-456-1111. To find your state senators and district representative, contact your state capital switchboard.

START:

1. Start to observe potentially psychopathic behavior in any who are in the limelight, including politicians, Wall Street, bank CEOs, or anyone, for that matter, who wields power over you. Your decision will give you a clue regarding where you can and should place your trust. For example, knowing that psychopaths are drawn to the financial industry in positions of power and that financial corporations are psychopathic by their very nature, I have moved all my banking needs to a credit union; the major banks still are not trustworthy.

2. Since civics is not taught in our schools any longer, start to acquaint yourself with our country by reading our Constitution. You may find and download it here: http://www.usconstitution. net/const.pdf.

3. Start your American civics lessons here: http://www. thedreyfussinitiative.org.

4. Start shaming and shunning, through advocacy, those wealthy, self-concerned corporations and d-rich individuals who insist on tax evasion. Start to see through the looking glass of branding

and/or public relations efforts designed to benefit the rich. It is astonishing that the d-rich see themselves as victims whenever we challenge their obscene riches and corresponding dominant overreach. Tom Perkins, who bemoans "the war on the 1 percent," diabolically strategizes to destroy Social Security. Learn who to shame and shun by joining Too Much, A Conversation on Excess and Inequality at: http://toomuchonline.org.

5. Start projecting Living-in-the-Black energies into your environment and your politics. Find and follow those who exemplify constructive and creative energies. My recommendation would be to check out Thom Hartmann at www.thomhartmann.com or view him on Free Speech TV. Mr. Hartmann consistently models Living in the Black energies and listens to all points of view. Also, to hear news you will not hear in corporate media, check out Ring of Fire at http://trofire.com.

STOP:

1. Stop thinking billionaires know more than you do or are somehow more exceptional than you are. They are not! In fact, 50 percent of them inherited their vast wealth. They know no more than you do about running the country; the bubble in which they live has insulated them from any grasp of reality.

2. Stop and control any apathy you might feel. Apathy plays into the hands of the powerful because it births abandonment. There are a dizzying number of organizations, associations, alliances, and campaigns to join. To help you decide which ones to focus on, ask yourself what inspires you to make the world a better place. After you identify the issues with which you resonate, consider joining several action groups. Although it is not an exhaustive list, here are a few good choices:

   - Action for the Common Good: http://populardemocracy.org/action-common-good
   - Alliance for a Just Society: http://allianceforajustsociety.org
   - American Family Voices: http://www.americanfamilyvoices.org
   - American Sustainable Business Council: http://asbcouncil.org

- Business for Shard Prosperity: http://www. businessforsharedprosperity.org
- Campaign for America's Future: https://ourfuture.org
- Center for American Progress: https://www.americanprogress.org
- Center for Community Change: http://www.communitychange.org
- Center of Budget and Policy Priorities: http://www.cbpp.org
- Citizen's Climate Lobby: https://citizensclimatelobby.org
- Center for Responsibility and Ethics in Washington: www. citizensforethics.org
- Citizens for Tax Justice: http://ctj.org
- Coalition on Human Needs: http://www.chn.org
- Daily Kos: http://www.dailykos.com
- Democracy Initiative: http://www.democracyinitiative.org
- Ed Schultz Podcast: http://wegoted.com
- Left Action: http://leftaction.com
- Left Forum: http://www.leftforum.org
- Main Street Alliance: http://www.mainstreetalliance.org
- MoveOn.org: www.moveon.org
- Move to Amend: https://movetoamend.org
- National People's Action: http://npa-us.org
- New Rules for Global Finance: http://www.new-rules.org
- Our Revolution: https://ourrevolution.com
- People Demanding Action: http://www.peopledemandingaction. org
- People for the American Way: http://www.pfaw.org
- Pocket Cause: http://www.pocketcause.org
- Political Research Associates: www.politicalresearch.org
- Progressive Congress: http://www.progressivecongress.org
- Public Citizen: www.citizen.org
- Ring of Fire Network: http://trofire.com
- Southern Poverty Law Center: www.splcenter.org
- State of Belief: http://stateofbelief.com

- Sum of Us: http://sumofus.org
- The Nation: http://www.thenation.com
- The Other 98 percent: http://other98.com
- Truth Out: www.truth-out.org
- United for a Fair Economy: http://www.faireconomy.org
- U.S. Action: http://usaction.org
- Voices for Progress: http://voicesforprogress.org
- Working America: http://www.workingamerica.org

3. Stop tuning out when newscasters or politicians talk in billions and trillions of dollars. It is real money. Translate the figure into actual currency and readily grasp that $1 billion really is 1,000 million dollar bills. When you remind yourself of the proportion, you will make better and more informed decisions.

4. Stop supporting politicians who refuse to fund projects to rebuild America's infrastructure. Advocate for a new version of FDR's Work Projects Administration. It is a no-brainer to match people who want to work with jobs repairing and maintaining America's failing roads, bridges, and other systems.

5. Stop adding to Living-in-the-Red energies in your life, in others, and in politics. Following those who exude these toxic energies is not what you need in your life, nor do we need such negativity in our country. Good decisions and choices are never made with red energies. There are many of us, many organizations, working for positive change, Living in the Black. Black and red energies are very real and exist simultaneously; choose the energies you want to inhabit and surround you.

6. Stop believing corporate publicity ads that say corporations have your best interests at heart. They have no heart.

One Marvelous Question

After reading this chapter, if you were going to do one thing marvelously well to move forward, what would that one thing be?

Can we be saved by who wins the battle of the Titans?

CHAPTER TWO

The Battle of the Titans: The Patriotic Rich v. the Contemptuous Dictators

"It takes just one star to pierce a universe of darkness."

Richelle E. Goodrich

The good news is that some millionaires and billionaires appear to have their heads screwed on straight, like those who have joined the Patriotic Millionaires organization. Sadly, though, we never see or hear them loudly challenging their greedy counterparts over the outrageous, selfish, and childish things they say and do. In fact, we do not hear much about them at all. In fact, I only discovered their existence when researching this book.

These thankfully responsible and moral individuals first came together during the lame duck session of the 2010 Congress to demand higher taxes on themselves and other millionaires and billionaires, for the sake of the country. They agree with James Madison, political theorist and the fourth president of the United States, who said, "There should be a limit to immoderate income." They understand the problem very well, as their website states:

> The Patriotic Millionaires are a group of more than 200 Americans with annual incomes over one million and/or assets of more than five million, who believe that the country's current level of economic inequality is both dangerous and immoral. They recognize that while there are many causes of inequality, the current level of economic disparity is largely the result of a multi-decade effort by wealthy elites to enact legislation designed to enhance their personal wealth and their political power. This is done with little or no regard for the negative consequences such policies have on the vast majority of Americans.

> The Patriotic Millionaires are dedicated to reversing these policies and to ensuring that the legislative capture that led to their adoption

comes to an end. To realize that goal, the Patriotic Millionaires focus on a set of issues that best illustrates the difference between legislation that serves the interests of the majority of citizens and that which enriches the few. These issues are taxes, wages, and the democratic process. Members expressly support legislation that directly yields:

- A fairer tax system that includes greater tax obligations for millionaires and major corporations who have benefited the most from the nation's resources

- Higher incomes, beginning with a minimum wage of at least $15 an hour, for wage earners, who are the foundation of our nation's economy

- Less political influence for those whose sole credential is the ability to pay for it.

  The Patriotic Millionaires' strategy relies primarily on public education. They seek to use their unique position to expose the ways privileged self-interests influence the country's legislative process. They also highlight specific policies that best serve the interests of the majority and that can promptly reverse growing levels of economic disparity.

When I discussed the uphill climb the Patriotic Millionaires have ahead, their political director, Justin Strekal, said:

> As I'm sure that your work will help illuminate how much of a fight there is ahead of us, and in concert with the work of the Patriotic Millionaires and the tens of thousands of others who are working hard to restore a semblance of fairness in America's political and economic systems, we'll get there. We didn't get here overnight, and we're starting at an organizational disadvantage against the moneyed interests that seek to protect and expand their power, but eventually we will win.

Visit the website for their free eBook, *Renegotiating Power and Money in America.*

Nick Hanauer is a vocal billionaire who espoused, in an op-ed piece for *Politico* magazine, that he foresees "pitchforks" coming for his fellow 1%ers if they do not recognize and address the severely growing income inequality. He further states that many billionaires are "entitled white men" who "feel persecuted." He recorded a TED Talk that "pulled back the curtain" on how billionaires think. According to Hanauer, billionaires sincerely believe they are the only people who matter, which fits with Senator Sanders's point that they believe they are the only "real citizens." He further states that Plutocrats must give up on the trickle-down theory, citing the example of buying two pairs of pants. He can afford to buy a 1,000 pairs of pants, but what would he do with them? He calls "zillionnaires" to wake up, because it cannot last.

Nick Hanauer is a billionaire who is attempting to explain to all of us the billionaire mentality: how they act and what they value, power and control, which they see as their God-given right. The people have been completely abandoned by those who either won the lottery of birth or have made an extravagant amount of money but feel no loyalty to we, the people who supposedly don't matter, or the country that provided them a home in which to experience their great success.

A battle of the titans is underway, rather than a healthy battle of ideas that would exist in a truly democratic society, and the *millionaires* do not appear to be winning, but I hope they do. There are 200 Patriotic Millionaires. Yet, at the same time there are 158 *billionaire* families who seem poised to run the country. Those 158 families are systematically and strategically distributing their limitless wealth into politics, especially in the 2016 election, to principally Republican candidates. An October 10, 2015 *New York Times* article by Nicholas Confessore, Sarah Cohen, and Karen Yourish, "The Families Funding the 2016 Election," stated, "Not since before Watergate have so few people and businesses provided so much early money in a campaign, most of it through channels legalized by the Supreme Court's Citizens United decision five years ago."

Not surprisingly, these extremely wealthy people are secretive. They do not want their actions to be made public, most likely because they would then have to endure accountability, shame, and shunning by the rest of us. This same article explained that the new political donor elite are profoundly private, and many donations are made from P.O. boxes and businesses or camouflaged through limited liability corporations and trusts. These methods exploit the new avenues the Citizen United Supreme Court decision provides to corporations, giving them even more ability to spend money on a candidate's behalf. To hide even more, the political donor elite, either for tax purposes or privacy, refuse to list themselves as the owners of their own homes, further concealing family and social ties.

The Koch brothers routinely hold secret meetings in Palm Springs, California, and other locales. In these gatherings, they and their disgustingly rich friends plan for their vision of future America, their kingdom in which there would be little room for the rest of us.

Recently, I saw a *NonSequitur* cartoon showing a guru sitting on his mountaintop with a sign that read, "Enlightenment." Another guru sat on the nearby mountaintop, in more magnificent surroundings, with bags of money all around him. His well-lit sign declared, in all its neon glory, "Entitlement."

Predominantly, the billionaire class has developed an entitlement culture without conscience. Most will say and do whatever they want, without hesitation, as long as it propels them to greater riches. The Koch brothers are prepared to spend an unlimited amount of money to re-create America into their anti-government, Libertarian utopia, to convince us to abandon out traditional American values so they may buy the so-called liberty to spend endless amounts of cash in order to selfishly syphon, pillage and plunder the country's people and resources like the greedy pirates they are.

There is a small minority of millionaires in New York who understand this unsustainable pillaging. Forty millionaires, through the Responsible Wealth project, an organization of rich Americans who support "fair taxes and corporate accountability," wrote a letter on March 21, 2016 to the New York governor and legislature, asking to be taxed more because they are deeply concerned about the state's struggling economy and ailing infrastructure. It is too early to tell, but I am hoping they will be successful in New York and shame the d-rich in the country into following their lead.

John Adams, our second president and founding father, was not optimistic about whether or not we could sustain our republic. He wrote that the goal of a democratic society is not to help the wealthy and powerful but to attain "the greatest happiness for the greatest number." Perhaps we would be doing better as a nation if our modern politicians had not abandoned this wise thinking long ago.

Disingenuous Do-Gooders

Some multibillionaires seem to want to *appear* that they are using some of their wealth for good. As Chrystia Freeland, a journalist and author, said in her *Plutocrats: The Rise of the New Global Super-Rich and the Fall of Everyone Else* (Penguin Random House), "Gates has become an evangelist for this idea that capitalism must do good, and do-gooders must become more capitalist. He even has a name for it: creative capitalism." This catchy phrase sounds too close to George W. Bush's concept of compassionate conservatism, but these terms are defined by their originators and, most likely, do not mean what we think they do. Chrystia Freeland goes on to say:

> "Strikingly, the ambition of the philanthro-capitalists doesn't stop at transforming how charity works. They want to change how the state operates, too. These are men who have built their businesses by achieving the maximum impact with the minimum effort – either as financiers using leverage or technologists using scale. They think of their charitable dollars in the same way."

I find this last quote frightening; personally, I do *not* find them admirable. I see billionaires as people who want to morph our country into an entity they can manipulate to achieve their desires, like the Koch brothers wanting to "ghostwrite the American story." Their desires, most probably, do not mirror those of we, the people, and they certainly are not the desires of the democracy our founding fathers had in mind when they wrote our Constitution. At a programmatic level, I am sure the money is welcomed by the organizations that receive it. At the 50,000-foot level, however, billionaires are remaking this country into something unrecognizable, an oligarchy, which is an abomination in the eyes of democracy. At the same time, they ironically and misguidedly believe they are do-gooders.

Often, we read about some billionaire do-gooder donating a million dollars to this effort or a couple of million to that one, and we are easily fooled and impressed. In reality, that is mere pocket change to them, not to mention that most contributions equal a tax deduction. If a billionaire has 79,000 million dollars, what are a few million donated here or there? That money will quickly be recouped, maybe many times over when their name appears on a brand or product and they are romanticized as a great benefactor, resulting in even more profits for them. As the saying goes, it takes money to make money. We need to start seeing this as obscene instead of impressive; all in all, the d-rich donate little of their wealth, and any lackluster charity they do pass along is usually handled through foundations of their own creation. In fact, much actually leaves this country via their foundations, though that is not to say the issues overseas are not urgent and crucial in their own right.

Mark Zuckerberg, Facebook phenom, was recently lauded in the media for his donation of two and a half billion bucks to the Silicon Valley Community Foundation. It looks good on paper and in that trending bar, but the fact remains that the money was not given without conditions; therefore, that money could not be used to address issues in the area or be administered by a nonprofit board of directors who could freely make decisions about its disbursement. Instead, Mark and his wife, Priscilla Chan, placed the money in a donor-advised fund, so they could call the shots. At the same time, they sneakily created a supporting organization, Startup: Education. On the surface, this appears to be a good thing, as they purported that their new organization will fund Bay Area schools. Maybe this is true, but who will receive the grants? Will they be earmarked only for cash-strapped public schools, or will charter schools, which have been siphoning funds from the public school systems into private enterprise, get their hands on the Zuckerberg's seemingly generous donation? Again, two and a half billion is not a big hit on the couple's net worth, but they could look like the good guys by contributing it, all while they keep the reins tightly clutched in their hands, so they can use the funds to support *their* vision and keep the money away from anyone who disagrees.

A foundation or charity created by a d-rich individual is really irrelevant. Why? Because that money is taken out of general circulation with an ulterior motive, for some particular purpose, identified and selected by the billionaire, and the funding may or may not benefit America. Please do not misunderstand: I certainly do not begrudge truly charitable work that has no undesirable or selfish ulterior motive. I do, however, begrudge that the enormous sum of money was accumulated in the first place, thus having a massive impact on economic inequality, adding to the abandonment of the middle class and the less fortunate. President Dwight Eisenhower's Republican administration tax rate on the wealthy was 91 percent, and the government built America's roads, bridges, and even the interstate highway system with the revenue; meanwhile, none of the d-rich at the time ended up living on the streets.

The Do-or-Die Paradigm Shift

How can we reignite our power and control? The only answer is that we, the people, must undergo a complete paradigm shift. Many of us, about 50 percent of the country, have been manipulated into thinking that what the d-rich want is also what is best, but we must stop voting against our own interests.

All of us have been victims of the multimillion-dollar branding scheme funded mainly by the Koch brothers but also by the 400 billionaires they gather regularly to plan the take-over of the country. They have financed numerous think tanks, media organizations, academic projects, and political candidates – from the presidency to school boards – to coordinate their antigovernment, Libertarian message; in doing so, they can more effectively manipulate and deceive us into voting for their d-rich interests and not our own. They have been succeeding at the polls and in half the states in the country. Many states, such as Kansas and Wisconsin, have had a complete takeover, from the governor's office to both legislative branches, which now implement Libertarian values. Both Kansas and Wisconsin, possibly along with a few more states, are now failing their citizens and the very essence of democracy.

Several years ago, I sat next to a nice gentleman on an airplane. The Tea Party, which was created and funded by the Koch brothers, was becoming well known at that time. During our trip, I learned that he considered himself a Tea Partier and was antigovernment. I also learned that his career consisted of working at Boeing, that he was on Social Security and Medicare, and that he'd just finished his part-time job as a census-taker. When I speak of requiring a paradigm shift of great proportion, I refer to someone exactly like that very nice gentleman on the plane. As far as I could determine, the government had treated him nicely. Boeing survives on federal contracts, so his pay came from the feds, in essence. His Social Security, Medicare, and census-taking positions were all government-coordinated and/or government-funded programs. Still, there he sat with Bill O'Reilly's *Who's Looking Out for You?* book on his lap. It seemed to me that the federal government looked out for him very well.

We all must experience a dramatic change in consciousness, and we must do it now. We, the abandoned people, must realize – as the Koch brothers, Sheldon Adelson, Donald Trump, and numerous other billionaires already clearly understand and exploit – that politics is of vital importance to our individual futures, as well as the future of our country. A paradigm shift of great proportion, a political revolution (sans guns), is required; we must collectively seek to manifest those Living-in-the-Black energies, those constructive, cohesive, and creative energies, to counteract the years of destructive, divisive, soul-destroying suppression the oligarchs have heaped upon us all. The behavior of the d-rich is a perversion of democracy and an impediment to manifesting the Living-in-the-Black energies we so desperately need to revive.

Donald Trump is an inheritance baby. Fred Trump, his father, was a New York real estate tycoon who provided his son with an elegant and fashionable youth, including private schools and the economic security of a multimillion-dollar inheritance. His father's success gave Donald a great advantage in the world, and because it takes money to make money, Donald Trump leveraged even more wealth on his own. In October of 2015, in response to a question asked at an NBC-sponsored town hall meeting by a Republican voter, "With the exception of your family, have you ever been told no?" Donald replied, "My whole life really has been a no, and I fought through it. It has not been easy for me...and you know I started off in Brooklyn. My father gave me a small loan of a million dollars."

Donald, understanding the importance of politics, is a multibillionaire running for president, and his entire campaign is built on Living-in-the-Red energies. He has garnered support from so many who saw Wall Street steal 13 trillion dollars ($13,000,000,000,000). If we were to put the cash Wall Street executives stole in a one dollar pile, it would reach 882,258 miles into the sky or it would wrap around the earth over 35 times. No one can tell me, not ever, that there is not enough money in the country to fund federal programs (including the Defense budget) and infrastructure projects. The issue is that it has been stolen and captured in private bank accounts, on and offshore.

Stunningly, a candidate for president of the United States of America, Donald Trump, openly exudes Living-in-the-Red language and ideas in his campaign. He channels anger and fear and uses them both to his great advantage. Unashamedly and unabashedly, he demonizes two entire cultures, Mexicans and Muslims. He promotes the building of a wall and claims he will force the Mexican government to pay for it. How? Does he plan to bully the Mexican government, yet another example of Living in the Red? And by the way, when has building a wall between two countries ever worked out very well in human history? Not only that, but who is going to pay for it when some brilliant souls someday cries, "America, tear down this wall"?

Protesting is a cornerstone of democracy, yet Donald Trump recently said of a protester at a rally that he wanted to "punch him in the face." He calls his campaign rivals liars and "sick," albeit, to be fair, all the 2016 Republican candidates are calling each other liars. He also said, "I could stand in the middle of Fifth Avenue and shoot somebody, and I wouldn't lose voters." Are you seeing red yet? I am! Red, red, and more red!

These observations are clearly not complimentary to his fans, but his supporters are not really thinking. This is exactly what Living in the Red does: It halts clear thinking. Ed Schultz, an American television and radio host, said on his February 24, 2016 podcast: "This is not a thinking man's election." This observational comment does not bode well for our country, a nation that desperately needs to experience a paradigm shift of great enough proportion that it will rescue us, as individuals and a country, from this mess. It is an illusion to assume that any billionaire will act for the benefit of the people, especially those who long to build walls.

Whether or not he wins, Donald Trump's candidacy sends chills up my spine. His campaign has unearthed a long-buried truth: An enormous number of people simply do not understand the role they have played – by their abandonment, neglect of responsibility, apathy, and utter negligence – in creating the country that now enrages them. The presidential office is the most powerful in our government, and electing someone to fill that position is not to be taken lightly. We cannot afford to seat someone who operates with raw, destructive, and divisive energies in our Oval Office, for this will not better our lives in any way. Since when has any negative energy ever improved things for anyone? Why would any voter believe that supporting a person who embodies such red energies would improve the country?

Each of us must decide in which environment, personally and societally, we want to live. Do we wish to live with anxiety, anger, hatred, aggression, fear, apathy, and cynicism swirling around us, or do we want to bask in trust, faith, hope, meaning, security, and achievement every day? The answer should be obvious.

The *Santa Cruz Sentinel* op-ed headline on February 21, 2016 read:

> Having belittled his Republican rivals as well as Democrats, Muslims, migrants, people with disabilities, prisoners of war, and uncountable celebrities, foreign leaders, women and journalists, Donald Trump trained his wellspring of venom on Pope Francis on the eve of the pontiff's trip to Mexico last week.

In the toxic red category, Politico reported in an article, "David Duke: Voting against Trump is 'treason to your heritage,'" that David Duke, former KKK Grand Wizard, announced a call-to-arms: "...voting against Donald Trump at this point is really treason to your heritage... Call Donald Trump's headquarters... They're screaming for volunteers. Go in there. You're gonna meet people who are going to have the same kind of mindset that you have."

Folks, this is your red alert! It is dangerous and frightening to see so many people drawn in by such hatred and venom. We must get a grip on our anger and channel it constructively. Restoring the middle class, the middle-class lifestyle, and assisting those less fortunate by reigniting our democracy will simply not be possible as long as we stagnate within these Living-in-the-Red energies drowning us. Our wounds will just fester and worsen, and we will tear ourselves apart even more. Are we even able to help ourselves? I think we can, once we admit and understand how manipulation by oligarchs works.

Donald Trump presents himself as an outsider, yet members of his billionaire class are currently the real citizens of our times. They and their hired lobbyists are the only people Congress listens to, and, because of this selective listening, the very people who support Donald Trump for president cannot see that he and his class are the reason Congress obstructs any justice for them. It is an irony of all ironies.

Thomas Frank, an American political analyst, historian, journalist, and columnist, in his book, *Pity the Billionaires*, says they present themselves as opponents of "entrenched power," yet, they *are* the ruling class. They *are* the entrenched power.

The d-rich are desperately afraid that we will wake up and pay attention. It is in their best interest that we do not, that we remain asleep while their toxic manipulations are perpetrated. They win if we do not participate in politics. *They* recognize how important politics are, or they would not be willing to spend whatever it takes to take our government captive, at the federal, state, and local levels. To capture our government means placing their cronies in the departments meant to protect the people.

If they do so, America's abandonment will be far worse than it is now. Regulations that keep the rich and powerful somewhat in check will be further erased; worker's rights, women's rights, civil rights, and even our right to vote could be wiped out, for this is already being attempted, via voter identification and suppression laws. Actions against the climate crisis will cease. There will be even more tyranny exercised by the minority, the billionaires, over the middle-class majority. There will be more government that a "small group [will exercise] control, especially for corrupt and selfish purposes."

Undeniably, our zeitgeist, the spirit and mood of our country, is currently Living in the Red. Interfaith Alliance Executive Director, Rabbi Jack Moline, put it this way on a State of Belief podcast:

> There is a climate of outrage in our country that ought to cause concern for anyone, but especially for people of faith. And when I say faith, I don't limit the term to people who are religious or even to those who consider themselves believers in God. Instead, I mean those of us with a worldview that includes a measure of hope.

Rabbi Moline went on to say:

> The anger that has animated so many candidates for so many offices – and so many of their supporters – is a reflection of the exhaustion of the American soul. The problems we face as a nation are no less critical than the problems we each face in our own lives, but neither are the blessings of America any fewer.

> It is time for everyone to take a deep breath and a step back so as to recognize the difference between heat and light. Faith is the way to achieve that sense of groundedness. The values we hold – whether they flow from the depths of our hearts or the Scripture we hold sacred or the teachings of a beloved mentor – give us hope, not the hope that is a magic wish but the hope that is an affirmation that tomorrow always holds the potential to be better than today when we seek the good and not the outrage.

The time is now! We must each "seek the good and not the outrage" and cause a do-or-die paradigm shift of great proportion in our areas of influence and recognize how important participating in politics is, not just to our democracy but to our very own lives.

Paul Krugman, Nobel Prize-winning economist, wrote in his *New York Times* op-ed column, *How Change Happens*, "The point is that while idealism is fine and essential – you have to dream of a better world – it's not a virtue unless it goes along with hardheaded realism about the means that might achieve your ends." We each must ask if we want to continue Living in the Red or move ourselves and our country to a more constructive, cohesive, creative reality.

Stand Up Activities

Below, for your consideration, are several suggested Stand Up Activities. For a further explanation of the Keep/Start/Stop organization tool, please see Chapter One. After reading this chapter, you may think of additional activities readers can implement. If you'd like to share your brilliant constructive, compelling and creative ideas, please do so at: www. facebook.com/americaabandoned.

KEEP:

1. Keep and cultivate your passion for our country and your fellow Americans. Numerous forces are striving to divide us and, therefore, control us. Divide and conquer works! Do not let those with position power convince you that you will be better off hating others; they strive to appeal to your lizard brain. Ask yourself what is in it for them to separate and alienate you from of the rest of society.

START:

1. When you see an opportunity or can proactively communicate with them, start supporting and acknowledging conscious wealthy people, such as the members of the Patriotic Millionaires organization, for their empathic efforts on behalf of the middle class and those less fortunate. They, too, are fighting an uphill

battle against the d-rich. It is shocking to think there are billionaires who are not rich enough to influence the billionaires who are unimaginably wealthy, such as the Koch brothers, with their combined wealth of $82,000,000,000. How will they ever spend it all?

2. Start to research whether any college or university in your community has accepted funds from the Koch brothers and what conditions were attached. The Koch brothers have been known to endow Economics Department chairs, so they can require them to profess Libertarian views to the students.

3. Start a petition at https://www.change.org. You have the power to change the country by reaching others who share your valid concerns.

STOP:

1. Stop navel-gazing! When we are completely focused on our personal universe, abandonment prevails. We miss many important things that might affect our lives when we operate with a narrow, narcissistic focus. In reality, we live in many worlds at the same time. This requires multitasking. In addition to our personal sphere, we live in neighborhoods, cities, counties, states, and a country and on a planet. Give yourself and your fellow humans the attention they deserve. Do not abandon them.

One Marvelous Question

After reading this chapter, if you were going to do *one* thing marvelously well to move forward, what would that one thing be?

When we get active, we will change the game, because the game, until now, has been a Velvet Coup.

CHAPTER THREE

The Velvet Coup Is Happening to You! Part One

"Power concedes nothing without a demand.
It never did, and it never will."

Frederick Douglass

Several years ago, I facilitated a meeting on "Information Literacy in the Czech Republic." There, I learned about the country's *Velvet Revolution,* a nonviolent upheaval and transition from a one-party Communist government to a parliamentary republic. Remarkably, the Czechs accomplished this monumental feat without firing a shot. Through demonstrations and protests, they successfully gained their independence from Russia.

Borrowing from Velvet Revolution, a phrase coined by the dissident's English translator Rita Klimova, who later became an ambassador to the United States, my theory is that America is experiencing a Velvet Coup. No gunfire has occurred in the name of it, but a four-decades-long billionaire and corporate coup have created this intestacy, which is nearing completion.

Throughout history, there has always existed a dynamic tension between the rich and powerful and the rest of us. In fact, our country was founded on this very dichotomy, after our ancestors left behind an oppressive monarchy. Once again, we are facing a critical moment in history by experiencing an intentional, multi-faceted coup by the rich and powerful corporations and the oligarchs who own them.

What precipitated the Velvet Coup? It was a reaction to corporations being affected by some tough policies from Congress, between 1969 and 1972— laws meant to protect the environment, improve workplace conditions, increase consumer rights, and so on. The wealthy and most corporate executives hated it. Why? Laws lead to regulations.

In essence, regulations are rules, the rules of the game for any specific industry. Corporations and the rich detest rules that seek to regulate. They desperately want to operate by their own rules or, better yet, no rules at all. To make or save money, they want to be free to pollute the environment, deal with workers, and treat customers however they deem necessary, and they do not want to be held accountable for any of their actions. Corporations are psychopathic by their very nature.

It gives me no pleasure to make the point that the main vehicle for corporations and billionaires to implement the Velvet Coup is the Republican Party. The party already aligns with conservative and Libertarian values, so it is a natural partnership. The corporations and billionaires send their lobbyists to influence and work with Republican politicians to draft laws to benefit them or push for the regulations they want eliminated. Republicans, by partnering with corporate lobbyists, never again have to worry about raising campaign funds in order to keep their elite positions in government. It is a symbiotic relationship.

That said, there are corporatist members of the Democratic Party as well. Bill Clinton's administration moved the party to the right, further from the working class and the democratic principles that supported them. The programs Clinton championed were Republican-light, and subsequent Democratic administrations have followed suit. A democratic group known as the Third Way, meant to advocate a bridge between right-wing economic and left-wing social policies, was, in reality, supported by Wall Street billionaires and corporate money.

Still, there is a clear difference between the two major political parties. The Republican agenda is steeped in money, which is brought to light when their candidates blatantly court and receive millions of dollars from billionaires such as Sheldon Anderson and the Koch brothers. These billionaires found the political party who will do their bidding; now, all that stood in their way was public perception.

Vice President Henry Wallace warned us about this. During WWII, the United States was caught in the throes of fighting fascism in Germany and Japan. Fascism was on everyone's mind, as terrorism consumes our minds today. Vice President Wallace wrote an article for *The New York Times* (April 9, 1944) about whether or not fascism could happen in America. It was his summation that an American fascist would not use violence but would poison our public information channels. He wrote, "With a fascist, the problem is never how best to present the truth to the public but how best to use the news to deceive the public into giving the fascist and his group more money and power."

Giovanni Gentile, an Italian philosopher and politician who also ghostwrote Benito Mussolini's "A Doctrine of Fascism," stated, "Fascism should more appropriately be called *corporatism* (emphasis added) because it is a merger of state and corporate power." Mussolini brought the reality of fascism to Italy when he dissolved the Italian parliament and created the Chamber of Fascist Corporations. Corporations were privately owned and openly in charge of the government.

Regarding the 2016 presidential campaign, an astonishing amount of money is coming from billionaires and corporations to buy candidates. Federal Elections Commission (FEC) Chair Ann M. Ravel shockingly stated, "The likelihood of the laws being enforced is slim." The commission is locked in a 3-3 tie, along party lines, and they realize that groups are violating election laws, but the commissioners are at each other's throats to such a degree that they are unable to protect the integrity of the election. The result? Corporations and the oligarchs who own them will have free reign.

Vice President Wallace went on to write:

> Still another danger (of American fascists) is represented by those who, paying lip service to democracy and the common welfare, in their insatiable greed for money and the power which money gives, do not hesitate surreptitiously to evade the laws designed to safeguard the public from monopolistic extortion.

The only entity standing in the way of their "insatiable greed for money and the power" was and still is the United States government.

The Velvet Coup chronology, as I have extensively researched, is delineated below. During the four-decades-long coup, many more events and prominent characters have been involved than what are outlined here; there are so many, in fact, that it would take an anthology to trace them all in entirety. To present my thesis, I have selected seminal moments and individuals in the following brief chronological overview:

1970s

- The Powell Manifesto

- Paul Weyrich, the American Legislative Exchange Council (ALEC), and the Heritage Foundation

- Republican President Richard Nixon resigns in shame, bolstering resolve

- *Buckley v. Valeo*: Money becomes a form of speech

- First National Bank of *Boston v. Bellotti*

1980s

- David Koch runs for vice president and presents Velvet Coup tenets in his platform

- Paul Weyrich, "Goo-Goo Syndrome" speech

- Council for National Policy founded

- Ronald Reagan elected president/ Trickle Down Economics

- Grover Norquist taxpayer protection pledge

- Repeal of the Fairness Doctrine

1990s

- North American Free Trade Act (NAFTA)

- Contract with America

- U.S. Chamber of Commerce hires Tom Donahue

- Repeal of Glass-Steagall Act by the Gramm-Leach-Bliley Act

2000s

- Supreme Court Selects George W. Bush for president

- Wall Street taxpayer theft

- Grover Norquist NPR interview

- Central American Free Trade Agreement (CAFTA)

- Caucus room conspiracy

2010s

- Citizens United Supreme Court decision

- McCutcheon v. FEC Supreme Court decision

While the above chronology begins in the 1970s, that does not mean 1971 was the beginning of the Coup's foundational structures of conservatism, corporatism, and Libertarianism. In 1953, Russell Kirk wrote *The Conservative Mind*, in which he delineated conservatism all the way back to Edmond Burke, an Irish statesman and member of the British Parliament in the 1700s.

Russell Kirk believed civilized society required "orders and classes." He also believed capitalism was kindred to Communism, and he was not a fan of either. He rejected democracy because of its "great tradition" in valuing that all men are created equal. He believed in a hierarchical class system.

The Velvet Coup, then, is the actualization of Kirk's rejection of democracy and the supplanting of a hierarchical system. What we must realize is that Velvet Coup proponents are instilling a hierarchical system of mega-corporations and multibillionaires to run the "orders and classes." This is made possible by the vast amount of wealth accumulated by both corporations and billionaires during the past several decades. What creates this universal tension between the rich and powerful and the rest of us is the scale of wealth that the rich and corporations now control. Proportionally, it is more accumulated wealth than any other time in history.

In his book *The Rise of the Counter-Establishment*, Sidney Blumenthal, an American journalist, activist, writer and former political aide to President Bill Clinton, wrote:

> ...the source of the counter-establishment's (conservatism) rise is more than a single cause, more than just the decline of party. Its ascendance was neither inevitable nor by chance. *The conservative*

elite has been built by individuals who believe strongly, plan strategically, and move collectively (emphasis added).

It is my view that those individuals, as well as those who lead and own the corporations, have planned strategically and moved collectively to enact the Velvet Coup of America.

The 1970s

There is an actual date and person associated with the launch of the Velvet Coup. It was August 23, 1971, when Lewis Powell, Jr., a corporate attorney who wrote a memo, also known as his manifesto, to Eugene Sydnor, Education Director of the U.S. Chamber of Commerce, entitled "Attack on American Free Enterprise System."

Notice the word "American." The more appropriate word would have been *Corporate*. It was Powell's position that business was under attack by Communists, New Leftists, Socialists, revolutionaries, college campuses, pulpits, media, intellectual and literary journals, arts and sciences, politicians, and Ralph Nader. Excerpts of the Powell Manifesto state:

> One of the bewildering paradoxes of our time is the extent to which the enterprise system tolerates, if not participates in, its own destruction.

And:

> The first essential – a prerequisite to any effective action – is for business to confront this problem as a primary responsibility of corporate management. The overriding first need is for businessmen to recognize that the ultimate issue may be *survival* – a survival of what we call the free enterprise system and all that this means for the strength and prosperity of America and the freedom of our people.

Powell's memo propagated victimhood and, in doing so, successfully scared the daylights out of corporate leaders and turned them into injured parties fighting for survival. In addition, the subtext message of Powell's manifesto was that the emasculation and victimization of business leaders was being perpetrated by the federal government.

Not long after Lewis Powell delivered his memo to the U.S. Chamber of Commerce, he was appointed by President Richard Nixon to the U.S. Supreme Court. Interestingly, the existence of the memo was unknown at the time of his confirmation hearing. Much later, it was leaked to Jack Anderson, a liberal syndicated columnist; upon reading it, Anderson questioned Justice Powell's objectivity in the high court and said: "[Powell] might use his position on the Supreme Court to put his ideas into practice... on behalf of business interests." Just a few years later, Lewis Powell and his fellow Supreme Court justices did just that, to an unimaginable degree, when they made a legal decision that would become a coup cornerstone.

A September 14, 2012 Moyers & Company article, "The Powell Memo: A Call-to-Arms for Corporations," observed, "The organizational counterattack of business in the 1970s was swift and sweeping – a domestic version of shock and awe."

Just like that, the Velvet Coup was launched.

Lewis Powell designed the playbook, but a prominent character in its implementation was Paul Weyrich, a conservative political activist and co-founder of several conservative think tanks, who would become a vital implementation arm of the coup.

In 1973, Paul Weyrich co-founded the American Legislative Exchange Council (ALEC) and the Heritage Foundation, the background of each may be found on the People For the American Way website, both of which have played integral and enormously effective roles in the Velvet Coup. They are billionaire-funded organizations whose employees contemplate tactics to make the rich richer and the powerful more powerful.

ALEC receives 98 percent of its revenue from corporations, corporate trade organizations, and corporate foundations. Their meetings are held in secret. As explained on the Center for Media and Democracy ALEC Exposed website:

> ALEC is a pay-to-play operation, where corporations buy a seat and a vote on 'task forces' to advance their legislative wish lists and can get a tax break for donations, effectively passing these lobbying costs on to taxpayers.

Today, elected representatives must spend a majority of their time raising funds for their campaigns. The high cost of campaigning has, in fact, dramatically affected the amount of time they have to read and write legislation and meet with constituents. ALEC has benefited from this and has stepped in with pre-written legislation. They approach a corporate-bought politician and advance their corporate agenda through state legislatures. There have even been cases whereby state legislators submitting a bill ALEC has lobbied them for have not been astute enough to remove ALEC's name from the draft!

As an example of their depth and breadth, ALEC Exposed tracked and stated, "Despite widespread public opposition to the corporate-driven education privatization agenda, at least 172 measures reflecting American Legislative Exchange Council (ALEC) model bills were introduced in 42 states in 2015." In addition, ALEC is extremely hostile to Social Security and Medicare. Their goal is to find ways to cripple the two programs so they may be privatized.

What is especially egregious is that ALEC is registered with the IRS as a nonprofit organization, while they are actually a corporate lobbying organization and a major tool of the Velvet Coup. The Center for Media and Democracy submitted testimony to the Senate Judiciary Committee delineating ALEC's many transgressions; that testimony recounted on the Center's website in an article, "Is a Corporate Lobby Masquerading as a Charity."

The Heritage Foundation was initially funded with a $250,000 donation from Joseph Coors, the son of Adolph Coors. If it is true that we may be judged by the company we keep, then the Heritage Foundation must be considered a true danger to democracy. From the Corporate Accountability Project website, an article titled "It's No Accident that Coors Is the *Right* Beer for America" provides this well-documented history:

> The Coors family has always had strong ties to neo-Nazis. Adolph Coors allowed KKK meetings and cross-burnings on brewery property in Colorado. In 1984, Bill Coors fought against passage of the Civil Rights Act, telling an audience of black businessmen that blacks don't succeed because they "lack intellectual capacity." After encouraging them to go back to Africa, he said that one of the best things slave-drivers did to American blacks "was to drag your ancestors over here in chains" because blacks in America

have greater opportunity than those in Africa. Joe Coors is a major contributor to the Moral Majority (note; Paul Weyrich also founded the Moral Majority), which has called for the imprisonment of gay persons with AIDS. The Coors family funds a right-wing sector of Christian fundamentalism, which seeks to replace democratic pluralism with so-called "traditional family values"; that is, an authoritarian, gender-based social order. They support groups that say homosexuals are an abomination and AIDS is God's judgment on sinners. They have supported Reverend Sun Myung Moon and Christian Reconstructionists, both of whom have called for the abolition of U.S. democracy and the establishment of a theocratic state (...one nation under God, *or else*).

The Heritage Foundation was once called "the General Motors of Conservatism." Sidney Blumenthal went on to say, "The foundation published a series of thick volumes detailing the policies it wanted implemented. The books were more than wish lists, as many of the proposals were carried out." In reality, they were Velvet Coup implementation blueprints. Today, there are numerous Velvet Coup implementation think tanks, all plotting and planning the demise of democracy and the corporate and disgustingly rich takeover of America. Money abounds to fund such groups. It is essential to research who funds and sits on the board of directors of any foundation or association so we may judge the caliber of the organization.

A seminal event that advanced the Velvet Coup was the Supreme Court's 1976 *Buckley v. Valeo* decision. Lewis Powell and his fellow justices in a landmark case on campaign finance law upheld limits to campaign contributions but struck down, based on the First Amendment (Freedom of Speech), spending limits by citizens and campaigns. It ruled that spending money to influence elections is a form of constitutionally protected free speech. We have all heard that money talks, and this decision gave it a voice, at least legally speaking.

Decades later, the *Buckley v. Valeo* decision would be foundationally used in the 2010 *Citizens United* case that removed restraints on corporations, allowing them to spend unlimited amounts of money advocating for or against candidates or referendums. Money is not free speech; rather, it is commercial speech, and it has undeniably bought politicians.

Wikipedia sites the decision's significance:

> *Buckley* set the United States at odds with the practice in most of the rest of the democratic world. For instance, under the European Convention on Human Rights, it was held in *Bowman v. United Kingdom* that equality of citizen voice was a legitimate purpose, and spending money was not the core of freedom of expression. A similar approach is taken in Latin America. In other Commonwealth countries, such as in the Canadian case, *Harper v. Canada (Attorney General)*, it is routinely held that rules designed to limit spending at elections are legitimate, because they prevent conflicts of interest and promote political equality.

The *First National Bank of Boston v. Bellotti* (1978), with Louis Powell still on the court, bestowed corporations free speech rights. As Wikipedia states: "As a result of the ruling, states could no longer impose specific regulations on donations from corporations in ballot initiative campaigns."

This Supreme Court decision vaulted corporations and the rich over the middle class. Now, coupled with the *Buckley v. Valeo* decision, whomever had the most money, also had the most free speech.

In 1974, Republican President Richard Nixon resigned in disgrace. The subsequent democratic victory was so large that it once again threatened the corporate oligarchs. Their resolve to implement the Powell manifesto was significantly intensified.

The 1980s

The 1980s comprised a prolific decade for creating structural organization and determining resonating ideas to foster the Velvet Coup.

In 1980, David Koch – who would be one of the richest men in the world thirty-five years later – ran for vice president on a Libertarian platform. That platform set up the tenets of the Velvet Coup, which Koch stated he would advocate and put into effect if he became vice president

- the repeal of federal campaign finance laws

- the abolition of Medicare and Medicaid

- the deregulation of the medical insurance industry

- the repeal of Social Security

- the abolition of the U.S. Postal Service

- the repeal of all taxation

- termination of all criminal and civil sanctions against tax evasion

- the abolition of the Environmental Protection Agency

- the dissolution of the Department of Energy

- the dissolution of all governmental agencies concerned with transportation

- the abolition of the Federal Aviation Administration

- the abolition of the Food and Drug Administration

- an end to all subsidies for child-bearing and tax-supported services for children

- the repeal of the Occupational Safety and Health Act

- the abolition of the Consumer Product Safety Commission

- the repeal of all states usury laws

- the separation of education and State and an end to government ownership, operation, regulation, and subsidy of schools and colleges

- the repeal of all taxes on income or property of private schools, whether profit or nonprofit

- the return of America's railroad system to private ownership

- the privatization of public roads and the national highway system

- the privatization of inland waterways and the distribution system that brings water to industry, agriculture, and households

He stated that he would oppose:

- compulsory education laws

- compulsory insurance to provide health services, including abortion

- personal and corporate income taxation, including capital gains taxes

- laws requiring "self-protection" equipment such as safety belts, airbags, or crash helmets

- all government welfare, relief projects, and "aid to the poor" programs

These, to me, offensive positions are still alive and well today and form the basis of the Velvet Coup in which we now live. I argue that America has become a Libertarian utopia, as demonstrated by Paul Ryan, a democratically elected United States House Representative who distributed the fiction novel, *The Fountainhead*, by Russian-born Ayn Rand, a Libertarian deity, to his congressional office staff for their indoctrination. More seriously, the poisoning of the residents in Flint, Michigan is the direct result of Libertarian doctrine implemented by its governor, Rick Snyder. The Republican messages and policy positions consistently present Living in the Red energies. In my view, when anyone or any organization lives in the Red habitually and ritually, something is really broken.

It is important to note that Ayn Rand's theories are the basis of Libertarianism, a philosophy of a person who ardently believed in the doctrine of free will, which we need in order to make choices for ourselves and about others. Unfortunately, Libertarian zealots often misinterpret free will as a right to behave *selfishly*. The thinking goes like this: *I'm free to do whatever I want, despite how it affects others or the environment.* Billionaires and corporations exemplify this mindset and, in doing so, abandon all that does not serve them.

Ayn Rand was an atheist and founded the philosophy of objectivism, which states that we should pursue our own self-interest rather than pursuing the greater good for others. Somehow, this should all be done in the name of *reason*; if we reason properly, then we will realize that our own self-interest is paramount to anything or anyone else. Ayn Rand's twisted belief system is a must-see, eye-popping experience and there are several You Tube videos that may be found of her explaining her bizarre opinions.

In her perverse world, selfishness is moral. How cunning it is to present a potentially immoral act as moral! This is a central, profit-motivating message espoused by politicians, billionaires, and corporate CEOs because it justifies abandoning any responsibility for employees, customers, the environment, governments, and even the country – so much so that today, corporations no longer possess any economic loyalty to America (outsourcing jobs/tax evasion). Free will does not come without responsibility, but the Libertarian application in our society is responsibility-free and is a prime factor of abandonment. Libertarian values foster abandonment.

Those who admire Ayn Rand and her Libertarian tenet that selfishness is good need to know something: Ayn Rand based her *selfishness is good* and her "Superman" concept and character in her novels on one of the most famous men in 1928, William Edward Hickman.

William Edward Hickman said something that captured Ayn Rand's psyche: "What is good for me is right." She zealously responded to this self-serving worldview by writing in her journal that he was "a wonderful, free, light consciousness," further explaining that Hickman was unrestrained of any understanding of "the necessity, meaning, or importance of other people. " She also commented, "Other people do not exist to him, and he doesn't understand why they should." She wrote these journal entries like accolades, something to applaud, as if these were good qualities of human character.

Among his many other deplorable acts, William Edward Hickman kidnapped a 12-year-old girl from school, demanded a ransom from her parents, and killed and mutilated his captive anyway. To make the girl seem alive in his car, he wired her eyes open, stuffed her with towels, and then, while escaping with the ransom, pushed her out of the car, forcing her father to forever be haunted by the visual of his daughter's body parts strewn all over the road. This condensed version is bad enough, but many of the gorier details may be found on a website by Michael Prescott, a *New York Times* and *USA Today* journalist.

Rationally, one would think that when Ayn Rand learned of this revolting crime, she would disavow the what-is-good-for-me-is-right philosophy. Nope. Instead, she wrote in defense of the sociopath in her journal, "The first thing that impresses me about the case is the ferocious rage of a whole society against *one* man. No matter what the man did, there is always something loathsome in the 'virtuous' indignation and mass hatred of the 'majority'... It is repulsive to see all these beings with worse sins and crimes in their own lives, virtuously condemning a criminal."

This woman, who many in positions of power follow today, thought the whole of society is comprised of people who have committed "worse sins and crimes" than murdering a child so horrendously for simple greed. She is the hero of many, while her own hero is William Edward Hickman, a child killer. She demonstrated no empathy for the child, the parents, or the society so revolted by the act. Is this not a reaction of a sociopath as well?

It is no wonder, then, that I am truly frightened of anyone who would knowingly follow the Libertarian ideology, such as the multibillionaires Charles and David Koch and our current speaker of the House of Representatives, Paul Ryan, who gave his congressional staff an Ayn Rand novel as his idea of their necessary indoctrination as to what they might ultimately do and are doing to our country. In my mind, these are followers of a sociopathic mindset, and this is a salient reason why we have lost our democracy.

In 1980, Paul Weyrich, the 1970s cofounder of ALEC, the Heritage Foundation and Moral Majority, gave a speech to the Religious Roundtable that began the voter disenfranchisement and suppression component of the Velvet Coup. Known as the "Goo-Goo Syndrome" speech (on You Tube), he was surprisingly honest about his desire that not everyone should be allowed to vote, the very antithesis of democracy:

> How many of our Christians have what I call 'the goo-goo syndrome': good government. They want everybody to vote. I don't want everybody to vote. Elections are not won by a majority of people. They never have been, from the beginning of our country, and they are not now. As a matter of fact, our leverage in the elections quite candidly goes up as the voting populace goes down.

The right-wing voter identification and suppression laws all have their roots in Paul Weyrich's speech. When voter turnout is low, the Republican Party wins. They know this to be true and are, therefore, always motivated to suppress democratic votes. For this reason, we must courageously stand up against their efforts. It is vital to them to win at all costs, but it is vital to democracy not to let them. Conversely, one would think Democrats would turn out in droves for every election, but they do not. I believe Democratic voters do not realize that their votes are being methodically stolen; if they did realize and believe this, they would turn out in droves for every election. What we do know is that they most likely want to play a decisive role, a component of a coup, in changing America to a far-right, Libertarian country.

In 1981, an exceedingly secret, extreme organization was created. To this day, not much is known about the innocuously named Council for National Policy (CNP); of course, if the intent was to pull off a quiet coup, the name is perfect. What we do know is that the CNP was founded by several ultra-conservative, religious fundamentalist individuals such as Tim LaHaye, who made a fortune as author of the *Left Behind* series of books. His novels told stories of a fictional Armageddon and fantasied that nonbelievers would be left behind while believers were carried off, without clothes, at the rapturous moment. Another founding member was Rousas John Rushdooney, a Christian Reconstructionist who believed in imposing Old Testament laws onto modern society – laws that, among other things, advocate the stoning of incorrigible children and adulteresses. Not surprisingly, Paul Weyrich was also one of the founding members.

Why is the organization super-secret? Members are told to never mention the organization's name, in spite of their sanitized website. They are never to tell others when they meet and what is discussed at those meetings. You cannot join the group without an invitation, and membership costs thousands of dollars. There is nothing like it on the left political spectrum.

Some information has been pieced together since 1981. We know the CNP meets three times a year. We know that six 2016 Republican candidates spoke at their meetings. We also know Chief Justice Clarence Thomas spoke to the group, as did George W. Bush when he was running for president. We know a majority of its members are wildly wealthy, such as those affiliated with the Coors Beer family. The Center for Media and Democracy has a 2002 director's roster and a 2001 membership roster on their Source Watch page that reveals who was part of the group at that time; of course, it may have changed since then, but the list is still rather telling.

Mark Potok, a leading expert on extremism and award-winning editor-at-large for The Southern Poverty Law Center (SPLC), in a June 3, 2016 Ring of Fire podcast, discussed a 2014 CNP directory they were able to secure.

It revealed 413 members, a perpetual who's-who in the conservative movement: major names such as Tony Perkins of the Family Research Council, an organization the SPLC has categorized as a hate group; Steve Forbes of *Forbes Magazine;* and Linda Bean of LL Bean. Other well-known individuals are Paul Teller, who became Ted Cruz's chief of staff, and Michael Peroutka, who served on the board of directors of the League of the South, a white supremacist group that wants to carve out a portion of the South to create a country of anglo-celts.

No one knows exactly what this secretive, multi-decade organization does, but it appears to be an opportunity for conservatives and religious fundamentalists to network with the d-rich to fund similarly aligned projects and a organizational platform for planning the Velvet Coup. Mark Potok cited the example of Frank Gaffney, Jr., Center for Security Policy, who provided the bogus statistics Donald Trump used to announce his proposal to ban Muslim immigration; out of thin air, Gaffney created the statistic that 25 percent of American Muslims support jihad against the United States. This so-called statistic has been proven false.

Why is it important to know about the Council for National Policy? They have been in trouble with the IRS, and its leadership forbids members to talk about who they are and what they do. They may be a legal organization, but they certainly are not a democratic one for the power they sway over policy that affects all of us. In an Alternet article, "Secret Society: Just who is the Council for National Policy, and why isn't it paying taxes?" explains who its founder is:

> CNP was founded in 1981 by Tim LaHaye, the right-wing, evangelical political motivator and author of the *Left Behind* serial, which chronicles a fictional Armageddon and second coming (in which the non-believers are left behind while believers are carried off in a rapturous moment without their clothes. It gives an eerie ring to the No Child Left Behind Act).

The election of Ronald Reagan in 1981 was a paramount Velvet Coup achievement. Within just one decade of Lewis Powell's manifesto, the corporations and oligarchs had their man at the top. In Reagan, the Velvet Coup found their launch pad.

Reagan quickly fired 11,000 striking air traffic controllers who dared to fight for pay raises, shorter hours, and better working conditions.

Historians believe this set the stage for the assault on labor unions, the one that continues today. When Ronald Reagan took office, approximately 30 percent of the workforce was represented by unions; that number has now fallen to a mere 11.1 percent. What most of us do not realize is that even if we are not in a union, our salary increased when a union member's salary increased, due to the economic pressure in the marketplace. It is vital in a corporate coup, then, to reduce union membership to remove market pressure and enable corporations to pay lower wages to their employees. So goes the unions, so goes the middle class.

What better way to start a coup than to break the back of a large, nationally valued union such as the FAA, a union that, in fact, *supported* Ronald Reagan's election and one we all depend on to protect our very lives? If that substantial, highly esteemed union was evil, then all unions are evil, right? Corporations and those who own them want to destroy unions and make more money by suppressing worker pay. Thus, Ronald Reagan employed the basic coup strategy of advantaging the wealthy by demonizing unions and, thus, disadvantaging the working stiff.

Taking from the poor and giving to the rich is another Velvet Coup goal. During Reagan's presidency, this was accomplished through a tactic called the *Reagan revolution*. A revolution is "the overthrow of a government by those who are governed." However, that was not what happened. We, the people did not revolt. Ronnie's election was not a revolution; in fact, it was a *decisive exercise of force in politics*, a component of a coup.

Selling the American public on trickle-down economics is an example of that decisive exercise of force and was a breathtaking Velvet Coup maneuver. *Wikipedia* defines *trickle down* as "a populist political term used to characterize economic policies as favoring the wealthy and privileged." Does anyone really want a trickle of anything? Ronald Reagan and his economic propagandists were able to convince enough people that they might see a little something, improve their lives just a dribble, if the rich got more money and corporations had more advantages. Unbelievably, a majority of the voting public believed this malarkey and voted him and his so-called revolution into office for a second term.

Trickle-down economics was another coup strategy that worked so perfectly that there are still people who believe in the theory. How much more obvious can it be, to tell people directly, give the money to the rich and the rest of us only get promises? Today, it is clear that this ridiculous

Jill Cody

theory does not work. In a United for Fair Economy article, "Trickle-Down Economics: Four Reasons Why It Just Doesn't Work," they document that: 1) Cutting the top tax rate does not lead to economic growth, 2) Cutting the top tax rate does not lead to income growth, 3) Cutting the top tax rate does not lead to wage growth, and 4) Cutting the top tax rate does not lead to job growth. All that was promised to us if we supported trickle-down economics. None of it happened.

In his second term, Ronald Reagan solidified the Velvet Coup further with his "nine most terrifying words," a devastating shot uttered on August 12, 1986: "The most terrifying words in the English language are: I'm from the government, and I'm here to help."

Why would he say such a thing? Why would he want to demonize the government? Why was he compelled to be so hypocritical? It did not seem to matter that that very government he insulted provided him with a federal employee paycheck (taxpayer funded), housing (taxpayer provided), safety (taxpayer-funded Secret Service), a lifelong pension (taxpayer funded), and fame. He said it with the intention of separating us from our government and manipulating us into abandoning it so corporations and their oligarch owners could step into the vacuum we would voluntarily create. Divide and conquer was a brilliant tactic because it worked, and it still works today.

Think about what Reagan accomplished in that short, *terrifying* sentence.

Without saying it directly, his underlying message was that profit-motivated corporations and the d-rich know better than we do, that they could bring order to the classes. He manipulated us into thinking that the government was problematic and untrustworthy. Are there parts of the government that pose problems and are untrustworthy? Of course there are, but the appropriate reaction is to root out the problem and solve it, not to destroy the program or privatize it. Talk about killing the goose! There is, however, no money to be made in solving problems. The only real money is in privatizing traditionally government-run programs. They are the new Wild West.

Astonishingly, this came from the head of that very government. The President of the United States, by inference, told us not to trust him or anyone else working for the government. This incited attacks on and hatred of governmental departments, programs, and employees and encouraged replacing many functions with private, profit-seeking businesses. This mentality became so pervasive that we privatized our voting machines. Voting is the foundation of democracy and should be managed by our democratically elected government, but we farmed it out.

Talking Points Memo, in a three part series, extensively researched and analyzed the privatization movement, titled: The History of Privatization – How an Ideological and Political Attack on Government Became a Corporate Grab for Gold. It is a frightening read about the privatization of our democratic commons.

I remember the demonization of our government all too well. I had been working for municipalities for twelve years before this negative shift of appreciation from the public occurred. Quickly, the public changed from respecting my efforts on their behalf to yelling at me at public hearings, saying things such as, "I pay taxes," or, "I pay your salary," or, "You work for me." These statements were always disappointing to hear, as it seemed no one realized that I paid taxes, too, and worked for an elected body. If they had, they might have understood how ridiculous they sounded to those of us working on their behalf.

Seemingly overnight, public servant-hood changed in the eyes of many; it went from being an honorable profession to one populated by scum of the Earth. Now, forty years later, many hate our government – our democracy – and want to destroy it instead of valuing it and trying to improve and work toward creating that "more perfect union." In Ronald Reagan, the corporations and billionaires certainly had their man in place to advance the coup.

With those nine words, Reagan instantly pitted one set of Americans against another by deftly utilizing an us-versus-them manipulation technique. He encouraged people to disrespect their government. It was easy to do. No one likes to pay taxes, even government employees, but those of us who desire a functioning free and civil society know it is the toll we must pay for a democracy. The intentional use of the word "terrifying" also played on another conventional manipulation technique: fear. Today, we are still living with the residual hatred and distrust of government he fostered. Thom Hartmann, an American author, blogger, and radio and TV host, wrote:

He [Ronald Reagan] turned compassion to the less fortunate to villainization...created the mythical 'welfare queen,' mocked AIDS patients, and let his fellow 'Christians' know it was okay to belittle the homeless. CEOs before Reagan made seventy-eight times their minimum-wage workers. Today, it is almost 3,500 times! Without Reagan, America might have had the same income distribution we had in the 1970s, which would mean we could be averaging *$120,000 annually* – not $40,000. Reagan was the realization of Barry Goldwater's failed dream that put the GOP on the path of Crazytown, where it is today. He somehow managed to blend selfish, plutocratic Ayn Randian economic philosophy with fundamental Christianity and wrap it all up in a cowboy, patriotic image...and we are still hurting.

Ronald Reagan had his most terrifying words and now I have mine. I believe for me, and the middle class, the most terrifying words now are, "I want my fair share – and that's all of it."

Investigative reporter, Greg Palast, when delving deeply into the Koch brother's role in wanting to crush the Osage Indians, located a transcript of a secret meeting when he was asked why he needed to squeeze a few hundred bucks from the Osage Indians, Charles Koch answered: "I want my fair share – and that's all of it."

Democracy is built on trust, at least to a minimal degree. The drivers of the Velvet Coup have been successful at creating a society that will not trust or expect from each other or our government anything that is well executed, with the subtle intent that someone or something else can better provide for the American people. Who better than the Velvet Coup beneficiaries, all those billionaires and corporations?

Connie Cass, an Associated Press reporter, in her article "Poll Reveals Americans Don't Trust Each Other Anymore" said:

For four decades, a gut-level ingredient of democracy – trust in the other fellow – has quietly drained away. These days, only one-third of Americans say most people can be trusted. Half felt that way in 1972, when the General Social Survey first asked that question.

She goes on to say:

> Does it matter that Americans are suspicious of one another? Yes, say political and social scientists. What's known as 'social trust' brings good things: a society where it's easier to compromise or make a deal; where people are willing to work with those who are different from them for the common good; where trust appears to promote economic growth.
>
> Distrust, on the other hand, seems to encourage corruption. At the least, it diverts energy to counting change, drawing up 100-page legal contracts and building gated communities.
> Even the rancor and gridlock in politics might stem from the effects of an increasingly distrustful citizenry, said April Clark, a Purdue University political scientist and public opinion researcher. "It's like the rules of the game," Clark said. "When trust is low, the way we react and behave with each other becomes less civil."
> There is no easy fix. In fact, some studies suggest it's too late for most Americans alive today to become more trusting.

At the feet of Ronald Reagan lies, disheveled on the ground, the trust we once had in each other, the empathy we had for the less fortunate, and the respect for the democracy our government once represented.

An integral component of a coup is to manipulate the media. In 1987, the Reagan administration's pro-corporate Federal Communications Commission (FCC) repealed the Fairness Doctrine that had been in place since 1949. The Fairness Doctrine was the FCC policy that required media entities that held broadcast licenses to present controversial issues of public interest in an "honest, equitable, and balanced" manner.

The Reagan revolution brought numerous anti-regulation extremists into his administration. One was a broadcast industry lawyer, Mark S. Fowler, who became the chair of the FCC. Fowler saw television as "just another appliance...a toaster with pictures." He was contemptuous about the idea that broadcasting corporations, who held licenses to use publicly owned airwaves, had any role or responsibility to ensure democratic discourse, and Mark Fowler vowed to end the Fairness Doctrine.

The motive behind the Fairness Doctrine was to protect a scarce public resource. Since there are more media corporations than there are licenses within the broadcast spectrum, media companies that received licenses were responsible for public interest obligations, in turn, for exclusive rights to their bandwidth; since cable infrastructure is privately owned, this obligation was not required of the cable media.

There are misconceptions about how the Fairness Doctrine worked, as Steve Rendall, Fairness & Accuracy in Reporting (FAIR) Senior Media Analyst, explained in his article, "The Fairness Doctrine – How We Lost It and Why We Need It Back":

> There are many misconceptions about the Fairness Doctrine. For instance, it did not require that each program be internally balanced, nor did it mandate equal time for opposing points of view...and it didn't require that the balance of a station's program lineup be anything like 50/50.
>
> Nor, as Rush Limbaugh has repeatedly claimed, was the Fairness Doctrine all that stood between conservative talk show hosts and the dominance they would attain after the doctrine's repeal. In fact, not one Fairness Doctrine decision issued by the FCC had ever concerned itself with talk shows. Indeed, the talk show format was born and flourished while the doctrine was in operation. Before the doctrine was repealed, right-wing hosts frequently dominated talk show schedules, even in liberal cities, but none was ever muzzled (*The Way Things Aren't*, Rendall et al., 1995). The Fairness Doctrine simply prohibited stations from broadcasting from a single perspective, day after day, without presenting opposing views.

Since the abandonment of the Fairness Doctrine, coverage of an important political issue or any other issue of public interest has declined significantly, at the local, national, and international level. Newsrooms have been shut down. Investigative reporting is nearly nonexistent. News and public programming budgets were slashed. We are left to watch the BBC, Free Speech TV and RT to learn about our own country.

By 2003, 25 percent of broadcasters had no news or public programming at all. Today, the news is silo-ed, and we lazily watch news that supports our viewpoint. We have placed ourselves in a self-value-affirming box, with no holes punched through to breathe in new information. Only a very bold and curious person who will poke holes into their self-imposed box and look for different opinions or, in some cases, the truth.

Robert F. Kennedy Jr. observed, "The FCC's pro-industry, anti-regulatory philosophy has effectively ended the right of access to broadcast television by any but the moneyed interests."

Stand Up Activities

Below, for your consideration, are several suggested Stand Up Activities. For a further explanation of the Keep/Start/Stop organization tool, please see Chapter One. After reading this chapter, you may think of additional activities readers can implement. If you'd like to share your brilliant constructive, compelling and creative ideas, please do so at: www.facebook.com/americaabandoned.

KEEP:

1. Keep the Velvet Coup concept in your mind when reading and watching the news and when voting.

2. Keep in mind what values fascism and Libertarianism disseminate.

3. Keep in mind that what benefits corporations and billionaires may not benefit you. Their interests are very different from yours. There is no such thing as trickle-down economics. It never happened and was a hoax so the rich could get richer.

4. Keep in mind Lewis Powell's manifesto as you watch corporate ads and activities.

5. Keep in mind David Koch's vice-presidential campaign platform. Do you agree or disagree with it? Your answer will determine your future actions.

START:

1. Start to understand how you may have been manipulated to abandon your right to vote. If you vote in every election, good for you! If not, vow to take care of yourself and your family better by

voting in all elections. Visit www.americaabandoned.com to find out what voter type you are.

2. Start to observe the actual purpose behind voter ID and suppression laws. Do not let the laws steal or suppress your vote. Get mad at legislators who pass these laws and show them that you will do whatever it takes to vote, regardless.

3. Start shining sunlight on organizations such as ALEC and the Heritage Foundation. See what they are advocating and whether or not you agree.

4. Start to learn who Ayn Rand was. Research her anti-democratic, Libertarian and still astonishing values that impact America today.

5. Start asking yourself what unions have done to improve your life, such as the forty-hour workweek, child labor laws, holidays, workplace safety, and fighting for better wages and benefits. Remember that you cannot achieve benefits, such as these, to improve your life single-handedly.

6. Start agitating for a 2.0 version of the Fairness Doctrine. We cannot give up on a fact-based media versus an opinion-based one. We must free journalists who are imprisoned in a bad, profit- and ratings-driven system.

7. Start to advocate for a 2 .0 version of the Glass-Steagall Act and, once again, separate investment and commercial banking. The abandonment of the Glass-Steagall Act was a major contributor to the 2008 financial crisis.

8. Start being active with Moved to Amend (www.movetoamend.org) and Issue One organizations (www.issueone.org). The Citizens United decision must be reversed before any of us will have our full rights as citizens returned.

9. Start being a citizen lobbyist. An excellent booklet to help you do this is The Citizen Lobbyist – A How to Manual for Making Your Voice Heard in Government or download The League of Women Voters free handout *The Citizen Lobbyist* here: http:// abandon.exposed/leaguecitizenlobbyistpdf. If we all became our own lobbyist, we would overpower the phalanx of lawyers and

lobbyists corporations and billionaires employ. Learn how to do it; advocate for yourself. We have the power to overwhelm them. As Ross Perot once said: *"The activist is not the man who says the river is dirty. The activist is the man who cleans up the river."*

STOP:

1. Stop being susceptible to the throes of fear, anger and propaganda. Take your power back.

2. Stop viewing government as the enemy. Ask yourself what purpose does this belief serve in a democracy? Ask yourself who benefits if you continue to believe our democratic form of government is evil? Vow, instead, to improve our government at every level. The anti-government mindset feeds right into the corporate and billionaire Velvet Coup strategy.

3. Stop getting your news from the same outlets and look for new outlets such as the BBC, and Free Speech TV. Poke holes in the box in which you unconsciously have taken up residence. Be curious and cautious about how you find your news and fact check issues of interest at sites such as www.factcheck.org, www.flackcheck. org, www.facethefactsusa.org and www.opensecrets.org.

4. Stop the monopolization of our telecommunication companies by being informed and communicate to the FCC your positions. Net neutrality is still under threat.

5. Stop, if your business is a member, being involved with the U.S. Chamber of Commerce until, one day, they decide to represent all businesses (large and small), not just the mega – corporations who fund them. It may be too late for the U.S. Chamber to change but we can hope. Until then, become a member of the alternative organizations.

6. Stop electing people who will not live up to their oath of office and who think being in power is more important than our country.

One Marvelous Question

After reading this chapter, if you were going to do one thing marvelously well to move forward, what would that one thing be?

As if that was not enough, a freight train was on its way.

CHAPTER FOUR

The Velvet Coup Is Happening to You! Part Two

"In the end, we will remember not the words of our enemies,
but the silence of our friends."

Martin Luther King, Jr.

The 1990s

A Velvet Coup freight train was the North American Free Trade Agreement (NAFTA). Adopted on January 1, 1994 and signed into law by Bill Clinton on December 8, 1993, it was less of a trade agreement and more of an investor agreement. Of course, what investors could actually play at that level?

NAFTA was promoted as good for America by the world's largest corporations and their phalanx of lawyers but good for whom? Billionaires and corporations, of course. We seem always to fall for the line that if something is touted, "good for America," it will be equally as good for the middle class. I do not believe anything in NAFTA was truly good for us. When trade agreements are written, we need to ask who it really benefits. What do we, the middle class, really get out of it? Many are asking that question now regarding the Trans-Pacific Partnership (TPP) agreement that has the United States partnering with countries that promote slavery, sex trafficking, and includes many corporate advantages. It has been dubbed the vehicle to achieve corporate global domination.

Those against the adoption of the NAFTA were labor, environmental, consumer, and religious organizations that did not have and could not afford a phalanx of lawyers to counter the deal made between Mexico, Canada, and the United States. It was extreme: Never before had an agreement been drafted between countries that were at such disparate levels of development. In the agreement, each nation was required to conform all of its domestic laws, bypassing voters and their representatives who had previously rejected the very same policies in Congress and legislatures around the country.

Public Citizen Trade Watch, in a report titled "NAFTA's 20-Year Legacy and the Fate of the Trans-Pacific Partnership" published in February 2014, stated:

> NAFTA was an experiment, establishing a radically new 'trade' agreement model. NAFTA was fundamentally different than past trade agreements, in that it was only partially about trade. Indeed, it shattered the boundaries of past U.S. trade pacts, which had focused narrowly on cutting tariffs and easing quotas. In contrast, NAFTA created new privileges and protections for foreign investors that incentivized the offshoring of investment and jobs by eliminating many of the risks normally associated with moving production to low-wage countries. NAFTA allowed foreign investors to directly challenge before foreign tribunals domestic policies and actions, demanding government compensation for policies that they claimed undermined their expected future profits. NAFTA also contained chapters that required the three signatory countries to limit regulation of services, such as trucking and banking; extend medicine patent monopolies; limit food and product safety standards and border inspections; and waive domestic procurement preferences, such as Buy American policies.

At the time, Ross Perot, an American multibillionaire business executive best known for being an independent presidential candidate, warned, in a 1992 presidential debate that if NAFTA passed, there would be a "giant sucking sound going south," and the country would be ruined. Sadly, he was correct. Due to outsourcing via NAFTA, America has lost 60,000 manufacturing businesses and the employment they generated. Recently, I purchased an American car; it was actually made in Mexico.

There have probably been many stories we don't generally know about NAFTA, similar to the following one. In 2015, the United States lost a lawsuit that cost American taxpayers one billion in order to pay Canada and Mexico for damage to the profits from the beef and pork industries. The lawsuit was over country-of-origin labeling (COOL). I think it is safe to say that we all want to know where our food comes from, and COOL informs us of where the beef and pork we eat are raised and slaughtered.

This issue was heightened after the mad cow disease outbreaks began in 1986. A *New American* article written by Clinton Alexander, said:

> The COOL labeling requirements, extremely popular with U.S. consumers, stipulate that packaged meat must document where the livestock animals were born, where they were raised, and the location of slaughter. However, the World Trade Organization has repeatedly called for repeal of the COOL laws, insisting that they discriminate against Canadian and Mexican meat imports.

Because of NAFTA – and the WTO, where disputes are decided – we will no longer know where our beef and pork is raised and slaughtered. The Republican-held House of Representatives has already passed a bill to repeal COOL, and it appears the Republican-held Senate will follow. We, as consumers, have no influence on the agricultural industries of Canada and Mexico. Not only are American corporations benefiting from the Velvet Coup, but multinational corporations of other countries are beneficiaries, too, and we are forced to abandon our right to know. More people die of food poisoning every year than those who died in 9-11. It can be said that NAFTA was the beginning of American corporations' economic disloyalty to the United States.

The year 1994 was a big one for the Velvet Coup. Not only did corporations win big with the passing of NAFTA, but that was also the year when Republicans presented their Contract with America. This contract was drafted, with input from Newt Gingrich, by the Heritage Foundation. The foundation's initial funding came from Joseph Coors, of the well-known beer empire, and, to this day, they receive funding from other billionaires such as the Koch brothers. This should be a hint to the motivations behind the creation of the document.

Nevertheless, the contract was a public relations success. It was previously focus-grouped so they knew what topics pleased the American people, but there were no real specifics or promises that anything would become law. The Republicans rode it into office anyway. It was a political document rather than a governing document, but it was presented to us as a treatise, an explanation of how they would govern if they took over the government. It was presented to the American people six weeks before the 1994 election, with the insinuation that if we elected Republicans, they would shrink government, lower taxes, increase entrepreneurial activity (euphuism for privatization), and implement tort and welfare reform. It further entrenched Velvet Coup values of reducing government, to the point that it is unable to enforce regulations that cost corporations money, to lower taxes on corporations, and to promote Congressional action in privatizing traditional government programs.

The Contract with America mentioned balancing the budget but did not describe how Republicans would cut the hundreds of programs that served the public to do so. It talked about cutting taxes and increasing the defense budget but did not explain how. It was especially harsh on single mothers who relied on federal aid to raise their families; after two years of subsidy, they would be required to report the identity of the child's father before collecting further benefits. It talked about fighting crime but said nothing about gun control. It did not address healthcare, except to state, "We don't need a government-run healthcare system with costly new entitlement programs. Instead, we need to facilitate efforts to keep families together." How they thought keeping families together was a healthcare policy is still a mystery.

When the Republicans took office based on their political and public relations ploy, leading anti-government types like Tom Delay (R-TX) vowed to attack regulations that harmed business, such as worker safety, environmental compliance, and labor rights laws. They changed the focus of public hearings from protecting the public to what they privately deemed "War Crimes Trials," to concentrate on imagined governmental regulators' criminal behavior in applying the laws to business. To this day, Republicans attack governmental programs meant to protect the public from corporate malfeasance, a major goal of the Velvet Coup.

After sixty-two years, the Telecommunications Act was updated. On the surface, it made sense. By 1996, communication systems like cable and the internet had been invented, and it appeared obvious that the original act was out of date, but the 1996 attempt to improve the act was another coup event. The proponents used the Libertarian mantra that removing regulatory barriers would open industry markets to healthy competition. In reality, it did not happen, and corporate consolidation ensued.

As David Rosen, a writer and business-development consultant, penned in his Filmmaker Magazine article titled "Murdock's Media Monopoly":

> The Telecommunications Act of 1996, signed by Bill Clinton, was enacted to ostensibly promote media and communications competition. The act was part of a larger Clinton administration effort to strengthen U.S. corporate interests in an increasingly

globalized marketplace. Thus 'competition' became the new code word for domestic corporate consolidation.

The 1996 Telecommunications Act was sold to the public as a vehicle to the creation of competition in our telephone, cable, newspaper, radio, television and internet services. We are taught that competition, in a capitalist economy, is to provide consumers with the best price for the best product. The *original* act outlined a monopoly-fighting framework in these industries. The *updated* act undid that framework and replaced it with significant deregulation, saying there would be more competition in the marketplace. Of course that never happened. Despite a tenet of capitalism, corporations do not want to compete unless forced to do so. America used to have over fifty news media outlets. Now, with consolidation there are only five or six. The competition was swallowed up like guppies.

By destroying regulations that protect the public from monopolies, telecommunication companies then started to merge for the purpose of – you guessed it – monopolizing the industry. The 1996 act did not increase competition and lower prices; in fact, it decreased competition and raised prices in many areas, especially for cable service.

Ten years after the passage of the act, the Maurer School of Law published an article in the *Federal Communications Law Journal* titled "The Failure of Competition Under the 1996 Telecommunications Act." That article stated, "Instead of the predicted nirvana of free and open markets with numerous options for consumers and flourishing technology, we have concentrated and little marketplace choice."

Now, twenty years later, we find that not seeing the promise of competition and lower consumer prices was the least of it. Mergers, acquisitions, and takeovers have created monopolies never seen before, and media cross ownership – in essence, big companies swallowing up smaller ones – has constricted the flow of information and increased the propaganda power and fact-free media of the corporate owners, the billionaires.

For example, one of the richest men in the world, Libertarian Amazon Founder Jeff Bezos, bought *The Washington Post* in 2003. In March of 2016, *The Washington Post* ran sixteen negative stories about Bernie Sanders in sixteen hours. The point is not that Bernie Sanders was the target; the point is that Jeff Bezos directly influences the news and what we read in *The Washington Post*. As a side note, when Jeff Bezos bought *The Washington Post*, many journalists with integrity resigned; they saw the writing on the wall. By the way, it was *The Washington Post* that broke the Nixon Watergate scandal. Now, it brings us a hit piece an hour. So, the rich became d-rich, corporations became mega-corporations (News Corp, Disney, Gannett, etc.), and our numerous communication channels and how we got our news were abandoned to corporate monopolies and billionaire ideologies.

From 1912 to 1994, the U.S. Chamber of Commerce was a conservative yet reasonable organization that valued consensus-building and worked on behalf of small and large businesses alike. During World War II, the chamber president actually said collective bargaining was "an established and useful reality."

However, the Republican freshman class who rode the Contract with America coattails into elected offices wanted nothing to do with consensus-building. Unless the chamber dropped its *reasonable* tone, Republicans would start a competing organization. The chamber fell for this bullying tactic and, three years later, in 1997, Tom Donohue was hired as president. Not long after that, he said he would "make life miserable" for a Congress member and that a union leader needed a punch in the mouth (red energies!). Tom Donohue also vowed to end the chamber's days as a "sleeping giant, missing in action from many important political battles." Louis Powell would have been proud. Obviously, the *important* battles would be Republican ones, since the U.S. Chamber of Commerce was now, metaphorically speaking, *owned* by the Republican Party.

Tom Donohue flies around the globe in private jets and is chauffeured in a Lincoln while seeking to raise five million dollars a week to engage in partisan politics. In one keynote address, he said the Chamber of Commerce must "defend and advance a free-enterprise system" when it "comes under attack." The Lewis Powell manifesto is alive and well forty-five years later.

Today, by budget, the U.S. Chamber of Commerce is the largest lobbying organization in the country. We might ask: Who do the members so enthusiastically represent? They are a lobbying and campaign juggernaut for massive industries, those with the most money, such as banking, fossil fuels, tobacco, firearms, etc. Sheryl Gay Stolberg wrote in a *New York Times* article, "Pugnacious Builder of the Business Lobby":

"The Donohue chamber is in full-time attack mode," said Robert Weissman, who runs the liberal advocacy group Public Citizen. "From their point of view they've been very aggressive in advancing the interests of their constituents. From our point of view, they have very aggressively expanded the corporate grip over policy making in Washington DC."

The chamber abandoned mom-and-pop small businesses long ago. It is for the mega-large corporations that the chamber became a Velvet Coup implementation tool.

Alyssa Katz, the author of an investigative book on the U.S. Chamber of Commerce, *The Influence Machine,* said we must only follow the money; however, this is no easy feat, due to loopholes in the nonprofit laws. These loopholes do not require disclosure of the funds the chamber utilizes for lobbying and promoting candidates in elections. She further states that the Chamber of Commerce "...fights regulations on behalf of companies that don't want to be publicly associated" with corporate agendas. In other words, the chamber is a front, to hide what their members really want to accomplish, another trait of coup behavior.

The chamber, in this front role, works to reverse environmental protection, destroy unions and worker protection, create *AstroTurf* movements to hide corporate agendas, deny the climate crisis, and promote a vitriolic ideological anti-government mindset. Alyssa Katz goes on to say that the chamber has created a "right-wing monster" that "even it struggles to control" and perpetuates a conservative movement that is "destabilizing American democracy as never before."

The U.S. Chamber abandoned its original purpose under threat that an alternative, competing organization would be created now; in fact, it is facing alternative, competing organizations such as the American Sustainable Business Council with 200,000 businesses and 325,000 executives, owners and investors as members. Ironic, huh?

Another key Velvet Coup accomplishment of the decade was the demise of an 82-year-old banking law known as the Banking Act of 1933, commonly known as the Glass-Steagall Act (named after Senator Carter Glass (D-VA) and Representative Henry Steagall (D-AL)). During the long doldrums of the Great Depression, it became apparent that the Depression was primarily caused by commercial and investment banking being implemented by the same bank. The banks risked and lost depositor funds and, in doing so, destroyed millions of lives and sent the country into a downward spiral that took many years and governmental action to repair.

In other words, the *investment side* of the bank (assisting profit-driven large companies to issue stock, bonds, and trading securities) gambled with the funds from the *commercial side* (individual checking and savings accounts) of the bank and lost their depositors' money. To fix this devastating problem so a Great Depression would never happen again, the Glass-Steagall Act was passed by Congress, separating these two very different banking functions. No longer could a bank gamble with depositor savings.

Of course, bank executives did not like this separation. It is probably impossible for bankers to see a large pot of depositor savings and restrain themselves from wanting to get their hands on it. So, in 1999, Congress passed and President Bill Clinton signed the Gramm-Leach-Bliley Act, which repealed a seven-decade, successful financial safety net for we, the people, a significant event that contributed significantly to turning us into we, the *abandoned* people.

It is not difficult to understand that the Great Recession was mainly caused by the banking industry, which was once again allowed to gamble with depositor funds. Were there other factors? Yes, not the least of which were the rating companies, (Moody's and Standard and Poor's) abandoning their fiduciary responsibility and rating the junk the banks were selling as AAA. This outrageous, psychopathic behavior brought the United States economy to its knees and left millions of us behind.

The 2000s

The decade began with a coup within the Velvet Coup.

The U.S. Supreme Court, in a 5-4 vote (meaning only *one* person made the critical difference), usurped the 2000 presidential election when it instructed the State of Florida to stop counting votes and selected George W. Bush as the forty-third President of the United States of America. That long, arduous process finally ended in a travesty of justice; if all the votes had been counted, our forty-third president would have been former Vice President Albert Gore. However, the Supreme Court intervened and installed the corporations' and their owners' second man into the White House. After all, it had been a couple decades since their last man was in office. This decision was a political one and enabled the Velvet Coup to move forward.

One of the biggest secrets kept from us was the relationship between the Bush administration and the Project for the New American Century (PNAC). The project was a neoconservative creation to increase right-wing power overseas and, if that increased power just so happened to end in wars (in the name of "military strength and moral clarity"), then the military industrial complex would profit handsomely.

PNAC and the coup achieved success when ten of the twenty-five individuals who had signed the organization's statement of founding principles (including Dick Cheney, Donald Rumsfeld, and Paul Wolfowitz), were placed in key Bush administration positions. It is shocking to note that PNAC had called for regime change in Iraq in the late 1990s, and stated that the American peace "must have a secure foundation on unquestioned U.S. military preeminence." They hit a particular prescient note when they said, "The process of transformation is likely to be a long one, absent some catastrophic and catalyzing event – like a new Pearl Harbor." Then, the attacks of 9/11 happened. Interestingly, the PNAC website has now disappeared. Recounts of it may be found in *The Politics of Empire: War, Terror and Hegemony* by Joseph G. Peschek and The Center for Media and Democracy.

George W. Bush and the PNAC-aligned appointments to his administration saw their opportunity to increase the "military preeminence" when George W. Bush developed his Doctrine of Preemption as a key concept underlying the National Security Strategy and, subsequently, invaded Iraq. When the war turned out to be a worldwide disaster, PNAC quietly went away, changed its name, and morphed into PNAC 2.0, now known as the Foreign Policy Initiative.

The Bush administration went on to support the billionaire corporate coup of America with tax cuts for the wealthy; destroying governmental rules wherever possible; denying climate change (he was an oil man, after all, and nothing was going to hurt the oil industry on his watch); appointing two political ideologues and corporate zealots to the Supreme Court; replacing nearly a million federal employees to unaccountable private corporations; privatizing voting machines, immigration services, and prisons; and turning the keys of the country over to Wall Street. Sadly, this is not an exhaustive list.

If the goal was to abandon us, our needs, dreams, and our pursuit of happiness, then Bush's presidency was a great success, so much so that Wall Street's legalized theft occurred and the Great Recession followed. On its tail was a taxpayer corporate bailout, at a level never seen before. Wall Street pulled off the largest theft in history and was never held accountable. What a coup!

As Naomi Klein, a Canadian author, social activist, and filmmaker known for her political analyses and criticism of corporate globalization and corporate capitalism, related in her article, "The Bailout: Bush's Final Pillage":

> Rather than open plunder, it [Bush Administration] prefers bureaucratic instruments, such as "distressed asset" auctions and the "equity purchase program." But make no mistake: the goal...a final frantic looting of the public wealth before they hand over the keys to the safe.

On the sidelines – but still worthy of note for his role in the Velvet Coup – is Grover Norquist, the founder and president of Americans for Tax Reform and a cofounder of the Islamic Free Market Institute. In an interview on NPR's *Morning Edition*, May 25, 2001, he said, "I don't want to abolish government. I simply want to reduce it to the size where I can drag it into the bathroom and drown it in the bathtub." He perpetuated the theory that taxes are evil, even though a democracy cannot function without them. But that is the very purpose of the coup, is it not? He also gave cover to corporations in offshoring their profit to evade them. His backstory is also significant. In 1986, Norquist drafted the Taxpayer Protection Pledge to muscle and bully legislators to support Reagan's tax reforms, the goal being to cut off the source of revenue that undergirds governmental programs. How better to abolish government?

Paul Waldman, a senior writer with *The American Prospect*, said *in a Washington Post* article titled *"Nearly All the GOP Candidates Bow Down to Grover Norquist:"* "Norquist has become a kind of high priest of tax purity, with the power to declare which Republicans have kept the faith and which are vile apostates who must be cast out of the temple." Many may remember that he bullied Republican politicians with his Taxpayer

Protection Pledge. Who was he really representing when the purpose was to cut the life-blood of democracy?

The Central Free Trade Agreement (CAFTA) expanded NAFTA by adding five Central American countries to the deal: Guatemala, El Salvador, Honduras, Costa Rica, and Nicaragua with the addition of the Dominican Republic. As expected in a coup, the agreement was signed on May 28, 2004, and passed the House by *one* vote in the *middle of the night*. It was sold as a plan that would bring prosperity to Central America, but the opposite occurred. Central American nations have experienced so much violence and drug-related crime that the United States, in 2014, saw waves of children fleeing their countries to escape being murdered and raped. The Citizens Trade Campaign explained at the time:

> CAFTA reflects a push toward corporate globalization that has proven to traumatize small communities, destroy livelihoods, and destabilize the most vulnerable members of society. CAFTA would lower living standards and labor protection in the region, cost jobs, harm environmental protection, restrict access to essential medicines, harm rural communities, undermine our democratic process, exacerbate our unsustainable trade deficit, and promote privatization and deregulation of fundamental public services in Central America and the Dominican Republic.

They went on to say:

> The [Bush] administration's push for CAFTA is part of a strategy to create a Free Trade Area of the Americas (FTAA) that would cover all of the Western Hemisphere except Cuba. NAFTA and its sister agreements, CAFTA and the FTAA, all embrace irresponsible trade practices that serve corporate interests over the wellbeing of citizens throughout the hemisphere.

Trade agreements such as NAFTA, CAFTA, and the currently proposed Trans-Pacific Partnership are vehicles to the global expansion of the Velvet Coup.

Sedition is defined by Merriam-Webster as "the crime of saying, writing, or doing something that encourages people to disobey their government." I share with many others the belief that fourteen Republicans committed sedition when they met at the Caucus Room restaurant on President-elect Barack Obama's inauguration night, January 21, 2009.

The purpose of the meeting was to plan Barack Obama's political failure and, in turn, actively cause failure in the country, just to undermine and destroy his legacy. The result of their secret meeting was to hurt the country to such a degree that history would define the first black presidency as a complete disaster. Interestingly, just a few months later, the Koch brothers held a meeting with their billionaire friends to determine how they, too, could bring this failure to fruition.

Robert Draper, an American writer, correspondent for *GQ* and a contributor to *The New York Times Magazine*, listed in his book, *Do Not Ask What Good We Do: Inside the U.S. House of Representatives,* those in attendance who may have committed sedition at the Caucus Room restaurant:

> Republican House of Representatives: Eric Cantor (VA), Kevin McCarthy (CA), Paul Ryan (WI), Pete Sessions (TX), Jeb Hensarling (TX), Pete Hoekstra (MI) and Dan Lungren (CA).

And:

> Republican Senators: Jim DeMint (SC), Jon Kyl (AZ), Tom Coburn (OK), John Ensign (NV) and Bob Corker (TN). The non-lawmakers present included Newt Gingrich, several years removed from his presidential campaign, and Frank Luntz, the longtime Republican wordsmith.

Notably absent were Senate Minority Leader Mitch McConnell (R-KY) and House Minority Leader John Boehner (R-OH). However, based on their subsequent behavior, they were onboard with the plan but needed plausible deniability. Senator Elizabeth Warren (D-MA) said of the Republicans that by "abandoning the duties they swore to uphold [they] would threaten both the constitution and our democracy itself." Senator Warren said this of the Congressional Republicans not allowing a hearing on a Supreme Court nominee; however, it is applicable to just about everything the GOP has done since President Obama took office.

The "oath of office" Senator Elizabeth Warren refers to is:

> I do solemnly swear (or affirm) that I will support and defend the Constitution of the United States against all enemies, foreign and domestic; that I will bear true faith and allegiance to the same; that I take this obligation freely, without any mental reservation or purpose of evasion; and that I will well and faithfully discharge the duties of the office on which I am about to enter: so help me God.

The Caucus Room conspiracy was an overt coup of our democracy. Could those attendees be considered domestic enemies? The hard truth is that if our elected representatives are not really interested in democracy (just its false trappings) but, in reality, support corporate and oligarch dominance, then they are actively participating in the Velvet Coup and "threaten both the constitution and our democracy itself."

The 2010s

Once again, in the first year of the decade, a coup within the Velvet Coup was achieved.

It is imperative to understand that in 1886, corporations achieved *personhood* based only on a Supreme Court clerk's notation. In his book, *Unequal Protection*, Thom Hartmann wrote, "...corporate personhood was never formally enacted by any branch of the U.S. government." This enormously important issue that set the stage for today's Velvet Coup was written as a *headnote* by a court reporter, J. C. Bancroft Davis. Headnotes are not law and they are not a decision. They are notes written by a commentator, in this case a court reporter, or book publisher. Yet, today, our corporate legal structure is based only on this headnote. Astonishing.

The conservative tax-exempt, nonprofit Citizens United state that they are "dedicated to restoring our government to citizen control." In reality, though, they appear to be dedicated to serving up our government to corporate control. The organization produces television commercials and web advertisements and has created twenty-one documentaries, all with a conservative, anti-government corporate spin.

Citizens United took issue with the Bipartisan Campaign Reform Act of 2002, also known as McCain-Feingold Act. The nonprofit had made a movie about Hillary Clinton and planned to advertise and release it before the 2008 presidential election. The Federal Elections Commission (FEC) determined that it was a ninety-minute campaign ad and was in violation of the Bipartisan Campaign Reform Act of 2002. A lower court agreed and upheld the FEC ruling, but Citizens United appealed the lower court's decision to the Supreme Court.

For real, human, flesh-and-blood beings, things went frightfully wrong in the Supreme Court. Taking a giant leap, the court built on a 1976 decision known as *Buckley v. Valeo* that awarded free speech rights to money and a 1978 decision known as First National Bank of *Boston v. Bellotti*, which awarded free speech rights to corporations. The end result was that, since corporations had already achieved personhood, corporations now had no limits when it came to campaign spending.

Justice John Paul Stevens stated, in his dissenting opinion:

> At bottom, the Court's opinion is, thus, a rejection of the common sense of the American people, who have recognized a need to prevent corporations from undermining self-government since the founding, and who have fought against the distinctive corrupting potential of corporate electioneering since the days of Theodore Roosevelt. It is a strange time to repudiate that common sense. While American democracy is imperfect, few outside the majority of this Court would have thought its flaws included a dearth of corporate money in politics

Nina Totenberg, an American legal affairs correspondent for National Public Radio, in an article titled, "When Did Companies Become People? Excavating the Legal Evolution," explained that corporations have no political speech and, in fact, that a corporate corruption scandal in 1907 caused Congress to pass a law banning corporate participation in federal elections, a law maintained for seventy years. The first so-called crack came in 1978, with a 5-4 Supreme Court decision *(First National Bank of Boston v. Bellotti)*, stating that corporations have the right to spend money in state initiatives. Then, Citizens United, in another 5-4 decision gave corporations free speech rights and full rights to spend money however they want on candidate elections, at all levels of government. She accurately assessed, "It thrilled many in the business community, horrified campaign reformers, and provoked considerable mockery in the comedian classes."

Next came a Supreme Court decision, *McCutcheon v. FEC*, which allowed individuals to spend an unlimited amount of money. In a 5-4 decision, the court determined that the aggregate spending limits by individuals was a violation of free speech, thus opening the door for billionaires to buy elections. Clarence Thomas was the fifth vote and stated separately in the decision that all contribution limits are unconstitutional. That statement indicated that Justice Clarence Thomas supports legalized bribery.

Shaun McCutcheon is a rich conservative who likes to send money to political candidates who will advance his right-wing beliefs. He thought it unfair that he was limited in the amount of money he could donate to a specific candidate, so he sued. Since money had free speech rights, he believed limiting the amount of money he could donate to his political candidates violated his First Amendment rights.

The FEC position was that limits on the amount of money an individual could give to a candidate fought corruption. In other words, campaign contribution limits suppressed bribery. Of course, our corporatized court agreed with Shaun McCutcheon, and an imbalance of speech was created; in other words, those with more money could talk more than those with less. Corporations and the d-rich win again

The Alliance for Justice produced a report titled "The Roberts Court and Judicial Overreach" that states in its overview section:

> It has been well-documented that the Roberts Court consistently pursues an agenda that favors powerful corporate interests and the wealthy at the expense of everyday Americans. What is less well known is that, in order to reach these preferred outcomes, a bloc of five conservative justices has proven strikingly willing to engage in judicial activism by overreaching and twisting the law. The Supreme Court's shift is the result of a decades-long campaign by special interest groups to elevate corporate profits and private wealth over individual rights and personal freedoms.

Woven together through the decades, the U.S. Supreme Court gave personhood to corporations, free speech rights to money, and the ability for corporations and the wealthy (even foreign investors) to spend unlimited amounts of cash to influence our politics. Five of the justices handed corporations and their billionaire owners nearly unlimited power. Even when given a second chance to change their disastrous Citizens United ruling, they doubled down and reversed a 100-year-old Montana corporate spending law, one Montana wanted to keep in place (so much for the Republican mantra of advocating for states' rights!), confirming that corporations are people with First Amendment rights. What more could a corporate coup want?

In 1971, the year the Velvet Coup was launched, there were 175 lobbyists. The numbers have grown steadily through the decades, and today, there are approximately 13,000 registered lobbyists. The money corporations spend on lobbying, $2.6 billion, is more than the Senate and House operating budgets combined. Many corporations have so many lobbyists that they can be everywhere they need to be, at the same time, fighting or supporting bills that either benefit or detract from their business.

Lee Drutman, a senior fellow in the program on political reform at New America and author of *The Business of America Is Lobbying*, related in his article, "How Corporate Lobbyists Conquered American Democracy":

> For every dollar spent on lobbying by labor unions and public-interest groups together, large corporations and their associations now spend thirty-four dollars. Of the 100 organizations that spend the most on lobbying, 95 consistently represent business.
>
> The self-reinforcing quality of corporate lobbying has increasingly come to overwhelm every other potentially countervailing force.

In 2006, I recall being shocked when I saw John Boehner (R-OH) handing out checks from tobacco lobbyists to colleagues on the floor of the House of Representatives, literally helping lobbyists sway and bribe votes. As noted by NumberOf.net, by 2010, there were nearly twenty-six lobbyists for every member of Congress not counting the Congress members themselves, like John Boehner. It makes one wonder how often something like this happens.

Each and every one of us has a personal decision to make: Do we want our elected representatives to make choices and laws that improve the quality of our lives, or do we want to abandon ourselves to the quality of life corporations will create in the vacuum we create by not keeping our elected officials accountable?

It is my argument that if someone like Donald Trump, Michael Bloomberg, or any other multibillionaire becomes president, these entitled authoritarians who do not see the world the same as we do or possess the same values as we do, will make the Velvet Coup completed. If we do not want this to happen, we must vote people into office who will reverse corporate personhood and the Citizens United decision and enact laws that benefit the middle class and not just billionaires and corporations.

In our current decade, the long game is nearly complete. The Velvet Coup's undisguised launch in 1971, with the Powell manifesto, has seamlessly marched us to the point that our democracy is in a precarious state. It is still possible to pull back from the brink of becoming a complete oligarchy, as long as we stand up and stand up now!

Stand Up Activities

Below, for your consideration, are several suggested Stand Up Activities. For a further explanation of the Keep/Start/Stop organization tool, please see Chapter One. After reading this chapter, you may think of additional activities readers can implement. If you'd like to share your brilliant constructive, compelling and creative ideas, please do so at: www.facebook.com/americaabandoned.

KEEP:

1. Keep aware of trade agreements and what they actually will do. This might take some work on your part, but trade agreements also have a tremendous impact on you, your job and your family.

2. Keep fighting to make Wall Street accountable for the theft they perpetrated on the middle class. Make the president and attorney general pursue indictments.

START:

1. Start to follow trade agreements. They impact your daily life, if not your job. NAFTA had a disastrous effect on our country, but the trade agreements with South Korea and China have been equally disastrous. One to especially watch out for and fight is the Trans Pacific Partnership (TPP). I am puzzled and disappointed by the fact that President Obama advocates for the TPP. It has been called "NAFTA on steroids," costing the United States more jobs. Shockingly, it was negotiated by corporations in secrecy and creates a court comprised of corporate attorneys who will hear disagreements between countries, the result being that the United States gives up its sovereignty to these corporate attorneys. The passing of the TPP will achieve corporate globalization (http://www.citizen.org/TPP).

2. A tragic example of how the United States has already lost quite a bit of its sovereignty, under NAFTA, is when the Congress passed a law to protect dolphins from being killed by the tuna industry. A handful of Mexican tuna millionaires claimed that the

requirement was an unfair "trade restriction" and the case went to the World Trade Organization (WTO) for resolution. What the Mexican government representing their wealthy tuna fishing industry wanted was to be allowed to chase, net and kill dolphins, as they fished for tuna, and still be able to claim the tuna to be "Dolphin Safe." A corporate court heard this issue at the WTO. The corporate attorneys assigned to the court sided with the tuna industry (surprise, surprise) and the United States lost the case. Now, even if you happen to see "Dolphin Safe" on a tuna can label, we really cannot trust that it is, in fact, true. What is particularly sickening, is when the dolphin pods try to escape the chase and the tuna nets, the baby dolphins are unable to swim as fast, so they are left behind, lose their mothers, their pod, and either starve to death or are eaten by sharks. Thousands of dolphins die each year because NAFTA was drafted so that the United States could not pass a law that would protect the dolphins over corporate profits. Issues like this will be much worse if the Trans Pacific Partnership trade agreement is approved by Congress. Goodbye, American sovereignty.

STOP:

1. Stop sitting on the sidelines, if you feel you are, now that you've learned about the Velvet Coup. It can only continue to succeed if no one knows about what has happened during the past several decades. Discover what lights the fire in your belly and seek out the organizations that share that fire.

One Marvelous Question

After reading this chapter, if you were going to do one thing marvelously well to move forward, what would that one thing be?

We need to be mosquitos.

CHAPTER FIVE

Abandon Your Vote, Ruin Your Country

*"If you think you're too small to have an impact,
try going to bed with a mosquito in the room."*

Anita Roddick

Instead of frogs, we need to be mosquitos.

Elections matter. Those who do not want us to vote desperately want us to believe our vote will make no difference, and they will go to great lengths to stop us. When I meet someone who says they do not vote, I ask them why are they throwing their birthright away? To date, no one has given me an answer, let alone a thoughtful one. They appear dumbfounded. They willingly abandon their citizenship birthright, browbeaten by the Paul Weyrichs of the world into believing that voting is not worthwhile. They have become cynical about politics. Danny Glover, a well-known actor and activist, wisely said, "Power wants to diminish expectations." The people in power want to do everything they can to diminish the importance of voting.

How will our country's politics ever improve or reach its potential when a large percentage of us abandon our democratic responsibility? Voting is a birthright that Americans who came before us fought and died for, and a birthright admired and desired by billions of people around the world. Founding father, Thomas Paine said, "Voting is the heartbeat of democracy." What is going on with the scant numbers showing up at the polls?

A Center for American Progress article, "Race and Beyond: Why Young, Minority, and Low-Income Citizens Don't Vote," explained:

> Civic engagement – best exemplified by voting – depends upon an engaged and informed citizenry. But in America, it's hard to be a

good citizen if you're poor, ignored, or vilified. Life is just too hard to worry about lofty issues such as public policies and partisan political intrigue. Indeed, among too many poor and minority Americans, voting and choosing elected officials just isn't viewed as essential to their lives.

Millions of the "poor, ignored, or vilified" have dropped out of the political process. I cannot argue that they do not have a right to feel cynical, for they are abandoned populations. For decades, powerful forces focused on taking all the fun out of being a citizen, and those forces have won.

As mentioned in Chapter Two, to win elections, it has been a clear Republican strategy, since the 1980s (see Goo Goo Syndrom) to stop as many people as possible from voting. Make it hard, uninteresting, and ineffectual. Make it confusing, discouraging, and boring. Make it frustrating. Most of all, make it seem useless, a chore, and a waste of time and effort. The more successful these strategists are, the more the d-rich and corporations will be able to take over our political system. Then, more of the "poor, ignored, and vilified" drop out. It is a vicious cycle, one that is unsustainable for our democracy. The billionaires and corporations understand how important it is to be in control of the United States government, but those battered by anti-voting subliminal messaging do not. The more they shamelessly manipulate people to voluntarily give away their power and keep branding voting as worthless, the more power the wealthy will possess. It is just that simple.

The decline in unions, as organization hubs, has also had an enormous and catastrophic impact on voter turnout and inequality. In an article written by Sean McElwee, a research associate at Demos, titled "One Big Reason for Voter Turnout Decline and Income Inequality: Smaller Unions," stated:

> The decline in unionization is due to several factors but research suggests that politics played the most important role. David Jacobs and Lindsey Myers, sociologists at Ohio State University, find that "reductions in union strength attributable to policies endorsed by Reagan and by later neoliberal administrations helped create the acceleration in inequality after 1981." Laws like so-called "right-to-work" legislation and Supreme Court rulings such as 2014's *Harris v. Quinn* have gutted union protections. The impact of this decline on widening inequality is clear, but the reason for this connection is not often clearly sketched. While conventional

wisdom holds that unions bolstered wages through collective bargaining, new evidence suggests that unions played an equally important role as the "organizing centers of the working class."

The empirical research on the impact of unions on inequality is clear. As the Economic Policy Institute (EPI) recently showed, there is a clear correlation between the decline in union membership and Gini coefficients (a standard measure of inequality ranging from 1, absolute inequality and 0, absolute equality) at the state level in the United States. In a 2012 study published in *The American Sociological Review*, Thomas Volscho and Nathan Kelly find that "the rise of the super-rich is the result of rightward-shifts in Congress, the decline of labor unions, lower tax rates on high incomes, increased trade openness, and asset bubbles in stock and real estate markets." However, their model shows that of these variables, union membership is the most significant factor.

Our Founding Fathers' Personal Sacrifice

Even though he is unaware of his influence, Thom Hartmann has been a mentor of mine since his days at Air America Radio. I have listened to his syndicated radio show almost daily for over a decade. After so many years of listening, one gets to know a person. He is a man of integrity, principles and is brilliant. I credit him with much of what I have learned about this country and the struggles so many of us experience, sometimes needlessly, at the hands of those in power.

I was surprised when I heard Thom become emotionally overwhelmed when reading a section of one of his books on his March 2, 2016, radio show, *Hour 2*. I had never heard him break down on the air like that before. The passage from *What Would Jefferson Do? A Return to Democracy* discussed what our founding fathers sacrificed to found this country and how disappointing it is that today, so many citizens choose not to vote or are unwilling to make the extra effort to overcome the roadblocks the d-rich and powerful have currently cemented into place.

Thom Hartmann wrote that the average age of the 56 signers of the Declaration of Independence was 33. They were idealistic, determined liberal radicals. The Boston Tea Party had initiated forces for a liberal democracy (sad that its name has been co-opted today by ultraconservatives). The conservatives of the day wanted to stay a British colony, but:

> ...these liberal radicals believed in both individual liberty and societal obligations. A nation must care for the lives of its own, guarantee liberty, and ensure its citizens happiness – a radical concept that had never before appeared in any nation's founding documents.

> The signers wrote in the declaration, "We mutually pledge to each other our lives, our fortunes and our sacred honor," and it was a simple statement of fact. The day they signed that document, each legally became a traitor and was sentenced to death for treason by the legal government that controlled their lands and their homes.

These brave men created a country the world had never seen before. The idea that people would govern themselves without an oligarch, monarch, or dictator in charge was revolutionary. However, binding together their lives, fortunes, and sacred honor turned out to be sadly prophetic for some of them:

- One of the wealthiest, Thomas Nelson (VA), died in debt at age 50 because he had mortgaged his home to pay for the Revolution, but the British seized his home and lands and damaged it so severely that he was unable to repay his mortgage.

- A Philadelphia merchant, Robert Morris, lost 150 ships at sea during the war that led to his ruin.

- Signers William Ellery (RI), Benjamin Harrison (VA), George Clymer (PA), Philip Livingston (NY), Lyman Hall (GA), and Francis Hopkinson (NJ) lost everything for their bravery.

- John Hart (NY) died alone and miserable three years later. His wife died soon before he signed the Declaration of Independence, and his thirteen children found themselves scattered among sympathetic families to hide them from the British and conservative loyalists. John Hart never saw any of his children again.

- Seventeen of our founding fathers were financially wiped out by the war they had begun with England because of their signing of the Declaration of Independence.

Thom Hartmann went on to explain:

> Altogether, nine of the men in that room died, and four
> lost their children as a direct result of putting their names
> to the Declaration of Independence. Every single one had
> to flee his home, and, after the war, twelve returned to
> find only rubble.

> After the war was over and the conservatives had fled to
> Canada and England, the survivors of the new American
> nation met to put into final form the legal structure of the
> nation they had just birthed. It was not to be a nation of
> cynical, selfish libertarians who believed the highest value
> was individual freedom and independence from society,
> or the greatest motivator was greed. It was not to be a
> kingdom. It was not to be a theocracy, where religious
> leaders made the rules (as had been several of the states).
> And it was not to be a feudal nation ruled by the rich.

After relating Thom Hartmann's story of our founding fathers' sacrifice, I
find that I, too, become teary-eyed for those men who lost their children,
their wives, their businesses, their fortunes, their homes, and their very
lives to birth this country. It was an act of love for a better future for their
generation and the generations of today. Many more of us should repay
our debt to them by voting.

Citizen Voter Types: Which One Are You?

Without question, there are "poor, ignored, and vilified" populations
that are just holding it together, but then there are those who are simply
not able to keep it together, such as the embarrassingly large homeless
population in this country. These citizen populations have had so many
cards stacked against them that, even though I would hope they would
vote to voice their desires and, thus, try to make a positive impact on
their circumstances, they cannot be blamed for being unable to do so. Our
society has abandoned them, and the barriers imposed by newly enacted
voter ID laws are too great.

I do understand that voter apathy is a serious issue. Why vote when there
are powerful political, religious, industry and ideological forces (PRIIF)

convincing us that we should give up this critical practice? The candidates are all crooks, right? The ballot issues have contorted descriptions: No might mean yes, and yes might mean no. There is also the lesser-of-two-evils predicament. Worse, Republican-held state legislatures may have rigged the system in ways that make it nearly impossible to vote, as Alabama did by requiring a driver's license to vote and then closing thirty-one motor vehicle offices in primarily black areas.

Many of us think our vote will not count, and that is a convenient excuse as to why we should abandon our responsibility to vote. Extending this rationalization to a broader interpretation: If everyone thought that, it would become a self-fulfilling prophecy. Obviously, if you do not vote, it cannot be counted, right? The Democratic Party in Mississippi knows otherwise.

In November of 2015, Representative Bo Eaton and Republican Mark Tullos were running for the seat in the District 79 state legislature. Each candidate received exactly 4,589 votes. As per state law, a tiebreaker game of chance was held, and Eaton (D), who drew the long straw, was declared the winner. Of course the Republicans were not happy about this, even though state law requires it, silly as it is. They challenged the result of their candidate drawing the short straw. After a convoluted process, by January of 2016, the Republican legislature unseated the Democrat and replaced him with the Republican, despite the fact that the Mississippi Election Commission and the Mississippi secretary of state had certified the election results. Since these manipulative games do happen, we must *always* vote. None of this drawing-straws business would have happened if the election had not been so close.

There are, however, a large number of people who just cannot be bothered to take the time to learn about issues or candidates at the local, state, and federal levels, so they willingly abandon their votes. This is when the Weyrichs of the world win. There are also those who have registered to vote, indicating some interest in participating in the democratic process, then stay home. Again, the Weyrichs of the world win. In addition, there are those who need to be truly excited about an issue or candidate before they are motivated to turn out or, in some cases, just mail in their vote. This also is yet another victory for the Weyrichs. The end result is that three populations willingly abandon their vital voting power.

After a recent local election, a newspaper article quoted the Registrar of

Voters forecast for the election, saying that only a 35 percent turnout was expected because "…there are not a lot of hot issues on the primary ballot."

This meant 65 percent of registered voters were abandoning their votes by staying home, staying at work, or believing their vote did not count, or else there were not enough "hot" or exciting issues to warrant their time. They totally missed the main point: Voting *is* the hot issue, because so many nefarious forces are stealing it. In fact, it is the hot issue of all issues in a democracy. In 1996, Taiwan had its first democratic presidential election with a 76 percent voter turnout. It was a spectacular level of voter participation. The same year, the voter turnout for the U.S. presidential election was 49 percent, and we invented the concept.

What would this country look like if America had a 76 percent voting rate? Would the multibillionaires be in control of Congress, the Supreme Court and, thus, the country, as they are now? Would programs that support the health and wellbeing of the people be constantly under attack? Would numerous tax cuts for the d-rich and the opposite strategy of austerity for the middle class ever have occurred? Would we never have abandoned our democracy?

"There are two types of Americans: Those that vote and those that don't," Bill Maher once proclaimed on his television show. After hearing this simple statement of fact, I felt it required further thought and developed four Citizen Voter Types:

- Courageous
- Concerned
- Casual
- Caustic

As you read further, try to determine where you fall among these types.

Courageous Voter

The Courageous Voter is the highest form of an American voter, a voter and an activist, with time available to them while they concurrently manage their lives. Marie Rutkoski, an American children's writer, said, "Happiness depends on being free, and freedom depends on being courageous." The Courageous Voter knows that being well versed on the issues, actively discussing those issues with others, and not missing an election, whether is it a midterm or presidential year, is the *ultimate* demonstration of "being free."

Courageous Citizen Voters are Living-in-the-Black voters who follow positive, purposeful, principled, and serious candidates. They possess enough courage that they will not be swayed by the entertainment news media and their ratings-driven stories meant to emotionally manipulate the voter. They are proactive with their emotions and know "a more perfect union" is only achievable by voting. They cannot be demoralized because they know the democratic process is more important than their ego and are motivated by intrinsic reasons. They take an inside-out approach to voting. They are more likely to be repulsed than persuaded by inflammatory candidate rhetoric, as they are keenly aware that policy issues at all levels of government determine the quality of their lives, not the bombast of rhetoric. They are continuous learners, open to new ideas, and they realize voting is simply not optional.

Courageous Voters have developed excellent information literacy skills, are sober-minded, and have fine-tuned internal radar for malarkey. They know elections have consequences and look up lies on fact-checking websites such as the Pulitzer Prize Politifact website for their "Pants on Fire" rating. They vote the entire ballot, even the judgeships, and do not just vote on so-called hot issues. They put their representatives' and senators' numbers and email addresses in their smartphones and do not hesitate to contact them on important issues. They are citizen lobbyists. They do not leave politics to politicians without their constructive democratic voice being heard when public policy is written. They firmly understand that our founding fathers wanted citizens to have individual liberty *and* societal obligations and, therefore, are angry that their freedom to vote is being methodically stolen. Courageous Voters understand that democracy is a not a spectator sport.

In April of 2016, the cofounders of Ben & Jerry's ice cream were arrested at the Democracy Awakening protest in Washington DC. Their website stated, "It all comes down to a simple idea that we believe in whole-heartedly: If you care about something, you have to be willing to risk it all – your reputation, your values, your business – for the greater good." They and everyone attending the Democracy Awakening protest are not spectators and exemplify the Courageous Citizen Voter.

Concerned Voter

The Concerned Citizen Voter votes in all elections because they are concerned about their future, their children's future, and the direction of the country. They stay on top of the issues throughout the year, are sober-minded, and recognize nonsense and crazy talk. They typically will not be swayed by inflammatory rhetoric and think it is sad that politicians do not exemplify better behavior. They fight demoralization, are motivated by intrinsic reasons, and also take an inside-out approach to voting. They educate themselves about policy, though perhaps not as deeply as Courageous Voters do. They will listen to political discussions with the intent to learn, and they discuss issues with others.

The Concerned Citizen Voter pursues an understanding of what is behind a ballot issue or the background of a candidate. They may also look for lies on issues and candidates. They may not conduct the same level of research as the Courageous Citizen Voter or be as proactive on the issues; however, they do understand the importance of being heard by their elected representatives. They may be concerned about private information becoming public and more reticent to become advocates because of it. They may hold their elected leaders accountable occasionally by calling their office or emailing on an issue. They will respond to emailed requests to sign petitions, via *armchair advocacy*, but they generally will not write original letters to their elected representatives on behalf of issues, except on rare occasions.

Predominantly, Concerned Voters Live in the Black and support serious and well-prepared candidates. They are not knee-jerk voters. They, too, understand that democracy is delicate and that voting is their primary expression of power.

During elections, my grandfather used to say, "Vote for me. I'll take care of you!" Courageous and Concerned Citizen Voters do not fall for the candidate who says what they want to hear, without specific policies to back it up, those who expect us to trust them only because they claim they can "take care" of us.

Casual Voter

The Casual Voter voluntarily suppresses their vote and does not vote in every election. Unknowingly, they are playing into the hands of those who do not want everyone to vote. They take an outside-in approach to voting. This voter type can be fooled by the strength of a candidate's charisma and will likely not take the time to ascertain the candidate's character or anti-character behavior. As I define it, *anti-character behavior* is an intentional act to not do what is right, but the act does not reach the level of criminality or, if it does, it is executed due to no perceived accountability will follow.

Casual Voters do not pay attention to politics or issues facing the country unless it is campaign season, most likely a presidential campaign season at that. I once heard someone say he was not going to vote simply because there was "not anything interesting on the ballot." Upon hearing this, I thought, *Good grief! It isn't a dinner menu!*

Casual Voters likely will not take the time to utilize resources that are easily available to them, such as the internet. They depend on political ads to inform them, so their knowledge about the candidates and issues is superficial at best. The Casual Voter will not look more deeply into whether or not an ad is telling the truth or who sponsored it. Lack of in-depth research leads to being misinformed because they believe and fall for the emotional manipulation contained within the ad. They may be also called Low-Information Voters. As President John F. Kennedy once said, "The ignorance of one voter in a democracy impairs the security of all."

It was the Casual Citizen Voters who lost the 2014 midterm elections for the Democratic Party, because they decided not to vote and preferred to stay home. These voters changed America that year. The Senate flipped from Democratic to Republican dominance and, many Republican governors were elected at the same time. It was the lowest Democratic voter turnout since 1942.

We can assume Casual Citizen Voters want to be good citizens because they registered to vote, but they only vote when it is convenient. The 2016 California presidential primary was an example. These registered voters reacted to a few influences and then, because of them, tossed their votes away. The Associated Press called the winner of the Democratic primary the night before the election; in my view, that is media malpractice. They could have waited a day and let the public vote in the seven states that held primaries that day. Shame on the media executives who made that call! Also, independent voters were confused about how to vote: Many probably did not take the time to realize they might not be able to vote in a primary election unless they were registered in a political party.

Paul Mitchell, President of research firm Political Data, Inc., may have described the Casual Voter best: "It kind of reminds me of the person who goes into a diner, starving, and orders fifteen pancakes, and then, when the food arrives, they have a cup of coffee and a piece of toast."

A real damage the Casual Citizen Voter can wield is not following through on their civic duty to vote for the candidates and issues on the rest of the ballot, known as the *down ticket* or *down ballot*. The casual nature of these voters affects local and state issues significantly. Since they were inspired by only the presidential campaign, they likely did not study the rest of the issues facing them, so they continue with their day and ignore the election. If they do vote, they may skip the hard ballot questions because they did not take the time to research all the issues, especially the judges; the Casual Voter most likely does not realize judgeships possess profound power over them and can have a direct impact on their daily lives.

They may also not understand our country's history and its applications for today. Many young voters fall into this category because they are more likely to vote for the top of the ticket but not the down ballot. They may be energized by a candidate and know their party affiliation, but other elections like judgeships and initiatives require proper preplanning and research to understand what is asked of them, and they are less likely to do the work ahead of time. In an article written by Jud Lounsbury, a political reporter and former press secretary to several politicians, "Young Wisconsin Voters Aren't in It Just for Bernie, Despite What the Media Says," he explains:

> The reality is that younger voters tend to not participate in down-ticket races, especially those like the Wisconsin Supreme Court race, which was nonpartisan and not marked with "D" or "R." The conventional wisdom is that, as voters age, they become more familiar with different office holders, and their participation increases.

When asked, Casual Citizen Voters may have an opinion about an issue, but they are not motivated enough when election time arrives to arrange their life to vote on that issue. They can fall into the knowing-doing trap of thinking they have *done* something about an issue because they have *talked* about that issue. The Casual Voter reminds me of the wisdom of Dr. Seuss: "Unless someone like you cares a whole awful lot, nothing is going to get better."

Caustic Voter

Caustic Voters are a danger to democracy because they vote with anger. They are Living-in-the-Red voters who are reactive, vindictive, or irrational and follow candidates – and other people in positions of power – who reflect those feelings. Caustic Citizen Voters do not move the country forward in a positive direction. They vote for candidates or issues that will also implement Living-in-the-Red policies that may hurt other people, such as wanting to deport immigrants who entered the country illegally but whose children are citizens, thereby separating children from their parents. Tough luck, kids!

The Caustic Voter can be fooled by the strength of a candidate's personality and may be willfully blind to their character or anti-character behaviors. They are drawn to their candidate or political issue because it hits an emotional or fear-based resonance within them. They take a reactive outside-in approach to voting. They will not research positions or potential lies (and probably would not recognize a lie anyway) because the new information could challenge their belief system. They are reactive, and it is Red emotion that feeds them. They fall prey to weaponized hate delivered by some politicians and media outlets. Politicians do this to foment their base, and the media does it for ratings. Neither is healthy for citizens or democracy.

Since Caustic Citizen Voters do not sincerely look at an issue, and they are particularly susceptible to authoritarianism or tribalism. I recently heard Norman Ornstein, a political scientist and resident scholar at the American Enterprise Institute, call these voters the "tribal electorate," as for them, what the tribe believes is more important than the facts. Amanda Taub, a reporter for Vox.com (Vox Media, Inc.), wrote in her article, "American Authoritarianism: The Political Science Theory that Explains Trump Rally Violence":

> Much of the answer can be found in academic research into political behavior that political scientists refer to as authoritarianism. According to this theory, authoritarians are a group of voters who prize order and conformity, and feel deeply threatened by social change, influxes of outsiders, and hierarchies being upended.

When threatened, authoritarians support strongman leaders who promise drastic, decisive action to cast out outsiders and restore order.

Those Americans who respond to hate-talk are also Caustic Citizen Voters. They are easily ginned up by anyone who manipulates them to hate someone or something else. Rush Limbaugh, fostering hatred toward a Democratic president, said, "Socks is the White House cat. But did you know there is also a White House dog?" He was referring to Chelsea Clinton, when she was a child growing up in the White House. The hate-oriented Caustic Voters laughed at that comment. It is easy for a manipulator to foster anger and victim mentality in these voters and direct that anger toward *the other*.

At this time, Donald Trump is campaigning for President of the United States. A joint survey by Public Religion Research Institute and *The Atlantic* magazine found that 65 percent of his supporters embrace "a leader willing to break some rules to set things right." Oh my! This is a perfect example of Caustic Voter thinking. Then, when the rules are broken, how can they be certain things will be made right the exact way they want them made right? One of the reasons "things" are not "right" is because people are not following the rules in the first place. Either that, or they are ignoring them or are lobbying to get them off the books. Since when do two wrongs make a right?

The one-issue voter can also be categorized as a Caustic Citizen Voter. Regardless of the issue at hand, a one-issue voter does not recognize the complexities of a democracy and is, therefore, corrosive to society as a whole. They may be good people with good intentions, but they choose to live in a more simplistic frame of reality. They may also have an equally corrosive impact on an election because they can tip it to a minority view when, at the same time, Casual Citizen Voters choose not to participate in an election.

There is another type of voter I could categorize as a Caustic Voter. The founding president of the Public Religion Research Institute, Dr. Robert P. Jones, calls them *Nostalgia Voters*. Once called Value Voters, these voters believe the country has declined since the 1950s, and they romanticize those times. They forget that the country lived with the threat of nuclear war (duck and cover!), the cold war with Russia, that vaccines and medicine were not as advanced, or that the cell phone and GPS system they utilize in their daily lives had not yet been invented, etc.

In regard to the 2016 presidential election, Nostalgia Voters believe yesterday was better than today. Thus, when presented with the "make America great again" message, they respond specifically to the "again." In so doing, they overlook that the candidate who promotes that branding was divorced twice, curses in campaign speeches, incites violence, and owns gambling casinos. The deep fear they possess about living in today's world causes them to throw reason to the wind and caustically vote for candidates who clearly are unqualified for the job.

Cynical Citizen

The Cynical Citizen is a nonvoter. In a workshop I attended, Stephen R. Covey said *cynicism* is a "wound of the heart." Cynical Citizens feel they have been unforgivably abandoned by their country, so their hearts are injured. They may very well be right in their assessment. Thus, they see no reason to participate in the political process. They are too distrustful, resentful, and bitter to do so. Tragically, the bottom-half earners of the working scale do not vote. They have given up. They are unable to see the extraordinary power they would possess over their lives if they collectively participated. Cynical Citizens consistently throw their birthright away, significantly aiding and abetting the Weyrichs of the country by willingly staying away from the ballot box. I recently read a cartoon, *The Duplex*, in which a car bore a bumper sticker that read, "Don't blame me. I never vote." By not voting, they unknowingly exacerbate the problems in our country and for themselves.

In the fiscal sense, they would be called freeloaders, individuals who take advantage of another's generosity without giving anything in return. In a democracy, someone who does not vote is a democratic freeloader, someone who takes advantage of living in a democracy without participating in return. Cynical Citizens, who have abandoned their right to vote, have become nonentities in our democracy. They are not citizens, in the full sense of the word. They may be citizens by birth, a gift from our forefathers, but they do not earn their citizenship by voting. When we do not vote, we do not count. It is as simple as that. Is this really what the Cynical Voter wants?

In discussing cynicism, I am not saying there is nothing about which to be cynical. There are numerous reasons to feel cynicism, not the least of which is the Citizens United Supreme Court decision. President Obama said of the decision:

> A reason that people are cynical is money in politics. The Supreme Court issued a ruling – Citizens United – that allowed super PACs and very wealthy individuals to just finance all these ads that you guys see on TV all the time. Half the time, nobody knows who's funding them…and that makes you cynical.

It is paramount for us to realize what cynicism is and how it feels so we may step out of its grip. By way of their cynicism, Cynical Citizens are Living-in-the-Red citizens who promote apathy in society: Why vote? Nothing will change. People will say anything or do anything to win, right? Their victim mentality, justified or not, is insidious because of their collective harm upon society. Instead of an inside-out or outside-in approach to voting, they have simply checked out on democracy, and because abandonment abhors a vacuum, powerful, self-serving forces, billionaires, and corporations move in where these American nonvoters have moved out. Henry Neumann, a British explorer, hunter, and travel writer, said, "To live heroically is its own compensation in which all can share. In every person, there is a slumbering hero." Cynical Citizens need to know they are slumbering heroes; my message to them is to not throw away their Nineteenth Amendment rights!

Bill Moyers, an American journalist and political commentator, said in his article "Voting Is Important: Here's Why" of the 2008 elections:

> We know tragically how bullets can change the course of history. Bullets cost us Lincoln, John F. Kennedy, his brother Robert, [and] Martin Luther King.

> But ballots change history, too, and when I say our votes matter, I speak not out of some mystical belief in "the will of the people" but because elections – imperfect as they are, twisted and smattered by smears and lies and counter-lies galore, subject to distortion and manipulation – elections offer an alternative to violence, they keep us from coming apart altogether.

> It does matter who is elected and that our votes just might make a difference in the outcome.

The 2016 presidential election has seen a record number of new voter registrations. This is excellent news. The question is: After the election, what voter type will they become? Are they only interested in the 2016 election for its reality show, bizarre characteristics? Post-election, will they become Casual Voters or even Cynical Nonvoters? Or will they commit to being a lifelong Concerned or Courageous Voter? One is easy; the other is hard.

It is important for me to say, at this point, that I am not talking about good and bad people. A Courageous Citizen Voter could be a jerk, and a Caustic Citizen Voter could be well liked and constructive in everyday life. My focus is on their approach to voting and participating in our democracy.

Stand Up Activities

Below, for your consideration, are several suggested Stand Up Activities. For a further explanation of the Keep/Start/Stop organization tool, please see Chapter One. After reading this chapter, you may think of additional activities readers can implement. If you'd like to share your brilliant constructive, compelling and creative ideas, please do so at: www. facebook.com/americaabandoned.

KEEP:

1. Keep in mind that we are citizens first – then shoppers, movie-goers, students, employees, church-goers, etc. Engage. Be the mosquito. Vote! A good friend of my father's passed away and, since I knew him, too, when I saw his obituary in the newspaper, I stopped to read it. To my surprise, written at the end was a statement explaining that he was a proud Democrat and that he asked everyone to vote. How important is it to vote? Important enough for it to be the last message from a caring person to the world.

2. Keep the faith and know that your vote counts, even though there are powerful forces who want you to believe otherwise and keep the pressure on your representatives after elections. The squeaky wheel does get greased. Chris Hedges, American journalist, author and activist, said: "It is our job to make the powerful frightened of us."

START:

1. Start now. Decide if you are primarily Living in the Black or the Red. None of us can live in either of these internal environments all the time, but where do you primarily reside? Your vote will follow.

2. Start reflecting on what Citizen Voter Type you are. Can you move up a notch?

   a. If you are a Courageous Voter, I commend you! Keep up the good work and passion for the democratic process. I still ask, though, can you move your advocacy up a notch? Can you add one more issue you are concerned about into your life and be the change for this new issue?

   b. If you are a Concerned Voter, can you move to being a Courageous Voter by adopting one or two issues you are passionate about and begin to take proactive action? A fabulous resource is *The Citizen Lobbyist – A How-to Manual for Making Your Voice Heard in Government* by Amanda Kneif.

   c. If you are a Casual Voter, can you move up a notch to a Concerned Voter and make it a priority to vote in every election, whether it contains hot issues or not? Can you promise to spend a little more time researching issues and candidates? Ask for advice from friends you know and admire, those who participate more than you do in the democratic process. I am sure they will be delighted to be of assistance to you. An excellent resource is the League of Women Voters, which is certainly not just for women. Since 1920, this nonpartisan organization has been dedicated to improving "government and engaging all citizens in the decisions that impact their lives."

   d. If you are a Cynical Citizen, can you repair your wounded heart and rejoin our democracy? It is of particular importance for the Cynical Citizen to realize what our founding fathers sacrificed and lost to form our great country. Reengaging is not easy. You are a slumbering hero. The issues may seem overwhelming, but as Dale Carnegie once said, "By becoming interested in the cause, we are less likely to dislike the effect." As recommended above, seek friends and nonpartisan resources to get started. Make sure you are not living in a news silo, watching the same television or streaming stations and news shows, reading the same newspapers or apps, and listening to the same radio stations day in and day out. Mix it up! You may not be receiving information that is in your best interest.

e. As Charles M. Blow, *New York Times* op-ed columnist, said in an op-ed titled, "We Should Be in a Rage," "There is an astounding paradox in it: Too many of those with the least economic and cultural power don't fully avail themselves of their political power. A vote is the great equalizer, but only when it is cast."

f. Besides, voting is our one superpower against the d-rich and powerful corporations. Register here: http://register. rockthevote.com. Thomas Paine said, "Voting is the heartbeat of democracy. [Without it], man would be reduced to slavery."

3. Start electing serious people when you vote. No matter what Citizen Voter Type you are, select serious candidates who will work for us all, not a smaller faction such as moneyed interests. We need more serious people in office. Serious candidates may have more boring political ads, but less-serious candidates have more bizarre ways to try to convince you, diverting your attention away from the issues, such as Carly Fiorina's "Demon Sheep" political campaign ad. We need serious people doing serious work on our behalf and the country. Serious people also do their jobs and do them thoroughly and well. Currently, one party is refusing to work (shutting down the government, not passing bills, not holding hearings for judgeships, etc.). What would happen if you showed up on the job but refused to complete your work responsibilities? You would be fired!

4. Start to make voting honorable again. Be excited. Know that this is your moment to have your voice heard. Encourage others. Hold

voter parties and discuss candidates and ballot initiatives. A great resource is the nonpartisan League of Women Voters, www.lgv. org.

5. Start advocating loudly for campaign finance reform. If we had meaningful campaign finance reform we would know our system was not rigged and we would feel more secure about how our country is run. Enter your representative's phone numbers in your smartphone. Call them and be the mosquito, buzzing about reform. Lack of reform is the root of losing our democracy and the rise of the corporatocracy. We must know where our politicians' money comes from, and until we do, we must cleverly research the SuperPAC and donors who provide campaign funds. Our vote will follow. Fight to overturn the Supreme Court's Citizens United decision. We must forbid corporations from funding elections. Corporations are not people. Join End Citizens United at: http://endcitizensunited.org.

6. Start recognizing *oppo dumps*, opposition research that is dumped a few days before an election in the hopes of confusing voters. This does work, as the misinformation is disseminated so close to an election that it cannot be refuted in time. It is not illegal and is a political manipulation strategy. Recognize it for what it is and ignore it.

7. Start your own research on the subject. An excellent resource that explains the voting process and the tools you will need is the book, *Me, the People,* by Lisa Fontana. Other sources are the Election, Public Opinion, & Voting Behavior website: http://community. apsanet.org/epovb/home and Citizens for Responsibility and Ethics in Washington (CREW) at: www.citizensforethics.org.

8. Start your own campaign. For Courageous Voters and aspiring Courageous Voters, an excellent place to begin is to summon the help of SumOfUs, a "movement of consumers, workers, and shareholders, speaking with one voice to counterbalance the growing power of large corporations." Find out how this global community can support you here: http://sumofus.org.

STOP:

1. Stop paying attention to political ads. Did you know these are not legally obligated to tell the truth? We have to seek the truth on each ad or ignore them altogether, knowing their message is very likely manipulation, distortion, or an outright lie. Politicians and advertising agencies know the number one human motivator is fear. Knowing this will keep you from falling for this manipulation. It is especially enlightening to research the "funded by..." notations at the ends of the ads, sometimes hidden in very small print or announced very quickly. Many of these organizations are nonprofits created for only the election season, quick to disappear afterward. The transient nature of political funding for campaign ads does not bode well for a well-informed citizenry.

2. Stop and consider carefully when researching candidates and issues. We are pummeled by a barrage of information during election season, particularly in presidential races, so we must be in control of the deluge. It is free speech and part of the democratic process, but it can be overwhelming.

3. Stop being a Caustic Citizen Voter and Living in the Red and responding to Living-in-the-Red messages. When you support Red candidates or issues, you do not hear anything but your anger reflected back to you. It is impossible to make a good, sound decision when you are in that emotional state. Decide to stop now. How can we make the right decisions for all if we are stuck in Red emotions and vote accordingly?

One Marvelous Question

After reading this chapter, if you were going to do one thing marvelously well to move forward, what would that one thing be?

To fully participate in democracy, we must take our power back.

CHAPTER SIX

We've Been Robbed: Voter Disenfranchisement Tactics Revealed

*"At first glance it may appear too hard.
Look again. Always look again."*

Mary Anne Radmacher

Voting is all about power. Voter suppression, therefore, has been diabolically fine-tuned by those who want to possess that power. Some of us willingly hand our power over to those forces out of apathy or ignorance, but many see that power stolen.

Even though it was once true that the Democratic Party demanded literacy tests and intimidated African-Americans from voting, it is now the Republican Party who cleverly creates numerous methods to suppress voter turnout. Tragically, in 2013, voter suppression was facilitated by a 5-4 Supreme Court ruling, *Shelby County v. Holder*, which revoked an indispensable provision of the 1965 Voting Rights Act that lifted requirements for states known for past voter discrimination to contact the U.S. Justice Department and receive *pre-clearance* before changing their states' election laws. A year later, the Brennan Center for Justice said:

- Section 5 no longer blocks or deters discriminatory voting changes, as it did for decades and right up until the Court's decision.

- Challenging discriminatory laws and practices is now more difficult, expensive, and time-consuming.

- The public now lacks critical information about new voting laws that Section 5 once mandated be disclosed prior to implementation.

Many states, such as Texas, North Carolina, Alabama, and Mississippi, immediately implemented voter suppression tactics after the court's ruling. Examples of actions taken by those legislatures may be found on the Brennan Center website in an article titled: "Shelby County: One Year Later." Recently, a few courts have exposed the charade behind voter suppression tactics, but it will be a slow and expensive process to overturn legislated suppression through the court system.

Curbing voter access, however, started even before that horrible Supreme Court decision. In a 2014 article for *The American Prospect*, Wendy Weiser, Democracy Program Director at the Brennan Center for Justice, wrote in her article "Voter Suppression: How Bad? (Pretty Bad)":

> For the first time in decades, voters in nearly half the country will find it harder to cast a ballot in the upcoming elections. Voters in twenty-two states will face tougher rules than in the last midterms. In fifteen states, 2014 is slated to be the first major election with new voting restrictions in place.

> These changes are the product of a concerted push to restrict voting by legislative majorities that swept into office in 2010. They represent a sharp reversal for a country whose historical trajectory has been to expand voting rights and make the process more convenient and accessible.

Why the shift? She went on to write:

> Partisanship plays a key role. Of the twenty-two states with new restrictions, eighteen passed them through entirely Republican-controlled bodies. A study by social scientists Keith Bentele and Erin O'Brien of the University of Massachusetts Boston found that restrictions were more likely to pass "as the proportion of Republicans in the legislature increased or when a Republican governor was elected." After Republicans took over state houses and governorships in 2010, voting restrictions typically followed party lines.

Without the full protection of the 1965 Voting Rights Act, and with the addition of concerted and targeted voter suppression tactics, synergizing for the perfect storm, 2016 will be worse – the first election without a functioning Voting Rights Act. Think Progress created an interactive map,"What Happens To Democracy After You Gut The Voting Rights Act, In One Map," highlighting the new voting issues the Supreme Court created. Think Progress also created a well-made, ninety-second You

Tube video about this very issue, "How Voting Restrictions Could Sway the 2016 Election." This short production quickly demonstrates how 114 million people, in 17 states, could have their vote stolen due to the years of planning beforehand to do so.

The Truth About Exclusionary Voter ID Laws

Voter disenfranchisement tactics are particularly pernicious because there are so many of them, like incoming cannon fodder, pummeling us with barriers to the ballot box. Such strategies include: shutting down Sunday early voting, which was originally instituted so people who attend church could register together after services; limiting early voting, which has been proven to work well to increase turnout; and requiring driver's licenses, then closing the motor vehicle offices where those licenses are issued. That especially shocking suppression hatchet job occurred in Alabama: The legislature required photo IDs, such as a driver's licenses, then closed thirty-one DMV offices. The counties in which every DMV office was closed were meant to serve an African-American population of 75 percent or more.

Many states now require voter identification with convoluted requirements. Mary Lou Miller was 101 years old and had voted since 1934, but in 2015, her vote was stolen away from her because her mail-in ballot was not forwarded when she moved to a different assisted-living facility. She then tried to vote in person, to no avail. Here is Mary's story, in her own words:

> With no mail ballot, I attempted to vote early in person. I do not possess a government-issued photo ID, and I have had none issued since I stopped driving when I was in my early 80s, over 20 years ago. One of the benefits of mail ballot is that a voter is not required to provide such a document.
>
> But on Monday of this week, I was driven to a Texas Department of Public Safety office, where I wanted to obtain a proof of identity. I did not have a Texas driver's license, issued within two years of expiration, no passport, no unexpired U.S. military photo ID, nor did I have an "advance parole document with photo." Sorry, but I never did time in the penitentiary, so I don't have that document. Had I had just one of these documents, I could obtain my proof of identity and be somebody.

105

Since I didn't have one of the primary identification documents, I could produce either two documents from the secondary identification documents list or one from the secondary list, plus two from the supporting identification documents. Sorry, but I have never seen my birth certificate, if, indeed, one was issued. I was born in Luxor, a very tiny, unincorporated coal village in southwestern Pennsylvania, and maybe they recorded my birth, but I don't have a copy. Nor was I born abroad, and I don't possess a certified copy of a court order indicating a change of name.

Aggravatingly, Mary Lou Miller had a Social Security card, a Medicare card, and a voter registration card from her previous address, but they were suddenly ineligible documents, and they would not allow her to vote in 2015. Mary Lou Miller was born before women had the right to vote, and suddenly, that right was stolen by the Texas Republican legislature, who decided that previous and significant documentation such as her voter registration card was no longer sufficient. Should proving you are "somebody" be so difficult? The most illogical voter identification law I have heard of was also on the books in Texas. The Texas Republican legislature passed a law stating that a concealed handgun license is valid identification to vote, but a state-issued student identification card was not.

In an article for the *New Republic*, political journalist Rebecca Leber wrote:

> Actual voter fraud, which is the problem that Republican legislation supposedly addresses, is difficult to find. Ginsburg noted that there were "only two in-person voter fraud cases prosecuted to conviction" in Texas in almost a decade. The consequences of voter ID laws, on the other hand, are much easier to track. According to the nonpartisan Government Accountability Office, existing ID requirements reduced turnout in some states during the last presidential election, particularly among young and black voters. Now, imagine the impact is even larger, because it is spread over the thirty-three states that now require some form of photo ID to vote. The same report found that the costs of acquiring the needed ID ranged between $14.50 to $58.50 for 17 of the states.

Remember ALEC? The American Legislative Exchange Council is the incredibly powerful conservative organization founded by Paul Weyrich in 1973. The group represents corporations and *lawmakers*. They were strategically instrumental in changing the voter ID laws by writing their Voter ID Act in 2009 and advocating its course of action to Republican politicians. With the assistance of sympathetic politicians, ALEC took that act, which delineates requirements with the intent to suppress the vote, to numerous Republican-led state legislatures. The consequences of this concerted effort can now be seen around the country.

In just a two-year period (2011-12), lawmakers proposed sixty-two photo ID bills in thirty-seven states, with more than half of lawmakers being members of ALEC. The other half probably (nudge-nudge, wink-wink) received copies of the act from those ALEC-member legislators. In an *NBC Investigations* news article, "Flurry of Voter ID laws Tied to Conservative Group ALEC," Jennie Bowser, Senior Election Policy Analyst at the National Conference of State Legislatures, said, "I very rarely see a single issue taken up by as many states in such a short period of time as with voter ID. It's been a pretty remarkable spread."

The Center for Media and Democracy exposed the document and summarized it by saying:

> This bill would serve to disenfranchise many low-income, minority, elderly, and student voters, many of whom do not have driver's licenses. While the bill provides for free IDs, in many states the offices that would provide IDs are not located near the communities that would have the greatest needs and/or keep irregular hours. Taking the time to get an ID would be burdensome and many individuals who might otherwise vote would not take the time or be aware of the need to get an ID in advance of the election date.

Why would ALEC write their own Voter ID Act, when there really was no problem to solve? Simple: The strawman of voter fraud had to be fabricated. To suppress votes, they had to *create* a problem to solve. Why has the spread of their Voter ID Act proliferation in state legislatures been so "remarkable?" ALEC and the Republican state legislatures were getting ready for the 2016 presidential election so the voters they do not want to vote, Democratic-leaning populations, were methodically suppressed. To make matters worse, ALEC is a nonprofit organization that receives a tax break from the American people, including the very people they do not want to vote, the Democrats.

ALEC's purpose is to increase corporate profits, decrease regulations, reduce corporate taxes, and attack the weak and vulnerable. Why? The corporate and their sitting legislators fear voters and an independent populace.

Regarding the reason Republican legislatures are adopting the ALEC Voter ID Act, one Wisconsin lawmaker spilled the beans. On election day, in a television interview, Republican State Representative Glenn Grothman unwittingly told the truth. When asked by a reporter why he thought a Republican candidate could become the first Republican to carry Wisconsin in a presidential election since 1984, Grothman said, "Now we have photo ID, and I think photo ID is gonna make a little bit of a difference."

On April 5, 2016, Wisconsin held its first election after sweeping voter identification laws were adopted, and it did not go well. Wisconsin citizens experienced numerous problems, such as long lines and difficulty in obtaining ID cards. Even though several studies determined that there was no voter fraud issue in Wisconsin, the Republican legislature and Governor Scott Walker pushed the law through. The only real result of the law, as Think Progress analyzed, was to cause the exact situation it created: a lowering in Democrat turnout.

Hidden Voter Purge

Smoke, mirrors, and a click of a button! Like vapor, an insidious voter suppression technique is being utilized by about twenty states. Kris Kobach, Kansas Secretary of State, has turned into a one-man voter purge ambassador. With his creation of the Interstate Crosscheck program, he has institutionalized the disappearance of individual voter rights that no one could possibly foresee. In the name of so-called voter integrity, thousands upon thousands are being accused of double voting in approximately twenty states.

The diabolical strategy is that when two names are nearly the same but are in different states, it is assumed that the name belongs to one individual who is committing voter fraud. It is not assumed that two people might have the similar or even the same name. Therefore, in the Crosscheck program, *both* names are purged. In Greg Palast's August 29, 2016 *Rolling Stone* article, he quoted Mark Swedlund, a database expert with clients such as eBay and American Express, to look at a confidential Crosscheck list that was given to Greg Palast by mistake but was extremely enlightening. Mark Sewdlund said the Crosscheck list used "childish methodology." He went on to say, "God forbid your name is Garcia, of which there are 858,000 in the U.S., and your first name is Joseph or Jose. You're probably suspected of voting in 27 states."

Interestingly, the last names that were most often purges were names that are ethnically derived. Stephanie Singer, a Philadelphia elections commissioner, gasped when she learned this and said, "There are going to be a lot of David Lees on that list." I find this particularly interesting, because my husband's longtime friend from kindergarten is named David Lee!

Greg Palast called Kris Kobach's system a "cruel and silent system" that is secretly purging a million democratic and minority voters off the voter roles by the November presidential election.

Kobach's Interstate Crosscheck program compares names among participating states but only uses first and last names and supposedly birthdays and Social Security numbers. In reality, that *crosscheck* is not happening. On the confidential Crosscheck list that Greg Palast received from Virginia, the Social Security numbers were not even on it. As a spokeswoman for the Republican State Leadership Committee said, "We want to make it easier to vote but hard to cheat." Is there any cheating? Where is there a lack of voter integrity?

Coupled with purging the so-called duplicate names, what also is happening is equating database *errors* with *fraud*. An *AXISPhilly* article, "PurgeMachine: A Republican 'Voter Fraud' Program Flags Many Voters, Detects Little Fraud," stated:

> To be sure, voter rolls across America contain erroneous and out-of-date information: Names are misspelled; addresses wrong; people who moved away from one address are still listed as being registered, mostly because few people moving think to notify the Election Board of their departure. Election boards are constantly updating their rolls, using computers to check them against death registries and change-of-address forms filed with motor license bureaus.

There are many reasons to find clerical errors on a state's voter roll. It is an imperfect list created by an imperfect process, but the result of deleting a name from voter registration rosters can be the permanent disenfranchisement of an American, and it may only be because they are unlucky enough to possess the same name and birthday as that of an entirely different voter in an entirely different state. That click of the button to make names disappear happens in an office by a faceless bureaucrat, without notice, and the voters may never know about it until they go to the polls.

Ohio Secretary of State John Husted claims the Crosscheck report works because he came up with hundreds of names with issues. However, when he sent twenty of those names to law enforcement, none resulted in charges.

Colorado Secretary of State Scott Gressler sent seventeen names to the Boulder County District Attorney. After an investigation, the DA reported that none involved fraud and called Scott Gressler's intent "politically motivated."

North Carolina, using the Crosscheck program, stated that they wanted to delete 35,000 names from their state rolls. The Virginia State Board of Elections, wanted their state legislature to throw out 57,000. Dick Morris, a Fox News commentator, blew things really out of proportion with unproven crazy talk in regard to the 2012 election, claiming, "Probably over a million people" voted twice.

One of the most egregious examples is Kris Kobach. When his activities were called "a poll tax and a national disgrace," he retorted by saying, "Every time an alien votes, it cancels out the vote of a United States citizen." There is no known proof that anyone from Mars has voted in an election, let alone an undocumented farm worker. The use of this offensive terminology that depersonalizes and demonizes says it all about his assumptions. Studies have repeatedly shown that voter fraud is a nonissue, a strawman, yet Kobach said, "We have had many, many cases of noncitizens registered to vote prior to our new law." Is that so? Of course he would say something like that, right? He never proved it, and tossing out the comment did not make it fact.

It is sorrowful that we have people in power who harbor such antidemocratic ideologies. Voters exercise power through election and Kobach, as well as all elected officials, are expected to be trustworthy and even-handed when wielding it. Voting should be a right and not abridged by the State. Yet, by employing his Crosscheck concept, Kris Kobach placed 22,000 registrations in limbo. An opponent, Jean Schodorf, when running against Kobach for Kansas Secretary of State, said some of the registrations were those of seniors who did not drive or could not find their birth certificates, stating, "They will never be able to vote again, and it tears them up." Even the Government Accountability Office, a trusted nonpartisan congressional research agency, reported that turnout in Kansas declined nearly 2 percent, directly due to the voter identification laws recently adopted. That 2 percent is enough to swing an election. Since voter ID laws disproportionally target students, seniors, and people of color, all who primarily vote for Democrats, they are restricted from the voting booth. Mission accomplished.

There is some hope though. Florida and Oregon have withdrawn from Kris Kobach's Interstate Crosscheck program, citing the data as "unreliable." Oregon will use a Pew Charitable Trust program instead, which comes with a fee. Meanwhile, Kris Kobach's program is free. What is that ol' saying? You get what you pay for?

What seems particularly outrageous is that many of the motivations of those in power who pass these disenfranchising voter identification laws are vilely mean-spirited. Don Yelton, North Carolina GOP Precinct Chair, said his state's voter ID law will "kick Democrats in the butt" and hurt "lazy blacks." This and several other nasty comments are recorded in Bill Moyer's "Unbelievable GOP Statement on Voter Suppression."

In addition, the article includes several videos that allow direct viewing of some of these statements, but the one from *The Daily Show,* featuring an interview with Don Yelton and Congressman John Lewis is not to be missed. As a postscript, there is some justice in the world after all. After *The Daily Show* aired its segment on voter suppression, Don Yelton resigned from his position as precinct chair.

I believe it is the meanness and lack of trust in many who came before them that has lost young voters, and we need them so desperately. Shenanigans, such as states not honoring their state-issued college identification cards, have disillusioned millions of young people. Many remember the message of hope and change in the 2008 election but did not see any real change for them. College is still unaffordable, and dream jobs are nearly unattainable.

Catherine Rampell, a *Washington Post* opinion writer, in her "Where Are All the Young Voters?" said of the hope and change mantra:

> This oversimplifies things, but it is true that over time young people have withdrawn from traditional social and political institutions, including everything from political parties to churches. In polls, millennials say they trust almost no authority figure to do the right thing most or all of the time: not Congress, not the president, not the Supreme Court, not the media, not Wall Street and definitely not federal, state and local government. Mired in debt, with scant job prospects, young people feel abandoned by the organizations that once claimed to represent their interests. Perhaps as a result, millennials have elected not to participate in the elections that grant such figures their authority. Only a third of young people say their vote will "make a difference" anyway, according to the latest Harvard Institute of Politics youth poll.

I despair when I think about our voting-age youth. How can we overcome such disenchantment? How can we regain the trust in our American institutions? Young voters cannot find a different Congress to trust. They cannot find different governments to trust. They cannot find a different Supreme Court who will make better decisions for their future. After all, this is their country. How can they be convinced that if they rejoin the democracy and vote like a swarm of mosquitos, they will be a dominant force and make an immense impact on creating the country they *do* want? How can we turn these Cynical Citizen Voters into concerned ones? I wish I knew.

Voter Fraud: Real or Imagined?

I was asked once what a *strawman argument* is. *Wikipedia* defines it as "a common form of argument...an informal fallacy based on giving the impression of refuting an opponent's argument, while actually refuting an argument that was not advanced by that opponent."

Mignon Fogarty at *Grammar Girl*, explains it better with an analogy:

> It's as if you took a flaming scarecrow, threw it onto the floor, yelled, "Look! It's my opponent's dangerous strawman," and then you appeared to save the day by dousing the flames with water.

All while your opponent mutters, "That's not *my* strawman. What just happened?"

Voter fraud is a strawman. The Republicans have thrown a flaming, fiendish idea out into the country by insinuating that there are millions of people who will intentionally abuse the system by casting numerous ballots – and driving all over the place to do it. They claim they can save the day by passing voter ID laws, leaving the rest of us saying, "That's not true. What just happened?"

The concept of voter fraud became such an overwhelming issue that the Bush administration conducted a major investigation between 2002 and 2007 and did not find enough evidence to prosecute one single person.

Ari Berman, author of *Give Us the Ballot: The Modern Struggle for Voting Rights in America,* said in an interview with *The National Memo*:

> The State of Pennsylvania, which passed a voter ID law in 2012 that was purportedly designed to stop in-person voter fraud, admitted in a recent court filing: "There have been no investigations or prosecutions of in-person voter fraud in Pennsylvania; and the parties do not have direct personal knowledge of any such investigations or prosecutions in other states." So this is really a phantom menace. Republicans are hyping voter fraud in order to mask the real purpose of these laws, which is to reduce turnout among Democratic-affiliated constituencies – namely, low-income, student, and minority voters – who are most negatively impacted by these new voting restrictions.

Kansas Secretary of State Kris Kobach, a rabid proponent of ferreting out voter fraud, found only three people who could be criminally charged with it. According to his official, certified August 2015 "Voter Registration Statistics," there were 1,705,537 registered voters in the State of Kansas. That means, out of almost two million people, he discovered only three. That speaks volumes, in and of itself, but further analysis is required to really see the strawman in this situation.

Two of the three individuals he criminally charged comprised a married couple, a Vietnam veteran and a volunteer domestic violence educator. They were retiring and, while living in Kansas, were building another home in Arkansas and often traveled to and from each property. They mistakenly voted in each state for the 2010 midterm election, not even a presidential, pursuant to confusion or just not remembering in which state they had voted. Trey Pettlon, their attorney, said, "It was a stressful time for them, and in the confusion, they made a mistake... They didn't intend to do anything illegal. They have a long track record of being good citizens." Think about this: This couple had to hire an attorney, shouldering the cost of defending themselves while they were trying to retire, and they became scapegoats for Kris Kobach's rabid agenda.

The third individual was also an older person, a 64-year-old who lived in Kansas and Colorado. He freely admitted that he voted in both states because he thought it was okay. He paid taxes in each, and the voter registration forms are at the state level rather than the federal. He believed he could vote only in one county of each state and did not realize he could not vote in each state. His so-called crime was one of ignorance, but his actions were not a calculated attempt to swing an election.

Since 2000, there have been 2,068 alleged cases of voter fraud. Most likely, many of these were similar to the situations in Kansas, mere confusion, yet the secretary of state used the issue as a political hatchet. For now, let us do the math. There are approximately 146,311,000 registered voters in the United States. If we divide 2,068 by 146,311,000, assuming that all those cases were manipulative people who actually wanted to waste gas driving around the country to destroy the American electoral system, the percentage of voter fraud in this country is 0.00001413, a number so infinitesimally small that it defies understanding.

In a blog post dated October 25, 2014, by LaFeminista, in an article titled: "Breaking: New Scary Chart Released," a very important point was made:

> The reason voter fraud is of an issue is purely political, and that reason is to suppress votes for one party alone. The new voter ID laws are anti-democratic and are, in themselves, a type of fraud. Fraud is:
>
> 1) a deception deliberately practiced in order to secure unfair or unlawful gain;
>
> 2) one who assumes a false pose; an imposter.

This basically says that, despite all the evidence to the contrary, voter fraud is a problem and is *fraud* (emphasis added) itself.

Yet, voter fraud tactics are successful in suppressing at least 8 percent of real, eligible voters, not imaginary ones.

Recently, there was a story about votes being cast by people who had already passed away. On the surface, this looks bad and feeds into the Republican meme of serious voter fraud, justifying their restrictive voter ID laws. However, looking more deeply – an act most will not do, as it requires time and thought – reveals that only 215 votes were attributed to dead people out of nearly 10 million registered voters. Those who support voter ID laws will cite the Los Angeles case but fail to mention how infinitesimal the real issue is in relation to the sheer size of Los Angeles County. That, my friends, is a strawman if there ever was one!

Voter Intimidation

Intimidating voters at the polls is not a new suppression tactic, but in our attempt to create a more perfect union, it has to be stopped. This methodology gives an obvious advantage to one party by keeping a segment of the voting population from casting their ballots, and it is often utilized against minority populations.

Recently, in a speech to his Pennsylvania supporters, Donald Trump said the only way he can possibly lose in the state was if the Democrats cheated. He insisted on his supporters and police being at the polls to keep this from happening. Talk about calling the kettle black! It is, in fact, the Republican Party that has a Department of Justice Consent Decree against them, banning them from doing this very intimidation tactic!

In the 1980s, a special election was held for governor of New Jersey. During that campaign, the RNC shamelessly sent out mislabeled mailers to black and Hispanic neighborhoods. When they were returned by the post office, due to the intentionally inaccurate addresses, they purged the names from the voter rolls. They then created the National Ballot Security Task Force and utilized off-duty police officers to monitor the polls, donning armbands and brandishing weapons, identified as the National Ballot Security Task Force.

There should never be cause in this country for police intervention in our voting process, yet there is a long history of it. In Selma, Alabama, police have been utilized to intimidate minority voters. In the past, they were often called in to enforce poll taxes and literacy tests; there are now laws against any police force being near polls just for this reason. In Pennsylvania, the very state where Donald Trump bellowed this absurd clarion call, a law is on the books that disallow police from being closer than 100 feet away from the polls, unless an emergency situation requires their assistance. Minorities exercising their right to vote is *not* an emergency situation for anyone other than Donald Trump.

In 2013, the RNC challenged, before the Supreme Court, the Consent Decree, demanding that they be allowed to continue using their National Ballot Security Task Force. The Supreme Court upheld the decree, so the Republican Party is legally forbidden from doing what Donald Trump just called upon his supporters to do. The Consent Decree is scheduled to expire in 2017, but if voter intimidation by Trump supporters does occur, the Department of Justice may very well extend the term of the ban.

Unfortunately, it may be too little, too late, as the damage may already be done. Donald Trump has publically encouraged his Caustic Voter supporters to be at the polls to intimidate those who want to cast their ballots on the opposing side. The very definition of *cheating* is "acting dishonestly or unfairly in order to gain an advantage." Bearing this in mind, which party is actually cheating?

Gerrymandering:
Houdini Districts that Cost Voters Their Voice

In the March 26, 1812, *Boston Gazette,* the word *Gerry-mander* was used for the first time. The article was about Governor Elbridge Gerry (pronounced "Gary"), who redrew the Massachusetts state senate election districts and redistricted them to benefit his Democratic-Republican Party, the name of the party at that time. When the new district lines in Boston were mapped, it looked like the shape of a salamander; hence, gerry-mander was born, though it was later mispronounced as "jerrymander" and has since lost its hyphen.

There is a real, constructive purpose for redistricting. We redistrict areas of a state to adjust for population increase or decrease to determine representation. This type of redistricting is foundational to democracy. Nearly all our elected officials at the federal, state, and local levels are elected from these geographical territories. However, gerrymandering is the manipulation of geographical boundaries to advantage one party or class, and it is now being used as a weapon to suppress votes. In addition, redistricting discussions by elected officials already in office take place behind closed doors. Further explanation may be viewed in the film *Gerrymandering 101*, at: endgerrymandering.com.

For example, in the 2012 election, House Democrats received 1.4 million *more* votes nationwide, yet the Republicans still held control of the House of Representatives. This was entirely due to Republican control of the House in 2010, when census data was used to reapportion the electorate and because Democratic Casual Voters stayed home and did not vote in the midterms. With the House of Representatives under Republican control, they redistricted not on population but rather, by how they could best gerrymander areas for their party's benefit. Therefore, in 2012, 1.4 million Democratic votes were suppressed by the Republican Party lines drawn in 2010. Unbelievably, gerrymandering for political advantage is legal and constitutional, probably because no one thought there needed to be a law against it, due to it being so flagrantly anti-democratic.

The problem now is that computer technology, coupled with intense motivation for power, whoever is in control of the federal government in a census year will not redistrict the federal elected offices based on population, its original purpose, but on cleverly and strategically remaining in power. The same will happen in the states.

Therefore, in the first year of a new decade, the winning party will redistrict according to their own agenda, to the greatest benefit of his or her party. The next census year, 2020, will be a powerful year for the controlling political party. Democrats are more likely to stay home during midterm elections, though I hope this will never again be the case, so Republicans have been the benefitting party in gerrymandering districts to stay in power. Until more states create nonpartisan congressional and legislative redistricting commissions such as California, Hawaii, and Idaho, politicians will be able to pick their voters instead of the voters being able to pick their politicians.

It happens so fast that it would make your head spin! Just hours – yes, *hours* – after the Supreme Court struck down Section 5 of the Voting Rights Act, Texas immediately reinstituted the very same redistricting plan that previous courts had already deemed unconstitutional. State Attorney General Greg Abbott defended the reinstitution, citing that it was not about racial discrimination. Rather, it was about not allowing Democrats to vote, which is entirely legal, by the way; if minorities just so happen to be caught up in the suppression, oh well.

North Carolina House Representative David R. Lewis was surprisingly honest behind the motivations of gerrymandering his state's districts: "I think electing Republicans is better than electing Democrats, so I drew this map in a way to help foster what I think is better for the country." When confronted about gerrymandering the North Carolina district maps, he directly admitted to rigging the system to favor the Republicans. Obviously, the purpose of districts, determining representation by population, had nothing to do with it. It was about what he *thought*, not what was intended by the system he confessed to rigging.

Stand Up Activities

Below, for your consideration, are several suggested Stand Up Activities. For a further explanation of the Keep/Start/Stop organization tool, please see Chapter One. After reading this chapter, you may think of additional activities readers can implement. If you'd like to share your brilliant constructive, compelling and creative ideas, please do so at: www. facebook.com/americaabandoned.

KEEP:

1. Keep a promise to yourself that you will do your level best to overcome the deliberate roadblocks to registering and voting. Read Thom Hartmann's incredible story, "The War on Voting Comes Home," about what he had to go through to get his new identification after he moved to Washington DC on Truth Out, Aug 2016.

2. Keep in mind, always, what our founding fathers sacrificed for you to be a citizen of our great country. Do not let their loss of life, fortunes, and family be in vain.

START:

1. Start learning about your state's voter ID requirements. Many have passed convoluted forms of voter identification, as advocated for by ALEC, so it is important to know clearly what is required. Do not trust that it will be the same for each upcoming election. To assist with the barrage of changes, Rock the Vote has a "Voter ID Requirement by State" webpage so you may learn what your state requirements are.

   For kicks and giggles, look up the State of California voter registration requirements, then take a peek at Texas'. When you see the disparities between the two states, you will see an area for advocacy, is to fight for a national voter eligibility standards that include specific prohibitions against voter restrictions designed to suppress voter types such as democrats, minorities, students, etc. Another resource is the American Civil Liberties Union (ACLU) "Oppose Voter ID Legislation" factsheet.

2. Start advocating for the reinstatement of the sections of the Voting Rights Act that the Roberts Supreme Court nullified in 2010. Find useful resources at Craig Connects, "5 Voter Rights Orgs You Should Follow."

3. Start fighting the gerrymandering of districts so we, the people can once again choose our representatives and not the other way around. Make gerrymandering districts illegal and insist that the only criteria for determining districts be based on geographical location. Sign up at IndependentLines.org. Learn the fascinating history of the word on Wikipedia.

4. Start advocating for election days to be a holiday. Did you know the president could declare it a national holiday? Also, September 27 is a National Voter Registration Day. For more information, visit the National Voter Registration day website.

5. Start protecting yourself. Just because you filled out a registration card does not mean you are, in fact, registered. Go online and check your County Registrar's office for their voter list. Find "7 Ways to Beat the Ballot Bandits" at www.gregpalast.com.

STOP:

1.   Stop ALEC! This nonprofit organization is pro-corporate and anti-democracy and behind the voter discrimination tactics adopted by many state legislatures. They are a tool of the Velvet Coup. They are a shadow organization for the oligarchs. Learn about the group at www.alecexposed.org. For voters new to advocacy, fighting ALEC tactics would be a great place to start.

2.   Stop staying home and not voting in midterm elections, if this has been your habit. Midterm elections are as important as the presidential years for your state, county, and municipality. Voting in a census-based year is vital.

One Marvelous Question

After reading this chapter, if you were going to do one thing marvelously well to move forward, what would that one thing be?

*There are so many diabolical barriers to voting.
Could there be even another?*

CHAPTER SEVEN

The Voting Machine Fiasco: A National Atrocity

*"Change is not a bolt of lightning that arrives with a zap.
It is a bridge built brick by brick, every day, with sweat and humility and slips.
It is hard work and slow work, but it can be thrilling to watch it take shape."*

Sarah Hepola

If we are successful in hurdling the diabolical barriers intentionally designed to either bar us from voting or make it so miserable and difficult that we willingly abandon it, and if we are successful in overcoming our own inertia in learning about candidates and issues, then, whether mail-in or walk-in voting, we may face other obstacles: decrepit voting machines, machines without paper trails (unlike our ATM machines), and hacking.

In an in-depth, empirical report from The Brennan Center for Justice, "America's Voting Machines at Risk," it alarmingly discovered that our nation's voting machines are derelict. These relics are at the end of their life span; they are not technologically current, are encumbered with old software, and it is difficult to find parts to fix them. Not only that, but the county governmental agencies that manage them do not have the financial resources to replace or keep them up to date.

The report also found that wealthier counties have newer machines than the counties without the same wealth tax base. This means the poorest communities and communities of color have the oldest, most derelict machines. Research determined that for the 2014 election, perhaps as high as half to three-quarters of a million votes were lost due to old voting machines. Now, the Brennen Center for Justice is raising the alarm that a voting machine meltdown is very likely for the 2016 election.

In 2011, the U.S. Department of Energy Argonne National Laboratory successfully hacked a Diebold voting machine with only twenty-six dollars' worth of parts and the know-how of an average eighth-grader. The team found that the Sequoia voting machine was susceptible to man-in-the-middle attacks, which can be done with a small, wireless machine that can interfere with vote tallies.

Beth Clarkson, a Wichita State University engineering professor and statistician, has accused Wisconsin, Ohio, and Kansas – states with Republican-held legislatures – of voting irregularities that could be indicative of tampering. In her article for the American Statistical Association, "How Trustworthy Are Electronic Voting Systems in the U.S.?" she states:

> I want to emphasize, as I always try to do, that statistics don't prove vote fraud. These statistics show that patterns exist in the data that correlate the type of electronic voting system in use with the percent (percentage Republican) vote changing with the total votes cast.

> Such patterns are examples of what we might expect to see if some voting systems were being sabotaged, but that doesn't mean that no other explanations are possible for these patterns. Voting machine manipulation is, in my opinion, the most likely explanation for these patterns. The most common pattern supports Republican candidates, but Democratic candidates are sometimes the beneficiary.

> The only way to prove vote fraud is through a post-election audit demonstrating significant deviations from the reported totals.

Another way to prove voter fraud is through a paper trail. Athan Gibbs, an accountant and inventor of the TruVote system, stated:

> I've been an accountant, an auditor, for more than thirty years. Electronic voting machines that don't supply a paper trail go against every principle of accounting and auditing that's being taught in American business schools. These machines are set up to provide paper trails. No business in America would buy a machine that didn't provide a paper trail to audit and verify its transactions. Now, they want the people to purchase machines that you can't audit? It's absurd.

It absolutely makes no sense to buy electronic voting machines that can't produce a paper trail. Inevitably, computers mess up. How are you going to have a recount or correct malfunctions without a paper trail?

To make matters worse, we have privatized counting our votes, and two Republican brothers own the industry. Bob and Todd Urosevich obtained financing from the far-right, Christian evangelical Ahmanson family in 1984 (also the primary funders of the Discovery Institute that fosters creation science education in California schools) to purchase the companies that eventually became Ohio-based Diebold and Nebraska-based ES&S. On the surface, they appear to be competing companies, but brothers who share the same ideological beliefs, much like the Koch brothers, are anything but competitive.

A 2012 *Harper's Magazine* article, "How To Rig an Election: The GOP Aims To Paint the Country Red," explained:

> Bob and Todd Urosevich are hardly household names. Yet the two brothers have succeeded in monopolizing American election technology for decades through a pair of supposedly competing corporations: the Ohio-based Diebold and the Nebraska-based ES&S. The latter was founded by the Urosevich brothers in 1979 and is headquartered in Omaha, where it has an Ayn Rand–flavored corporate address on John Galt Boulevard. It is also, let us recall, the same company that may have won Chuck Hagel his Senate seat.

> Diebold became the most infamous name in the industry in 2003, when its CEO, Walden O'Dell, a top fundraiser for George W. Bush, made a jaw-dropping public promise to "deliver" Ohio's electoral votes to Bush. The following year, California banned Diebold's touchscreen system, and Secretary of State Kevin Shelley blasted the company as "fraudulent," "despicable," and "deceitful." O'Dell stepped down in 2005, right before the filing of a class-action suit that accused Diebold of fraud, insider trading, and slipshod quality control.

> Concerned about its tarnished brand, the company removed its label from the front of voting machines. Then Diebold went one step further and changed the name of its voting-machine division to Premier Election Solutions.

As far as I can tell, nothing has changed. The issue with the reliability of counting our votes has flown under the radar since 2004, when a number of anomalies were detected throughout the country. We simply cannot trust corporately owned voting machines. As Dr. Bob Fitrakis, a political science professor and senior editor of *The Free Press*, wrote in his article, "Diebold, Electronic Voting, and the Vast Right-Wing Conspiracy":

> Athan Gibbs wonders, 'Why would you buy a voting machine from a company like Diebold which provides a paper trail for every single machine it makes except its voting machines? And then, when you ask it to verify its numbers, it hides behind 'trade secrets.'"

> Maybe the Diebold decision makes sense, if you believe, to paraphrase Henry Kissinger that democracy is too important to leave up to the votes of the people.

Whether it is consistent and informed voting or the condition of our voting machines and the integrity of our vote count, Thomas Paine, one of our founding fathers, said, "Those who want to reap the benefits of this great nation must bear the fatigue of supporting it."

If we are a voter and an advocate, we must continue being that change agent and hold courageous conversations with others to inspire them to participate more fully in the democracy they inhabit. If we know, in our heart of hearts, that we can do more, then we must reignite that honorable feeling when voting and find the one passionate issue to advocate and fight for. If you have abandoned our birthright, then reclaim it for yourself, in honor of our founding fathers and their sacrifice. All of us must fight the fatigue threatened by powerful forces.

There are people fighting the fatigue of defending our vote. Election Protection at 866ourvote.org, is one of those organizations. As they say, they are working 365 days to advance and defend our right to vote. There are many solutions to our miserable voting experience. Senator Ron Wyden (D-OR) has proposed legislation to create a nationwide vote-by-mail process, based on the successful experience in Oregon. Through it, no one has to take time off work or fight for their constitutional rights at a designating polling place. Georgia is ending its ninety-day blackout period after registering to vote. In addition, Vermont, Oregon, California, and West Virginia have programs that enable citizens to automatically register to vote when applying for a driver's license, and twenty other states are currently considering this process.

In his April 20, 2016 podcast, Ed Schultz, an American television and radio host, held a discussion with John Nichols, National Affairs Correspondent for *The Nation* magazine, who said:

> We just can't get voting right in America for some reason. Is their hanky-panky everywhere? Is there wrongdoing everywhere? Why can't we get this right? I mean, these complaints were taking place in 2000 and 2004. It is 2016, and we're still talking about it.

John Nichols pointed out that we have not yet established a set of core standards nationwide that states may not fall below. There are extremely different rules in each state, and this becomes a serious issue when electing a national candidate. Some states hold open primaries, some have closed primaries, and others have caucuses. This inconsistency affects both parties dramatically, but is only brought to our attention during national election years.

We must find a way to recapture our integrity in counting the votes. We must fight and advocate for voting machines that are owned by our Registrar of Voters, not by private, for-profit companies. We must ensure the integrity of those machines with a proper paper trail.. We must find a way to more efficiently and more effectively vote across the country, so everyone is secure in the validity of election results. Is that too much to ask for our democracy to thrive?

Stand Up Activities

Below, for your consideration, are several suggested Stand Up Activities. For a further explanation of the Keep/Start/Stop organization tool, please see Chapter One. After reading this chapter, you may think of additional activities readers can implement. If you'd like to share your brilliant constructive, compelling and creative ideas, please do so at: www. facebook.com/americaabandoned.

KEEP:

1. Keep in mind that voter fraud is a strawman argument, and the use of voter fraud concept is to suppress eligible voters.

START:

1. Start learning which type of voting machine your County Registrar of Voters utilizes at the polls and to count mail-in ballots. Is there a paper trail? How old are the machines? If you do not like the answer, find out who your county supervisor is and scream! The last thing you want is to complete your candidate and issue research, talk to friends, have voting parties, then lose your vote to an old, hackable, rusty relic of a machine without the accountability of a paper trail.

2. Start actively participating in organizations such as 866ourvote. org.

3. Start fighting for a core set of federal voting standards.

4. Start listening to experts in the voting machine issue such as Greg Palast, Investigative Reporter, at gregpalast.com and Brad Friedman at bradblog.com.

STOP:

1. Stop believing voting machines are accurate. They are not! Consider using a mail-in ballot, as this is the best option until voting machines are improved. Mail them in early. If you wait to submit them at the polls or a few days before the election, they may not get counted.

One Marvelous Question

After reading this chapter, if you were going to do *one* thing marvelously well to move forward, what would that one thing be?

What else do we need to thrive?

CHAPTER EIGHT

Sustaining Citizens: We Are the Government

"Let us never forget that government is ourselves and not an alien power over us. The ultimate rulers of our democracy are not a president and senators and congressmen and government officials but the voters of this country."

Franklin D. Roosevelt

In a democracy, a functioning government is dependent on citizenship. *Citizenship*, as defined by Dictionary.com is "the character of an individual viewed as a member of society; behavior in terms of the duties, obligations, and functions of a citizen." Now, remember the definition of *abandonment*: "to withdraw one's support or help from, especially in spite of duty, allegiance, or responsibility; desert." My point in comparing the two definitions is that they both reference "duty." As it relates to our form of government, abandonment abdicates our duty toward it, and citizenship requires embracing it.

Government is citizenship – at least in our form of government, because it requires self-rule. We often use the term "democracy" when speaking of the United States, but our form of government is actually a *republic*: "a state in which supreme power is held by the people and their elected representatives, and which has an elected or nominated president rather than a monarch," as Ben Franklin said when they formed the government that they gave us a *republic*.

As self-governing citizens, we must work together to determine our common good and design the path to achieve it with the ultimate outcome of shaping our collective destiny. Determining the common good and our collective civic virtue requires Living-in-the-Black energies and the rejection of anti-character behaviors. Citizenship is more than self-realization, what we want for ourselves; rather, citizenship is self-transcendence, what we should all want for us all. An American who brings constructive, compelling energies to the dialog and transcends their personal agenda for the public good is, in my view, a *Sustaining Citizen*.

Sustaining v. Syphoning

A Sustaining Citizen is more than a voter. They are the individuals in our society who sustain democracy and continuously build a sense of belonging for us all. They are the ones who join organizations because they feel a responsibility to something greater than themselves. The organizations in which they participate improve our collective soul. They reject Living in the Red. They are oriented to the whole, as well as to their private pursuits. They foster membership in our democracy and know citizenship does not end after an election. They are sober-minded and make fact-based decisions. They are both Courageous and Concerned Citizen Voters. Sustaining Citizens know government is incomplete but strive to finish it. They know how to stand up and cause action constructively. How they go about doing this is as unique as their individual DNA. They are the underpinning of civic life.

Sustaining Citizens are citizen lobbyists. For example, Adam Green, Cofounder of the Progressive Change Campaign Committee, was arrested, along with 400 other citizen activists, in April of 2016, during the Democracy Spring civil disobedience to protest a corrupt campaign finance system and rigged voting laws, an exercise meant to shame politicians who support getting the most money possible into politics and whose goal it is to implement voter disenfranchisement tactics. The police who made the arrests said it was one of the biggest mass arrests that have ever seen at the Capitol building; they literally ran out of room to process the activists. These Sustaining Citizens exercised their right to civil disobedience with Living-in-the-Black energies, and, because they did so, the police treated them with respect.

As a reminder, Living-in-the-Black energies are constructive, compelling emotions, while Living-in-the-Red energies are destructive and repelling. As individuals, we might find ourselves feeling Red energies from time to time, but Sustaining Citizens predominantly present constructive energies in their approach to improving our democracy.

We require more Sustaining Citizens and Organizations. Therefore, it is an imperative realization that everyone in America must possess an education in civics. Richard Dreyfuss, an American actor and activist, became so concerned about the lack of knowledge and understanding that he created a Sustaining Organization, The Dreyfuss Institute to "revive, elevate, and enhance" the teaching of civics.

Conversely, those who suck up money, resources, and obfuscate facts belonging to or that may be more appropriately used for the common good are what I term Syphoning Citizens. These implement a personal agenda, one that results in less and less money, resources, and truth being available to our society and existence; thus, they starve our economy, infrastructure, government, and our ability to make fact-based policy decisions.

If we are to become good little worker bees, why would we need civics education? That is the prevailing corporate mentality. Job applications do not require a test on the Constitution or knowing how our government operates, but perhaps they should. Running a mega-corporation does not require this either. Consider Chipotle CEO Montgomery Moran, who makes $13,489 an hour or Starbucks Founder and CEO Howard Schultz, who makes $10,285 an hour, based on a 40-hour workweek.

In a *USA Today* article, "Maximum Wage! How much CEOs earn an hour," which compared the hourly wages of 13 top executives, the average hourly salary was reported to be $5,859, and many of these CEOs fight against giving their hardworking employees a meager $15 hourly. In 2008, the Burger King CEO fought over paying a cent per pound more to the tomato-pickers and used his daughter's computer to spread disinformation to the media. I would hope that even the most Ayn Randian conservative would find this hourly disparity between CEOs and workers obscene, because these individuals, unwittingly or purposefully, are Syphoning Citizens. I only say "unwittingly" because I am certain this class of Americans would consider themselves good citizens and capitalists. They likely do not take a broader view on whether or not what they take from the economy is *sustainable*. These hourly salaries are not economically sustainable and, therefore, they are *syphoning* our democracy and the political and social equality of all Americans.

Sadly, there are many in power who want to starve the government and 99 percent of the public for their own personal benefit. Grover Norquist is most famous for this, with his "drown the government in a bathtub" Those who brought the concept of economic austerity to our country (how to drown government in a bathtub) as how to make America better exemplify the Syphoning Citizen. *Austerity*, by definition, entails "conditions characterized by severity, sternness, or asceticism" and requires avoidance of all forms of indulgence. PRIIF forces used and are still using economic austerity to starve programs such as Head Start, food for lower income children, and even governmental programs meant to ensure public safety (forms of indulgence in their minds), as a charade to advance their political, private, and profiting agendas.

In 2016, the 100-year anniversary of the National Parks System, the "drown the government in a bathtub" crowd has been so successful over the Velvet Coup decades that the system now suffers from chronic and staggering neglect. These are public commons treasured by everyone, but now, to accomplish the maintenance necessary for public safety, animal life, and infrastructures, they are considering, for example, plastering our beautiful, protected national parks and monuments with branding such as the Nike Swoosh, the Starbucks logo, and Target's bullseye.

By the way, proponents of austerity want us to believe there is not enough money in the country to fund needed programs for the citizenry, and they are right. What the privatization faction is not telling us is that there is plenty of money in America, but it is held in just a few d-rich hands or offshored in private and corporate bank accounts.

Michael J. Sandel, an American political philosopher and Harvard professor, penned *Democracy's Discontent: America in Search of a Public Philosophy*. In it, he wrote of Republican President Theodore Roosevelt:

> For Roosevelt, Progressive politics was emphatically an enterprise of moral uplift. "The prime problem of our nation is to get the right type of good citizenship," he asserted. Democratic government could not be indifferent to the virtue of its people. "In a democracy like ours we cannot expect the stream to rise higher than the source. If the average man and the average woman are not of the right type, your public men will not be of the right type."

Hourglass Government

I want to be very clear here: Government is *not* a business. A great lie has been perpetuated on the American people so corporations could convince decision-makers to hand over public resources and programs, allowing companies to expand their reach to generate more profits. I wish I could dismiss this as a fad, but the concept has been far too dangerous and damaging to the foundation of our democracy. So much of our public commons have been handed over to psychopathic, greedy, private corporations that nearly our entire judicial system has been privatized. Even more distressing, the march toward our public school system, Social Security, and post office system is strong and on its way.

Time and time again, we've seen that big business is nothing that deserves honor and glory here. The Wall Street theft and the near collapse of the world economy tells us that, but it was also evidenced when a private energy company blew up a neighborhood in San Bruno, California because it was cheaper to avoid maintaining gas lines than be concerned for a neighborhood's safety. As if we need more proof of the sinister and bottom line-driven intentions of big business, Delta Airlines recently experienced a complete meltdown of their computer system, delaying flights for days. Why? Because it is more cost effective, at least in the short term, to not bother with a back-up computer system, just in case the primary one fails. Contingency plans that would ensure good customer service are deemed too costly to be a priority, and this shows us, loud and clear, where their focus is.

We have been sitting on a two-legged stool for decades, wondering why we are not a stable country. Business is one leg of the stool; nonprofit organizations and religious institutions are the second; and government is the third. Government, though imperfect and requiring constant vigilance, is the only leg we, the people have to stand on to keep corporate power in check.

Government is citizenship at every level. As in an hourglass, we have several levels of government, with the federal government at the top (Congress, the president, Supreme Court, and federal employees). Then, moving down toward the center of the hourglass, are our state (governors, legislatures, elected representatives and staff), county (county executives, board of supervisors, and employees), municipal (mayors, city councils, city managers and staff), university (presidents, provosts, faculty and staff), and school districts (district administrators, school boards, teachers and staff). The people who work in these lower echelons of government have chosen to be public servants; in a democracy, this is also considered a civic duty. Somebody has to run things, or else we would all drown in chaos. Without individuals stepping up to serve the public – and not pursuing a for-profit, nonprofit, or religious career – we would not be able to manage our democracy. Public employees are an integral component to self-rule and deserve our respect.

Believe me when I say it is not easy to work for the public. I spent many years serving in several municipalities, and even though many I came in contact were very nice people, often doing civic duties themselves by volunteering on boards or commissions, quite a few were just horrible. The hate created by Ronald Reagan's nine words (I'm from the government and I'm here to help) played out for decades in the public arena, and it is still playing out every day. My only guess for this abhorrent behavior was they thought their civic duty was to yell, manipulate, and be disrespectful to publically employed individuals at every turn. What I have witnessed at City Council meetings would make your hair stand on end, and most City Council members are also volunteers, fulfilling a civic duty.

Democracy requires healthy skepticism, but the destructive force these Americans wielded was far beyond skepticism. They tossed into the public arena Living-in-the-Red emotions and victimhood. One might say that, as public *servants,* we deserved to be treated as inferior. Really? In my view, people who behave in this manner are not only disrespecting the individual who is trying to do the job for which they were hired but also the very democracy they live within. We do not have to like each other, but we must be civil (thus, civics) with each other for democracy to thrive. In our discourse, I fear civility has long been abandoned, and inflamed rhetoric constantly swirls around us. Civility does not suppress free speech as some might purport; on the contrary, it encourages it. It is generally difficult for people to voice their opinion when they are being bullied and pummeled with Red emotions and flaming rhetoric. We must make every effort to bring civility back, or our republic is in real trouble.

As citizens, we are the center of the hourglass. At an individual level, we vote and follow the rule of law that is foundational to democracy. We are the ones who hold our government in esteem or in dishonor. Are we going to choke off the moving sand or allow it to pass through to the other half of the hourglass? The other half is, after all, equally important. It holds our profit and nonprofit organizations, unions, clubs, associations, and religious groups. Like the sand in a flipped hourglass, we rise and fall together.

Still, there are those who want to break the glass and see us abandon each other. Who benefits from we, the people being torn apart? Who benefits from the gridlock when we cannot work together? Who benefits when *compromise*, a pillar of democracy, is demonized? Government is how we come together. Who benefits when we are at each other's throats? Corporations and the disgustingly rich, that's who – all our Syphoning Citizens and Corporations that so readily starve the majority of us so their minority may possess nearly all the money and resources of the country. They also stuff enormous amounts of money ($1.3 trillion) in offshore accounts with the calamitous effect of syphoning our governmental coffers and economy. Did you know that sixty-two individuals worldwide own wealth equivalent to that of half of humanity? The world's hourglass is so tilted that nearly all the sand is caught at the top.

Regarding Syphoning Corporations, in an April 14, 2016 report titled "Broken at the Top," Oxfam America stated:

> Tax dodging by multinational corporations costs the U.S. approximately $111 billion each year and saps an estimated $100 billion every year from poor countries, preventing crucial investments in education, healthcare, infrastructure, and other forms of poverty reduction. U.S. policymakers and a broken international tax system enable tax dodging by multinational corporations, which contribute to dangerous inequality that is undermining our social fabric and hindering economic growth.

The same report went on to talk about the Syphoning Citizens, as I call them, those who take for themselves to starve others. Teddy Roosevelt referred to them as "not the right type" of citizen. The Oxfam report continued:

> The gap between rich and poor is reaching new extremes. The richest 1 percent have accumulated more wealth than the rest of the world put together. Meanwhile, the wealth owned by the bottom half of humanity has fallen by a trillion dollars in the past five years. Just 62 individuals now have the same wealth as 3.6 billion people – half of humanity. This figure is down from 388 individuals as recently as 2010. These dramatic statistics are just the latest evidence that today, we live in a world with dangerous and growing levels of inequality.

This inequality is fueled by an economic and political system that benefits the rich and powerful at expense of the rest, causing the gains of economic growth over the last several decades to go disproportionately to the already wealthy. Among the most damning examples of this rigged system is the way large, profitable companies use offshore tax havens, and other aggressive and secretive methods, to dramatically lower their corporate tax rates in the United States and developing countries alike. This practice is called "tax avoidance" or "tax dodging." Ironically, these same companies, which retain a multibillion-dollar army of lobbyists to influence federal policy, are among the largest beneficiaries of taxpayer funded support.

The hourglass in which we all live is nearly shattered. What will keep it from completely shattering is democracy, not a corporatocracy or oligarchy. Courageous and Concerned Voters can save it! Sustaining Citizens can save it! For this reason, more of us must now move into these categories so our republic can be saved. It has become imperative that we elect Sustaining Citizens to what is now, sadly, a FUBAR Congress.

The FUBAR Congress

In recent history, the United States Congress approval rating has been as low as 9 percent and as high as 22 percent. That means that 78 percent to 91 percent of Americans (atrocious disapproval ratings), regardless of political party, think Congress is not worth the paychecks they take home, along with numerous other perks. Congress is not just broken. Rather – poof! – it has vaporized! No longer does Congress function as a branch of government. Taxpayers are currently funding a complete boondoggle, formerly known as the United States Congress. Even though we likely want to fire them all, though, we cannot. On the other hand, they do need us to rehire them. Voting for the right people for the right reasons – not out of anger or with a throw-the-bums-out attitude but with a hire-the-right-bums attitude. Electing serious, intelligent candidates is paramount. As President Theodore Roosevelt said, we need the "right type of citizen[s]" holding elected office.

Currently, Donald Trump is running for president, and his hyperbole attracts the Caustic Voter Type. Also, in my view, if a billionaire becomes president, the Velvet Coup will be complete. Most Trump supporters are angry at Congress for not working on their behalf. They want to throw the establishment (the bums) out, not realizing that the party in control of Congress is the Republican Party. They support a Republican to become president, the nominee from the same party that created the dire mess in which we find ourselves. The Caustic Voter may think they are voting for the individual who says what they want to hear, but at the same time, they are voting for the party and what that party stands for; for your reference, I have placed a list of what each political party generally stands for below. It really does not make any sense, but when the Caustic Voter is angry, reasoning goes out the window

It must be said, though, that Caustic Voters have every reason to be angry, but it is the reaction to the anger that must be strategic, not just a jerk of the knee. The 133rd Congress only passed 286 bills. In addition, Congress has only conducted business for 154 days out of 431 since that Congress began. President Truman called the 80th Congress the "do-nothing Congress," yet that Congress passed 906 bills. Our current Congress, passing only 286 non-consequential bills, really needs to be called "the FUBAR Congress," as in f**ked up beyond all recognition.

All we, the people have left, since our elected representatives are no longer representing us, is shaming, shunning (our voice), and voting. Our limited options are another reason why Americans are so angry, but we must shame, shun, and vote strategically. We are not helpless. Shaming, shunning and voting activities work when enough of us get together on an issue. We cannot succumb to the red meat language tossed out from the podium: "Build a wall! Ban Muslims! Regulate who can use what bathrooms!" We cannot waste our votes on hate-talk manipulation, for hate is Living in the Red, and we will not recapture our democracy with Red talk, Red emotions, or Red actions.

Fortunately, there are a few special, constructive representatives serving in Congress. Most of us are aware of Senator Elizabeth Warren (D-MA), who fights every day for the middle class and started the Consumer Financial Protection Bureau. There also is a freshman House Representative and an acquaintance, Tulsi Gabbard (D-HI), who fights for the middle class and improving communication between the two parties. When speaking publically, she often uses the *aloha spirit* as an analogy. She explains that most people think *aloha* means paradise, wonderful people, nice weather, and beautiful beaches but it really means much, much more. The word has two roots: *Alo,* "to share"; and *ha,* "breath of life." To live in the aloha spirit, then, means to live a life that is honest, truthful, patient, and always striving to humbly give respect to all people, regardless of where they come from. In the deepest sense of the word, she says, it allows us the opportunity to see each other truly as people transcending the boxes and labels in which we find ourselves Tulsi Gabbard and Elizabeth Warren are two examples of the "right type of citizen," the kind of people we must replicate in Congress.

What has forced Congress to abandon serving and representing we, the people is the gargantuan amount of money in politics. The Citizens United Supreme Court travesty created a destructive force in this country that has never been seen before by allowing corporations to secretly spend as much money as they want to support or attack politicians and legislative initiatives. We, as individual citizens or even citizens joined by unions, associations, or nonprofits, could never combat the money corporations have to spend. Most likely, that was the point, if you ascribe to the Velvet Coup argument as I do. Sadly, the current president, by executive order, could take a significant step to bring the dark money out of hiding by requiring companies that do business with the federal government to disclose their political spending. Congress could pass legislation to do the same or more. They certainly would have time to pass the needed legislation if they wanted to, because Congress is on schedule to work fewer days this year than they have in sixty years. Then again, I guess if they are not working, they do not have to even show up.

The majority political party's budget proposals, while dry material, are immensely important to us. In that one document is everything we need to know about the priorities of those governing us. Who gets ahead? Who is abandoned?

The federal budgeting process begins with the president sending his budget proposal to Congress. Congress is then to hold hearings. In 2016, this has not been the case. Why? Because the Republican-held Congress refused to hold budget hearings, after a four-decade track record. Gallingly, they made this decision *before* the president sent the budget to Congress. This act puts a sharp point on their temper tantrum and blind refusal to do any work, such as not holding hearings on a Supreme Court nominee, the Senate Banking Committee refusing to act on any presidential nominee for fourteen months, or the eleven-month delay on approving a head to the Treasury Department Terrorism Section. Their latest temper tantrum put the country at huge risk. Why did they not appoint a head to the Terrorism Section? By his own admission, Richard Shelby (R-AL) faced a primary challenge, and they did not want him to look bad to his constituency. Really? This is what Congress has devolved to? Is this what some constituencies have devolved to as well? FUBAR!

Due to abandoning their responsibility to the American people, the Republican Party is in an existential crisis and is now being taken over by a carnival-barker, self-indulgent, cruel billionaire. They do not like it, but the Law of the Harvest, reaping what one sows, governs. Unfortunately, the Democratic Party is not far behind, due to their waning ability to hold on to and fight for their once-held populist principles.

Republican Consultant Alex Castellanos may have said it best in regard to the Republican identity crisis, in an article written by Tom Hamburger and Matea Gold, titled "GOP Strategist Castellanos: Time To Rally Around Trump, too Late To Ask Mommy To Step in and Rewrite the Rules." They quoted Alex Castellanos to say:

> If our self-indulgent Republican Party establishment had really wanted to prevent a takeover of the GOP, they should not have gorged on political power while they failed to do anything to prevent the decline of the country. Our leaders could have led. They could have done more than say no to Democrats while offering no alternative."

Not surprisingly, a recent Gallop poll determined that card-carrying Republicans hold a more negative attitude toward Congress than Democrats do, even though the Republicans hold both houses in Congress.

Ian Millhiser, a Center for American Progress senior fellow, wrote "The Future of the Democratic Party Will Be Decided by the Supreme Court." In that article, he made the point that the Democratic Party has fallen from grace because they abandoned their previous fifty-state strategy, and now, "Republicans dominate the other (not the presidency) levers of American government." The Republicans hold 70 percent of state legislatures, more than 60 percent of gubernatorial positions, and 55 percent of attorneys general and secretaries of state. When Republicans are in office, the party tenets and belief system is also. This involves many things, like poisoning an entire city's water supply (Flint, Michigan) or passing union-hostile right-to-work (for less) legislation that decimates democratic organizations, or gerrymandering state districts to ostracize typically democratic populations such as people of color, students, and senior citizens.

The Supreme Court is to blame for the ability of any political party to gerrymander districts, but since the Republicans hold an overwhelming majority of state-level positions of power, they benefit the most from the *Vieth v. Jubelirer* decision in 2004, when the judges forbade federal courts from hearing challenges to partisan gerrymanders. That resulted in state lawmakers being free to draw up maps that enrich their party and lock out the other, even though such maps violate the First Amendment rights of voters. As Millhiser, "The Future of the Democratic Party Will Be Decided by the Supreme Court," relates:

> ... many states are extraordinarily gerrymandered at the state legislative level. Virginia, for example, has a Democratic governor, yet the Republicans enjoy a 67-32 supermajority in the state's House of Delegates. Similarly, Pennsylvania also has a democratic governor, but Republicans enjoy a 120-83 majority in the state House and a 30-20 majority in the state Senate.

Supreme Court Indifference

The current Supreme Court, led by Chief Justice John G. Roberts, Jr. (who served as a private lawyer working on behalf of George W. Bush in the *Bush v. Gore* case before the Supreme Court in 2000) has been receptive to business and corporate interests more than any other court before it. This Supreme Court, which has a record of primarily 5-4 decisions, has abandoned the people. A study prepared for *The New York Times* by scholars at Northwestern University and the University of Chicago analyzed 1,450 decisions since 1953. That study demonstrated that the Roberts court ruled for business interests, with a "statistically significant" difference, more than previous courts. In other words, America's Supreme Court, under Chief Justice Roberts, has abandoned the people for the corporation.

Chief Justice John Roberts is the justice whose court will be known as the court that abandoned democracy. *Citizens United v. Federal Election Commission* was not seen as a particularly important case, as the issue itself was one of narrow focus: The McCain-Feingold campaign finance law prohibited corporations from running television commercials thirty days before primaries. Citizens United, a nonprofit, wanted to run a documentary critical of Hillary Clinton within that thirty-day period. Thus, the FEC prohibited its broadcast under the law. Citizens United challenged the decision, and it did not appear to be much riding on the outcome.

Individually, Justice Roberts will be known in perpetuity for the disastrous Citizens United decision because he caused the case to be broadened from its narrow focus of whether or not the documentary could be shown within the thirty-day window to allowing limitless, undisclosed private money to be spent on political campaigns and, in doing so, abandoned precedence and generations of campaign-finance law. The Roberts Court guaranteed that d-rich interests, either by individuals or by corporations, now have the freedom to spend any amount of money from any source, including foreign governments, at any time, to try to win any election of their choice. In the name of freedom and free speech, the Supreme Court created an unfathomable imbalance between corporations and the d-rich and individual citizens because more money now equals more influence, more freedom, and more free speech. Those with less money – all the rest of us – now possess none of those things.

Senator Sherrod Brown (OH) recently made the observation that the Citizens United decision now allows well-heeled interests to just "threaten" elected individuals or campaigns and their limitless wealth; if they don't toe the line, it will be used against them. These threats are never made public, and when they threaten congressional members on a specific vote or bill, it will never be disclosed. He said it is a "terrible mess poisoning democracy" and "fundamentally wrong," all brought to you by Chief Justice John Roberts.

To complicate matters, there is a new breed of lawyers on the rise, those who specialize in Supreme Court advocacy and who have been extraordinarily successful in persuading the Court to hear business cases and to also rule in their clients' favor. Adam Liptak in his article, "Justices Offer Receptive Ear to Business Interests" explains that we know about the phalanx of lobbyists who advocate and pressure our congressional representatives, but now we have specifically bred lawyers whose job it is to lobby the Supreme Court.

Also, the U.S. Chamber of Commerce is a very powerful influence on the court. In many cases, the chamber files briefs supporting large corporations, and their success rate is over 80 percent. This indicates that the Roberts Court holds corporate interests powerfully over the interests of the people. After learning this fact, my husband renamed the court, the Supreme *Corp.*

In a *New York Times* article titled "Justice for Big Business," Erwin Chemerinsky, Dean of the University of California, Irvine law school, identified a "disturbing trend" that the Roberts Court "ruled in favor of big business and closed the courthouse doors to employees, consumers and small business seeking remedy for serious injuries by their decisions on affirmative action, voting rights and same-sex marriage." He went on to say, "A majority of the justices seem to believe that it is too easy to sue corporations... The court affirmed that it consistently favors manufacturers over consumers...and the court continued to sharply limit class-action suits against companies.

In his blog, Thom Hartmann began by saying, "The Supreme Court doesn't give a rat's patootie about you and me," an example being the Keystone XL pipeline. A lawsuit was filed by a group of five teenagers and two nonprofits representing thousands of young Americans on the legal principle held in Public Trust Doctrine, which intends for our government to do everything in its power to protect and maintain survival resources (air, water, etc.) for future generations. The Supreme Corp refused to hear the case. As Jeffery Toobin, Staff Writer for *The New Yorker* stated, "In every major case since he became the nation's seventeenth chief justice, Roberts has sided with the prosecution over the defendant, the State over the condemned, the executive branch over the legislature, and the corporate defendant over the individual plaintiff."

Individually, several members of the Supreme Court have abandoned the people because they are actually right-wing political activists and not impartial judges at all. In addition to Chief Justice Roberts:

- Justice Sam Alito attended an *American Spectator* fundraiser, headlined by Michele Bachman, a right-wing flamethrower, and the RNC chairman to assist the organization in raising tens of thousands of dollars. It was not Alito's first time to attend such a partisan event, as he was also a speaker for the same organization a few years before to help raise big dollars. His intent was to damage the Reputation of Vice President-Elect Joe Biden, as a serial plagiarist. The point about these type of actions is that we have a Supreme Court Justice who is blatant in his politics and would obviously not be a fair judge to more than half of the people in this country.

When Justice Alito was asked by a *Democratic Underground*

reporter why he thought it appropriate to attend a highly political fundraiser with the Republican Party, due to his position on the Supreme Court, Alito replied, "It's not important that I'm here." When confronted about helping to raise funds for the Republicans a couple years prior, he reiterated, "It's not important," then walked – or maybe ran – away. His actions clearly declare that he does not wish to be accountable and that he did not want to talk to them because he is a coward. Justice Alito also patronizingly and negatively shook his head when the president was explaining to the American people in a State of the Union Address the impacts of the Citizen United decision.

• Justice Clarence Thomas listens to Rush Limbaugh while exercising. What more do you need to know? Actually, there is much more to know. *The New York Times* reported Thomas's longstanding relationship with Harlan Crow, a Texas real estate developer who got his start in his father's business, Trammell Crow Company (another inheritance baby). He was a founding member of Club for Growth and sits on the board of the American Enterprise Institute, both extreme right-wing organizations, and he provides millions of dollars to Republican candidates and organizations. Harlan is most notable for funding the anti-John Kerry Swift Boat Veterans for Truth, an untruthful hit job on a Democratic candidate running for president. This close, good friend of Justice Clarence Thomas's chooses to decorate his back yard with replicas of dictators: Mao Zedong, Vladimir Lenin, Fidel Castro, and Joseph Stalin. These are the types of individuals Harlan Crow reveres? Does not every mother warn her children that they will be judged by the company they keep?

By now, everyone should know the scandal behind Justice Thomas's appointment and the charges levied against him by Anita Hill, who accused him of sexual harassment. It is important to note that Clarence Thomas is very fortunate that social media had not yet been invented, or the truth would have been more widely known at the time. However, today, we know much more about who he is.

Thomas owns an amazing bust of Abraham Lincoln made by a famous sculptor, Adolph Alexander Weinman, in 1914. The Lincoln bust was given to him by Christopher DeMuth, President of the American Enterprise Institute. In the years following, as of 2011, the American Enterprise Institute has filed briefs to the Supreme Court on three separate occasions; on each occasion, Thomas has ruled in their favor, even going beyond the scope of what they were seeking. In addition, Thomas regularly attends fundraisers sponsored by the Koch Brothers, in support of right-wing media outlets, think tanks, and organization. How can this justice be counted upon by the people when he brazenly flaunts his politics?

In Clarence Thomas's case, his wife, Ginny, must also be discussed. With money from the dictator-stature-loving Harlan Crow, Ginny created Liberty Central, now Liberty Consulting, an advocacy group with the goal of destroying the Affordable Care Act. The conflict of interest for Justice Thomas is blatant, yet he does not recuse himself when the Supreme Court is required to review sections of the act. More amazingly, Thomas failed to disclose nearly a million dollars of income earned by his wife; when confronted with this fact, he said, "Oops! Didn't understand the paperwork." What? How is this man sitting on the highest court of the land if he cannot understand IRS paperwork or know to hire someone who does? My sense is that he knew exactly what he was doing, but who is there to hold him accountable? Clarence Thomas is a prime example of an anti-character individual made only more frightening due to his position.

• Justice Antonin Scalia recently passed away, but his judicial legacy will live on for decades. Therefore, it is important to know who he was. To begin to understand him, we must first learn who is father was. Eugene Scalia sent his son to a military school where they had to pledge allegiance to Mussolini, and his father was founder of the American Fascist Party in 1934. Scalia's father had a large impact on his thinking, and he was known as a strong conservative at the young age of 17. In 2004, Scalia went on a hunting trip with Vice President Dick Cheney in Louisiana. That trip raised numerous questions about the propriety of a Supreme Court justice going hunting at the exact same time when Scalia was hearing a case involving the vice president being required to make public who served on his Energy Task Force. Scalia did not recuse himself, the court ruled in Cheney's favor, and the public will never know what decisions were made behind closed doors.

In a blog by Vegasjessie titled "Scalia's Fascist Roots Run Deep," the writer refers to Scalia as a "staunch enemy of most democratic principles... It's easy to see why. His father's allegiances lie with people who were sympathetic with the ways of the Nazis, who basically believe every function of government should be run by private corporations, that government should be strictly authoritarian, and that there should be no freedom for people within a country... A corporatist, a segregationist, and a big advocate of state's rights, he may as well be a plantation owner in the Antebellum South. I don't think his interpretation of the Constitution is what it's supposed to be. He has a conservative agenda and will always rule for the wealthy corporations." Jeffery Toobin said on March 4, 2015, "...Scalia looks ever more like a Fox News justice, who seems to get his talking points from popular culture rather than from the law."

- Justice Kennedy, in the first term of the Roberts Court, voted with right-wing justices 94.1 percent of the time. In one year, there were twenty-four blockbuster decisions regarding abortion, affirmative action, and freedom of speech and religion. Justice Kennedy voted, 100 percent of the time, to make them 5-4 votes for the political right.

The sad reality is that our Supreme Court justices are partisan. Most of us have been taught to believe judges weigh the facts, regardless of political party, then even the scales of injustice. In his book, *Justice v. Justice,* Bernard Schwartz , law professor at New York University School of Law, said of an earlier Supreme Court, "The Supreme Court does not work in the ... purely logical way many people think it does, but...through the personal as well as the legal give-and-take between the justices." He further said, "Surely, it is better for the court and country that this be made known than kept concealed behind the red velour curtains." So, it is best that we are aware of how partisan they can act. This Roberts Supreme Court has abandoned jurisprudence for the middle class to the benefit of corporations and conservative, partisan politics. Astounding...and sad.

I could go on and describe the backgrounds of the other four justices —,Breyer, Ginsberg, Kagan and Sotomayor — but one would be hard pressed to find numerous Living-in-the-Red energies such as tax evasion, fascism, dictator-revering friends, corporate zealotry, or blatant political theology in their personal histories.

Stand Up Activities

Below, for your consideration, are several suggested Stand Up Activities. For a further explanation of the Keep/Start/Stop organization tool, please see Chapter One. After reading this chapter, you may think of additional activities readers can implement. If you'd like to share your brilliant constructive, compelling and creative ideas, please do so at: www.facebook.com/americaabandoned.

KEEP:

1. Keep in mind President Roosevelt's words: "Government is ourselves and not an alien power over us."

2. Keep in mind that there is nothing the average citizen can do about the caliber, personality, and political belief system of a Supreme Court justice, yet, these justices have immense power over our everyday lives. The power of appointment lies in the hands of Congress and the president. Realize, your vote for Congress impacts the Supreme Court. At this time, with the death of Justice Scalia, the Republican Party is refusing to uphold their constitutional duty to hold a hearing for a replacement on the court. FUBAR!

START:

1. Start reflecting on whether you are a Sustaining Citizen and if you are involved with Sustaining Organizations.

2. Start analyzing whether a candidate running for office is a Sustaining or a Syphoning Citizen. The Sustaining Citizen candidate will work on the public's behalf. A Syphoning Citizen candidate will work on their own behalf and the behalf of those who fund them.

3. Start considering running for office yourself or becoming involved in your local political party. Both parties need changing from the inside.

4. Start educating yourself on national politics and issues by subscribing to the free or paid version of the *Ring of Fire* podcast at: www.trofire.com. They cover news and issues that directly affect our lives, things we will likely never be privy to through the corporate media.

5. Start to sign up for online news sources such as Six: State Innovation Exchange at: https://stateinnovation.org. This source quickly informs you about what is happening at the state legislative level. This is important, because what happens in one state may happen in others. Listen to Six Executive Director Nicholas Rathod and the inside story of ALEC in *The Good Fight*, Episode 39, at: http://rss.thegoodfight.fm/.

6. Start joining Sustaining Organizations such as the American Constitution Society for Law and Policy, https://www.acslaw.org. A copy of the Constitution is on the site.

STOP:

1. Stop thinking government is bad or worthless and electing candidates who hold this belief. How can a candidate improve a government they do not believe in? In effect, if you believe government is worthless, that very thought is a reflection on you, your friends, and your neighbors. In a democracy, "Government is ourselves and not an alien power over us." In my opinion, it is this Red belief system that has caused much of our current state of affairs in this country.

2. Stop making political decisions out of anger.

One Marvelous Question

After reading this chapter, if you were going to do one thing marvelously well to move forward, what would that one thing be?

In our two-party system, could Newton's Third Law apply?

CHAPTER NINE

Two-Party System: Government Yin and Yang

"When you tell a lie, you steal someone's right to the truth."

Khaled Hosseini

There is a dichotomy I cannot resolve in my mind. As Americans, we revere the concept of we, the people. We understand the nature of community in that statement and recognize the power of our democracy in those words. Many of us celebrate the diversity held within the phrase, knowing our strength as a country comes from a collection of ideas. Nevertheless, there is a significant, vocal faction who hates our government, people who despise our vital institution that forms the country in which we are so very proud. I understand being skeptical of our government; it is a required trait of citizens in a republic and how we weed out the problems and fix them. But should we hate it?

Another dichotomy exists in the political party belief systems. The Republicans, right-wingers, believe government cannot do anything good and want it drowned in a bathtub; that murderous metaphor demonstrates their hate of government. Democrats, left-wingers, believe it is possible for government to do good things. That is simplistic enough, but where did the concept of left and right wings come from? We can thank the French Revolution, when politicians met in a National Assembly to organize themselves into two different groups: those who supported the Revolution and those who supported the French King. Subsequently, in the 1930s, the British House of Commons split, using similar definitions as the French while debating the Spanish Civil War into the conservative Right and the liberal Left.

In his book, *The Web of Government*, Scottish Sociologist Robert M. MacIver explained, "The right is always the party sector associated with the interests of the upper or dominant classes, the left the sector expressive of the lower economic or social classes, and the center that of the middle classes."

David McCandless, a London-based author and designer, created a website to assist us to visualize data and complicated subjects and ideas, *Information Is Beautiful*. An extremely helpful infographic, visually depicts our two-party system and their respective views on government society and culture. It is a must-see.

Two-Party System Defined

I admire political cartoonists, deep-thinking artists who are able to succinctly capture a striking cultural issue with their ink and paper. Signe Wilkinson created a three-panel cartoon, each panel containing a version of the American flag that visually demonstrated the existing division between our two political parties. The first was labeled "Red States," and the flag bore only the red and white stripes, with no blue panel or white stars. The second, "Blue States," showed only a blue flag with the white stars and no striped section whatsoever. The third panel showed Old Glory in all its glory, labeled "*United* States." Needless to say, the first two flags looked ridiculous, sad, and rather pathetic. Even more pathetic is that currently, our political system in these not-so-United States is operating as those incomplete flags.

Understanding our political system is imperative to our civics comprehension. Basic information may be found on Wikipedia under "Federal government of the United States" and "Two-party System." Numerous issues could be discussed about our political party system; however, I am most interested in those who manage the two-party system.

I use "manage" because we and our country are being managed, not led. It is easy to confuse the meaning of the two words. To define the word *manage*, concepts and words such as "be in charge of, run, be head of, direct, control, govern, rule, command, administer, organize, conduct and guide" are used, and the ability to lead is inferred. To explain the word *lead*, concepts and words such as "be in charge of, be the leader of, be the head of, preside over, head, command, govern, rule, control" are used. The definitions of these two words are basically synonymous.

Subtly, meaning changes a bit when the word *leadership* is used. To define it, words such as "guidance, direction, control, management, supervision, governance, administration, rule, command, power, and influence" are used. In practice, however, there is a flaw in the definition as it pertains to government and leading our country. The definition does not reference leadership as being for the common good or in the pursuit of happiness or fighting for democratic equality.

Many years ago, I was enrolled in an Organization Development Academy. The instructors stressed that, in reality, there is a significant difference between managing and leading. Simply put, they said one manages *things* and leads *people*. *Leadership*, they said, is "the ability to envision a better future (for a company, nonprofit, government) and inspire people to achieve goals required to achieve that improved future." It is my theory that those who think of themselves as leaders of our political parties are only managing their respective parties; even worse, their managing is dictated and focused on money, not people. Also, for whom are they envisioning a better future? The lack of a leadership frame of reference in decision-making has dire consequences for the country and our democracy.

When I was beginning my research for this book, it was my complete intention to be as even-handed as possible when discussing each of the political parties. As my research progressed, I found it harder and harder to maintain a balanced approach. I know both political parties have misguided issues to address, but there is no equivalence between the two. As I learned more about each party and what they stand for, the more progressive I personally became in my own principles and values.

I will anger some readers when I say the Republican Party has been at the root of many of the struggles in which the middle class finds itself. Both political parties have been corrupted by money, but the Republican Party has corrupted itself willingly. In addition, it is philosophically against social programs that benefit the middle and lower classes, to such an extreme that it has become a theology. In fact, the Republican Party has completely abandoned the middle and lower classes and are so corporate friendly that they are intentionally seating corporate friendly judges in our America judicial system, which has led to numerous decisions that hurt the middle class. The Democratic Party is also corrupted by money because the Citizens United decision created legalized bribery and will not stand up to corporations and their demands. Still, having said that, Democrats are more likely to value social programs and attempt to fight for them.

Having completed my research, I have come to ask: How can the Republican Party be trusted to run a government that they hate? Now, when I hear someone say, "The parties are both the same," I want to scream, "No they aren't! Not by a long shot!"

The Authoritarian Parent: Republicans

Republican /ri-puhb-li-kuh n/: 1. of, relating to, or of the nature of a republic (adj), 2. favoring a republic (adj), 3. a person who favors a republican form of government (noun), 4. a member of the Republican Party (noun). (The Free Dictionary)

Re·pub·lic /rə' pəblik/: (noun) a state in which supreme power is held by the people and their elected representatives, and which has an elected or nominated president rather than a monarch. (Oxford Dictionaries)

In the 1960s, UC Berkeley Professor Jack Block and his wife, fellow Professor Jeanne Block began tracking 100 nursery school children for a long-term personality study, "Nursery School Personality and Political Orientation Two Decades Later." Even though conservatives took issue with the results, there is no reason to think the results were swayed, because assessing future politics was not a component of evaluating 3- and 4-year-olds at the time.

The Blocks followed the same children for decades and discovered, quite accidentally, that the whiniest were inclined to become conservative and turned into rigid young adults who followed closely to traditional gender roles and were uncomfortable with ambiguity. Even though Dr. Block agreed that Berkeley is not representative of the entire country, he still stood by his results of his sample, and of course conservative adults like to whine and complain about his results. He reasoned that insecure children look for the reassurance provided by tradition and authority and find those traits in conservative politics.

The Republican Party today is way beyond whiny. They have gone from complaining to bewailing, bemoaning, bellyaching, blocking, and bullying. When I searched for *complain* synonyms it listed four columns of Living-in-the-Red energies that represent the party's abandonment of its own definition of "favoring a republic." Even *New York Times* Op-ed Columnist Thomas L. Friedman, in his June 7, 2016 column, "Dump the GOP for a Grand New Party" stated, "If a party could declare bankruptcy, today's Republican Party would be in Chapter 11." He goes on to say that America requires a healthy two-party system, and he further states that our current Republican Party is "...an ethically challenged enterprise that enriches and perpetuates itself by shedding all pretense of standing for real principles." They do not make decisions that support the "state in which supreme power is held by the people." They have been wholly purchased by corporations and the d-rich and have alternatively placed the supreme power in their hands. The Republicans in office today are not *leading* the country by inspiring us to create a better future. Republicans do like to think of themselves as conservatives. By definition, true conservatives oppose change and possess a disposition for preserving what is already established. Conservatism philosophy espouses maintaining existing order and opposing change and innovation. Under such a value system, I cannot see how the Republican Party will ever be capable enough—or truly willing—to lead America into the future. Instead, they force austerity ideology, which generates frustration and fear in people, so they may *manage* the movement of taxpayer money to their benefactors.

Ironically, 2016 Republican presidential candidate Donald Trump does not represent typical conservative desire to maintain existing order; rather, he pontificates, in the most Living-in-the-Red terms, blowing up and undoing the entire foundation of our entire democratic principles. As the Block Study revealed, Trump appeals to adults who find ambiguity disturbing and are looking for an authoritarian father figure, a strongman who tells them the world is a dangerous place and that only he can save them. Astonishingly, Donald Trump used this exact mantra in one of his campaign rallies when he arrogantly announced, "Only *I* can do it."

President Franklin Delano Roosevelt, while touring the South in 1932, said, "The Four Horsemen of the GOP are Destruction, Delay, Deceit, and Despair." I worked for many years with municipalities, and one primarily important lesson I learned was that a governmental budget represents the politicians' program priorities." In other words, budgeting and spending money is, in reality, prioritizing human and community needs. Budget documents are dry and boring, but what they represent is highly important and can have serious impacts on all our lives when it is converted into legislation. Take, for example, the Republican's 2015 budget proposal. In one extremely important document all Four Horsemen are running at a full gallop.

As Paul Krugman wrote in his article, "Trillion-Dollar Fraudsters," "The modern GOP's raw fiscal dishonesty (Deceit) is something new in American politics...and that's telling us something important about what has happened to half of our political spectrum." The GOP's budget proposal (remember that these are priorities for legislation) savagely cuts food stamps, as well as savagely cuts Medicaid and Medicare (Destruction). It freezes Pell grants for college education and scales back other educational programs (Destruction). The Republicans continue to toss millions of Americans off health insurance, leaving them medically vulnerable once again (Destruction).

Despite the Republicans overreacting and hyperventilating for years about deficits, their 2015 budget does nothing about it (Delay). Their budget proposal leaves in place tax loopholes (Delay) for the d-rich and corporations while convincing the middle class that this plan will benefit them (Deceit). They say to the American people that when the rich get richer and the corporations get bigger (made possible by the actions of Republican Congress members), it will trickle down to the poor and middle class (Deceit).

This warped trickle-down economics theology did not work when Ronald Reagan adopted it, and it has not worked since, yet they keep promoting it anyway (Deceit) because it benefits those who give them money. The GOP-proposed budget, which represents their priorities, transfers more wealth to the d-rich and pays for it by cutting programs for children, seniors, students, and nearly everyone else in the poor and middle classes because they will not do anything for roads and bridges. Recently, the director for the Center for Disease Control went before the Republican-held House of Representatives and begged – yes, begged! – for 1.8 million dollars in research funding to develop a vaccine for the Zika virus, which causes heartbreaking birth defects. The Republicans refused. These are not Sustaining Citizens. They are terrifying citizens when it is possible for them to deny funding meant to save babies from debilitating defects. Pro-life is apparently a term used loosely.

In addition, their budget increases defense spending. America spends more money on defense then the next eight countries on the list. This country already spends $600 billion on defense, and the Republicans, in their 2015 budget, asked to increase that by $35 billion more, or $635,000,000,000, without paying for it, just like their Iraq war budget (Delay). Take a minute and think about what thirty-five billion dollars could do to remedy some of the needs of this country (infrastructure, education, healthcare, etc.). Paul Krugman ended his article by saying, "Look, I know that it's hard to keep up the outrage after so many years of fiscal fraudulence, but please try. We're looking at an enormous, destructive con job, and you should be very, very angry." The result of knowing their budget priorities and who they work for has caused a complete abandonment of we, the people by the Republican Party.

Will this Dickens-like budget be passed? Probably not but the ideologically based ideas will keep returning and it will have a serious impact on what does pass, as well as future legislation that will govern the country. It also speaks volumes about who the Republicans are and what they stand for. What also speaks volumes is their adept use and funding of the lie machine, with the sole purpose of the product of paralysis.

As Ari Rabin-Havt wrote in his book, *Lies Incorporated: The World of Post-Truth Politics,* there is a "growing force in American politics that creates and disseminates lies designed to disrupt the public policy process for money and ideological gain." This force is hired on behalf of corporations and right-wing conservative organizations, and there is no equivalent on the left. Ari Rabin-Havt relates that the quintessential individual who created paralysis as a product is Richard Berman.

Richard Berman, as related in *Lies Incorporated,* creates a labyrinth of bogus organizations to hide what corporation is funding which lie and has done so for decades, with his greatest of achievements being "the way he effectively blurs the lines between political operatives, corporate lobbyists, and the think tank world, sowing confusion on behalf of his clients." Ari Rabin-Havt continued:

> For each of these groups [Berman's organizations], the goal is often not simply to advocate for their point of view. As Berman explained during a surreptitiously recorded speech to a room of industry executives gathered at the Western Energy Alliance conference in June 2014, he works to confuse the public so they "don't know who to believe," putting them and the policymakers they represent in a position of ideological "paralysis."

Ari Rabin-Havt goes on to say:

> "Yet focusing solely on them [paralysis-producing businesses] obscures a fundamental truth: our democracy has been hacked, manipulated by political practitioners who recognize that as long as there is no truth, there can be no progress."

It has been the Democrats who have been on the receiving end of this product of paralysis for years, suffering the verbal abuse it causes. They have not stood up for our democracy; they have abandoned it for short-term pain relief.

The Nurturing Parent: Democrats

Democrat [dem-uh-frat}: an advocate of democracy (noun), 2. A person who believes in the political or social equality of all people (noun), 3. A member of the Democratic Party (noun). (The Free Dictionary)

Democracy: (noun) 1. government by the people; a form of government in which the supreme power is vested in the people and exercised directly by them or by their elected agents under a free electoral system. 2) a state of society characterized by formal equality of rights and privileges. (Dictionary.com)

Referring back to the Block study, in addition to identifying the personalities of small, whiny children, who tended to become Republican, those who were more fearful and were more comfortable with authoritarian leadership, the Blocks also discovered that confident children turned out to be liberals, bright, nonconforming adults with a wide array of interests. He also found that more confident children were eager to explore alternatives to the status quo and found liberal politics more compatible. These children grew up to be introspective, life-contemplative, perceptive, and esthetically responsive.

I read an article many years ago that hit me right between the eyes. It answered why I was so frustrated and disappointed with the Democratic Party. They did not seem to fight hard enough, to be an equal, counteracting force against the opposing party. They also did not fight hard enough against the Bush administration when the war in Iraq was contemplated. As Senator Robert Byrd said at the time, while standing on the Senate floor, the chamber was "ominously silent." He called out his own party, as well as the Republicans, because no other Democrat was on the House floor, challenging the premises for the war. For decades, the Democratic Party has fought tepidly for its principles and lag behind of their potential.

The article that grabbed my attention, was written by Mel Gilles, currently Zero Waste Specialist at Eco-Cycle (Boulder, Colorado) and author of *The*

Last Myth. That article was titled "The Politics of Victimization," and it explained the problem. In my view, she nailed it. She described how the Democratic Party leaders responded to the shellacking in the 2004 election, in which they said they should have been more likeable, more appealing, that they should have tried to be better and learn from their mistakes. As written in her article, that was an *introspective, life-contemplative, perceptive, and esthetically responsive* post-election position to take to a fault. Mel Gilles also powerfully stated, "Ask anyone who has ever worked in a domestic violence shelter if they have heard this before. They will tell you, 'Every single day.'"

A stunning example of Democratic silence, as an abuse victim would respond, was when forty-seven Republican Senators wrote a letter to Iran, saying the United States cannot be trusted to follow through on the nuclear negotiations the Obama administration had completed with them, basically threatening that it could be undone by the next president. It was an unconscionable act by an American political party. However, in my view, it was more unconscionable that the Democratic Party did not respond with any principle or opposing force. That letter, a clear intent to sabotage the Republican Party's own government, was in direct violation of the Logan Act, but the Democratic Party ignored it.

The Logan Act is a federal law that was passed in 1799. It forbids unauthorized citizens from negotiating with foreign governments who have a dispute with the United States. Its intent is to prevent undermining a governmental position, the exact intent of the Republican Senators who wrote it. Any violation of the Logan Act is supposed to be a felony. Shouldn't the Senators be aware of this law? Of course. They are United States Senators! If they did know about it and wrote the letter anyway, they committed a reprehensible, felonious act. Still, neither the Democratic leadership nor the attorney general did anything to hold those forty-seven accountable for their actions. As we all know, if people are not held accountable, they are emboldened.

Another example of the Lie Machine and the following incessant verbal abuse was the trigger phrase, "death panel" and the unrelenting lie that the Affordable Care Act (ACA) had a provision to force recipients to die sooner. They basically accused it of attempting to kill Grandma! On the face, it was simply absurd, but those against President Obama and the ACA used the Lie Machine – businesses, individuals, and media outlets willing to prostitute themselves to hammer the "death panel" meme until it could not be ignored by the Democrats. The Democrats, though, instead of fighting the lie with equal force or refusing to be pummeled into submission, did what abuse victims do to stop the pain: They caved and removed the end-of-life counseling provision from the laws, a provision even openly supported by the American Association of Retired Persons (AARP). The purveyors of paralysis achieved their goal, to confuse enough people so they would become enraged and fight to remove a benefit that may be of help to them in the future, with the additional ideological benefit of diminishing President Obama's signature legislation in the public's mind.

The rise of the Third Way faction of the Democratic Party was, I believe, a direct response to long-term abuse from the right-wing media, politicians, and corporations. Third Way pulled the Democratic Party away from representing the middle/lower classes and unions to a pro-growth message (code for pro-corporation) and underplayed the seriousness of wealth inequity. After all, we can't make the billionaires unhappy! They abandoned the populist platform that led to a four-decade-long trust between the middle class and the Democratic Party. Some Democrats have even supported and taken money from the payday lender industry, whose entire business model is to charge high interest rates to middle and low-income individuals and families who live on the edge every month, thus ensuring a cycle of financial dependence on the industry.

According to CJ Atkins's articled titled "Third Way Democrats Preparing To Challenge the Left for Factional Control," "By shifting attention away from the systemic failures exposed by the Great Recession, their hope is that the anti-austerity and social justice movements will be derailed and lose steam."

None of what Third Way stands for looks anything like the FDR Democrats who brought seventy years of prosperity to the country. How can democracy survive when an entire party is corporate and billionaire owned and a large portion of the opposing party is as well? As Ted Kennedy said at the 2008 Democratic National Convention, "You cannot know the difference between a minor concession and a major betrayal of principle unless you know what your principles are." What does the Democratic Party stand for today? Is it for FDR populist principles or Third Way corporate pro-growth, an inequality-ignoring message?

In Thomas Frank's *Listen, Liberal...or What Ever Happened to the Party of the People?* he said something frightening when it comes to our hopes for continued democracy. In my view, this will only be changed if we shame, shun, and vote, but he said:

> "...While there are many great Democrats and many exceptions to the trends...by and large, the story has been a disappointing one. We have surveyed this party's thoughts and deeds from the seventies to the present, we have watched them abandon whole classes and regions and industries, and we know now what the results have been. Their leadership faction has no intention of doing what the situation requires.
>
> It is time to face the obvious: ...the direction the Democrats have chosen to follow for the last few decades has been a failure for both the nation and for their own partisan health. "Failure" is admittedly a harsh word, but what else are we to call it when the left party in a system chooses to confront an epic economic breakdown by talking hopefully about entrepreneurship and innovation?... When the party of the common man basically allows aristocracy to return?"

A major lesson from Senator Bernie Sanders's campaign was that it showed us how to respond to and not fall prey to the abuse syndrome cycle. He tamed PRIFF forces by exemplifying the courage to stand on principle. Katrina vanden Heuvel, an American editor, publisher, and part-owner of *The Nation*, in her article, "Clinton May Take the Nomination, but Sanders Has Won the Debate," explained his captivation of millions: "And he did it so less with personal charisma than with the power of his ideas and the force of his integrity demonstrated by spurning traditional deep-pocketed donors in favor of grass-roots fundraising."

When it comes to our two-party system, I think a *Non Sequitur* cartoon by Wiley Miller said it well. The cartoon was an illustration of two people approaching a crossroads in front of a brick wall. On top of the wall, there was curled barbed wire and two signs, pointing in the opposite direction of one other. One sign said "Trepidation," and the other said, "Fear." Which path (party) will we choose?

Could Newton's Third Law Apply?

Newton stated, "For every action, there is an equal and opposite reaction." However erroneous, I am going to try and equate our two-party system to Newton's Third Law. In essence, it states that in every interaction, a pair of forces (two-party system) acts on the two interacting objects (each political party). The size of the forces on the first object (one party) equals the size of the force on the second (the opposing party). The direction of the force on the first object (one party) is opposite to the direction of the force on the second (the opposing party). Forces always come in pairs, an equal and opposite action-reaction force.

In an attempt to stretch the law to further apply to politics, it would be due to Newton's Third Law that the forces (each political party) would be assumed equal. Therefore, to always win or to tip the scales, one force has to cheat. One party might lie and manipulate (gerrymandering, voter suppression tactics, the product of paralysis, etc.) to make their force unequal. The resulting unequal force then creates an unequal reaction (domestic abuse syndrome, hoping the other party would play nice). In this analogy, it is due to Newton's Third Law that a third political party has never become a real force in American politics because as one political party directly opposes the other political party, how does a third force enter into the action-reaction equation? The law of physics would not allow it.

Political Party Rundowns

I present below a partial list relating each political party's core tenets and positions. They are stereotyping, and there are certainly exceptions from time to time. However, scanning the lists will provide you with an overview of each political party's general directional momentum when wielding power. The difference between the two parties is astonishing. By reviewing each rundown, we can clearly decide which party fits our personal view and how we envision the future of America. It is clear that we are in a struggle for the heart and soul of our country.

The Authoritarian Parent Republican Party Rundown

- Core tenet: Do not trust the average citizen. Rich and powerful know better. (This is the basis for cutting programs and suppressing votes.)

- Core tenet: No regulations. (This is the basis for eviscerating rules by which to function.)

- Core tenet: Politics is war. (This is the basis for believing Democrats are the enemy.)

- Core Tenet: Their world-view is the correct and only worldview.

- Engages primarily in the politics of personal destruction.

- Stands for outsourcing jobs to increase profit for companies/shareholders.

- Seeks governmental failure (drown in a bathtub) and against funding.

- Government programs: Starve the beast to cripple them, then announce that the government does not work.

- Stands with the National Rifle Association (NRA), without reservation.

- Stands for privatizing any and all governmental programs and services.

- Has shut down the government and held it hostage to force political agenda.

- Does not want every eligible citizen to vote. Works to privatize the voting process.

- Stands for one party rule.

- Dominates hate-talk radio.

- Stands with the 1 percent.

- Works to privatize and eradicate public schools. Funds charter schools with taxpayer money.

- Stands against unions and collective bargaining.

- Stands against the Consumer Financial Protection Bureau, the United States Post Office, Social Security, Medicare, and Medicaid.

- Stands against science and the climate crisis and with the fossil fuel industries.

- Stands with corporate and business zealots who want to privatize the profits and socialize the costs.

- Stands with Citizens United (unlimited money in politics).

- Stands with Wall Street.

- Stands for tax cuts and business loopholes for corporations and the wealthy. Stands against raising taxes on corporations and wealthy

- Stands against affordable college education and vilifies higher education and teachers.

- Stands against the fifteen-dollar hourly minimum wage.

- Stands for a flat tax that would benefit the rich and hurt middle- and lower-income citizens.

- Stands for privatizing the commons (police, fire, road maintenance, water, sewer, parks, Veterans Administration, education, prisons, etc.

- Advocates economic austerity to shrink government to trickle-up taxpayer money.

- Stands with Ayn Rand Libertarianism.

- Stands for blocking, filibustering, and obstructing opposing party and government, to the extreme.

- Abandons good faith, compromise, and "loyal opposition" concepts and practices.

- Worries about unbridled government.

- Political operatives childishly call the Democratic Party the Democrat Party (with an emphasis on the *rat*)

- Stands against a woman's sovereignty over her own body.

The Nurturing Parent Democratic Party Rundown

- Core tenet: Average citizen is trustworthy.

- Core tenet: Reasonable regulations (rules) to level economic activity and public and environmental safety are mandatory.

- Core tenet: Politics is the art of compromise.

- Engages primarily in the politics of issues

- Stands for manufacturing jobs in America and wants to bring them back.

- Believes it is possible for a well-managed government to do good things.

- Stands with 92 percent of voters who want gun background checks.

- Would never and has never shut down the United States government.

- Stands with eligible citizens to vote. Stands for government owned and operated paper-trail voting machines.

- Stands for a functioning two-party system.

- Few progressive radio outlets.

- Stands with the 99 percent and the middle class.

- Stands with the public school system.

- Stands with unions.

- Stands with the Consumer Financial Protection Bureau, the Post Office, Social Security, Medicare, and Medicaid.

- Respects science.

- Keenly understands that the human-caused climate crisis is a real and an existential threat to civilization.

- Corporate and business friendly, while knowing regulations are important to a capitalistic economy.

- Stands against Citizens United.

- Stands against outsourcing jobs.

- Stands for holding Wall Street accountable.

- Stands for closing tax loopholes and raising taxes on the wealthy.

- Stands for affordable college education and respects higher education and teachers.

- Stands for the fifteen-dollar hourly minimum wage.

- Stands for a progressive tax (taxed proportionally based on income).

- Stands for the commons (police, fire, road maintenance, water, sewer, parks, Veterans Administration, education, prisons, etc.

- Understands that economic austerity disproportionally impacts lower and middle classes.

- Stands with democracy.

- Understands good faith, compromise, and "loyal opposition" concepts and practices.

- Worries about unbridled corporations.

- Political operatives call the Republican Party the Republican Party, not childish, derogatory names.

- Stands with a woman's sovereignty over her own body.

Abraham Lincoln famously said, "A house divided against itself cannot stand." Our political divisions are so deep that our democracy is crumbling. Is this extreme division what we really want?

Stand Up Activities

Below, for your consideration, are several suggested Stand Up Activities. For a further explanation of the Keep/Start/Stop organization tool, please see Chapter One. After reading this chapter, you may think of additional activities readers can implement. If you'd like to share your brilliant constructive, compelling and creative ideas, please do so at: www.facebook.com/americaabandoned.

KEEP:

1. Keep in mind that there is an immense Lie Machine running at all times, operated by professionals at confutation. You must develop and utilize your information literacy skills to identify truth, as the news media can no longer be trusted for this. The truth has been lost to corporatocracy and ratings, and our media only exists for the ads; everything else is just filler.

START:

1. Start to ask yourself a question you may not have considered for many years: Why are you a member of your political party? Does your political party represent *you*? Independent and Decline to State are growing categories. The challenge in identifying yourself as such is that, depending on the state and their election rules, you may not be allowed to vote in the primary.

2. Start paying attention to annual congressional budget documents. The federal government operates on an October 1-September 30 calendar year. That means the proposed budget for the upcoming year is released in the summer. They present moral (or immoral) priorities of the political party in charge of our government. These, if adopted, can and do affect your daily life, so it's best to know what is being proposed beforehand so you have time to be a citizen lobbyist and call your representatives.

STOP:

1. Stop the cliché thinking that both parties are the same. A quick review of the rundowns in this chapter will clearly demonstrate the opposite. The two major political parties are not the same; they differ in numerous important and philosophical ways.

2. Stop ignoring political party platforms. They may not be religiously followed, but they do speak volumes about each party's priorities. The platforms are as different as the two presidential conventions were. Republicans hammer down on our troubling times, rehashing the failings of everyone currently in office. They purport that the world is a dangerous, fearful place, and they suggest that only they have the solution. As Paul Krugman, in a New York Times article

titled "No, America isn't a hellhole", explained that "None of this is actually happening ... Basically American cities are as safe as they've ever been ... crime has plunged." On the flipside, the Democratic National Convention spoke of hope, suggesting that our government really can improve the quality of people's lives and that America's best days are ahead. I encourage you to seek out each party's 2016 platforms. The different potential impact for the people living in America is staggering.

If one watched the 2016 presidential conventions, one would see an excellent example of what Living in the Red energies (Republican Convention) and what Living in the Black energies (Democratic Convention) look-like in action. Bill Barrow, an Associated Press reporter, commented on this phenomenon in his article, "Why do Republicans say the sky is falling? Is it?" He explained that the Republican National Convention depicted the world as a scary place plagued with "economic upheaval, political dysfunction, runaway immigration, violent streets and existential threats from abroad." They paint a bleak and fearful reality. Remember the Block study? When, in reality, unemployment is lower, the economy has grown, the country is out preforming most of the other advanced economies, and that Americans are much less likely to become victims of domestic or international terrorism than Europeans. Annually, more people are killed in car accidents than in acts of terrorism.

One Marvelous Question

After reading this chapter, if you were going to do *one* thing marvelously well to move forward, what would that one thing be?

Politicians like to tout "American exceptionalism," but who made America exceptional?

CHAPTER TEN

Middle Class No More

"The art of being helpful is behaving as if everything we do matters, because we never know which things might."

Gloria Steinem

In the history of the world, a country with a middle class is a unique and wonderful thing. Most of the world has been and still is led by monarchies, dictators, and authoritarian regimes of one sort or another. America became a beacon on the hill because of our middle class. Those living in other countries, who were oppressed by the rich and powerful, envied America's middle-class lifestyle. They saw that beacon's light shining all around the world and wanted to come here. Our middle class was an achievement, a social contract with one another that had not been seen before. The majority of our population, the middle class, could enjoy a nice, educated, safe life. The creation of the middle class made democracy a living reality.

Now, there is a real force in our country that wants to unravel that social contract we have with one another. They want us to abandon each other as Americans. The Velvet Coup culprits are causing the middle class to disappear. We have seen their cleverness in pitting one American against another. First, it is imperative to remember that it was the middle class who has been the economic engine behind this country's prosperity for the past fifty years. It was the ability of the middle class to pay taxes, due to earning salaries that sustained a middle-class living that funded our federal, state, city, and community services, that made us the envy of nations.

A middle class also offered hope to those who strove to be included. If you were responsible for yourself and your family, if you made sure you and your children were educated, if you demonstrated good character and put in every effort to work hard and responsibly move up the ladder, you would achieve the rank of middle class and would have earned a better life for you and your family. It was the American Dream. Do you hear anyone talking about the American Dream anymore? The PRIIF forces in this country create an economic divide and are growing stronger, while the organizations that helped create the middle class are growing weaker.

When President Ronald Reagan was elected, 30 percent of the American workforce was in a union. Unions built the middle class. Even though not everyone was a card-carrying union member, union negotiations for the 30 percent positively impacted the salaries of non-union employees. As of 2015, only 11.1 percent of the American workforce is represented by a union, so union impact has been eviscerated. NPR's "50 Years of Shrinking Union Membership, In One Map" says it all.

The only way people can stand up to corporations or the d-rich are through a union of workers. An individual cannot stand up to the rich and powerful; only a union can try, and the rich and powerful know this. The d-rich, corporations, and the Republican Party have done a marvelous job of demonizing unions. They have done an exemplary job of destroying them in the private sector so that even middle-class people are angry towards other middle-class people who may be in a union that still negotiates a good salary and benefits for their members. What a marvelous manipulation on their part. They pitted one American against another, getting us to do their dirty work for them while they sit back and watch us tear ourselves apart.

Remember the old adage "divide and conquer?" Well, the d–rich and powerful in this country are reaping the benefits of a divided middle class. They say it cannot be helped and blame globalization and technology, but they are wrong. This belief negates any responsibility on their part and creates the story that we are all victims of uncontrollable forces, that we must be tossed about, just going wherever the wind blows. America, once a leader and the envy of the world, is now a conglomeration of hapless, helpless victims of the times? Absurd.

In The American Prospect article by Harold Meyerson, an American journalist and opinion columnist, "How to Raise American's Wages," the author says:

> What corporate apologists won't acknowledge is that workers' incomes have been reduced by design. American business has adamantly opposed workers efforts to organize unions. Millions of jobs have been outsourced, offshore, franchised out, re-classified as temporary or part-time, or had their wages slashed,

in a successful, decades-long campaign to increase the return to capital.

He further says:

> The transfer of income from labor to capital, then, is chiefly the consequence of capitalists' design. But precisely because that transfer has been so thorough, reversing it will be exquisitely difficult.

The Velvet Coup in action.

Another method the middle class was destroyed by design was placing mandatory arbitration clauses in nearly every contract in which we enter, from healthcare to those with our cell phone providers. The Supreme Court, at the behest of corporations, has forced us into mandatory arbitration, with a ban on class-action suits, instead of being able to exercise our right to a trial before a jury. Who selects the arbitrator? The corporation does. If an arbitrator finds for the customer too many times, do you think they will be rehired for future arbitrations? The most galling part about this maneuver to undermine our rights is that if an arbitration decision goes against us, there is no appeal process. The Economic Policy Institute published a briefing paper, "The Arbitration Epidemic Mandatory Arbitration Deprives Workers and Consumers of Their Rights" on the issue that is well worth reading.

First, capitalists abandoned the middle class. Then, they trained their sights and came after them.

The middle class is not a natural consequence of capitalism. A report from the Center for American Progress, "The Middle-Class Squeeze: A Picture of Stagnant Incomes, Rising Costs, and What We Can Do to Strengthen America's Middle Class," highlighted the calamity that took place between 2000 and 2012. For a middle-class family of four, the cost of housing, daycare, healthcare, saving for college, and retirement increased 32 percent. Thus, in just twelve years, one-third of their buying power was lost. The result? Fewer and fewer Americans could build a life or work toward the American Dream. All the while, the rich got richer, singing the praises of capitalism. Why not? It worked for them, and they wanted more. How do they get more? Through a political party that is willing to give it to them by not spending money on the masses.

For example, on December 28, 2013 the Republican-held Senate caused 1,300,000 unemployed Americans to lose their unemployment benefits and another 2,000,000 Americans to stop receiving assistance. Merry Christmas! The assumption the Senate made was that these people were "takers." They demonized, polarized, and pitted American against American, breaking the social contract and the very spirit we had for each other through the unemployment insurance program. Even though millions of people lost their jobs to the capitalist design to destroy the middle class, our own Congress was a tool in the continuation of that plan. It is un-American to abandon fellow Americans who are in need, or at least it once was, but destroying the social contract was paramount in creating an oligarchy.

Conservative economic policies, by their very design, abandon the middle class. The past thirty-five years of Reaganomics has slowly eroded our unique and wonderful middle class to a staggering level. The middle class was created with a progressive tax structure, a sliding scale based on ability to pay, and a portion of the resulting revenue funded the Servicemen's Readjustment Act, of 1944, also known as the GI Bill. It was the underpinning of the middle class.

It is fascinating that conservatives seem to want to return America back to the 1950s and 1960s, the boom years for reaping benefits of passing the GI Bill, because it was a period of successful so-called socialism. The GI Bill was a socialistic tool that honored our veterans and provided them with low-interest mortgages, cash support for high school, vocational, and university tuition and, believe it or not, living expenses while going to school. The GI Bill also provided low-cost loans to start businesses and created unemployment insurance for a year. It created the American middle class that was envied around the world. Could we have a healthy, vibrant middle class again today, with that kind of government support? Of course we could! The GI Bill recipients and their families received a hand-up, not a handout.

Today, Republicans and the d-rich think just about any social program, like those offered by the GI Bill, as handouts to takers who they deem are undeserving of governmental support. The Republicans are right to want to return to the 1950s and 1960s, based on the economics of that era, yet they refuse to pass any legislation or amend their ideology to create those economic successes again for the twenty-first century. They now religiously believe social programs are socialism.

We should take another look at this theology that social programs equates with socialism. For the mind that wants simple answers, this is an easy belief system, since "social" shows up in both. However, we must understand the difference between *the commons* in a democracy and socialism. This is a subtle difference, and the two concepts are easily confused because of their complexity. To complicate the issue further, the concept of socialism has been demonized in this country, as well as intentionally misapplied to the commons of a democracy.

As we previously discussed, the United States was formed as a republic, a country governed by elected representatives and an elected leader. A republic is a government in which the power resides in a body of citizens who are entitled to vote for their elected representatives. The elected representatives, then, are responsible to their citizens and govern according to law. We also use the word "democracy" to describe our republic because it is characterized by the doctrine that everyone is to be treated equally and should possess equal rights.

The democratic doctrine requires us to come together as citizens to govern ourselves. Led by elected representatives, we must differentiate between the things we can do for ourselves from those we can do together, for our mutual benefit. What we do together is known as the commons. For example, I cannot personally start, manage, hire, or equip a police or fire department, sewage treatment plant, a post office, or a parks system. Therefore, as citizens, we must come together to provide these services equally for all. This is not socialism; on the contrary, it is democracy in action.

As an interesting side note, our country's Pledge of Allegiance was written by Francis Bellamy, a Baptist minister who thought of himself as a Christian socialist. Among other things, he believed that capitalism is idolatrous, rooted in greed, and is the underlying cause of much of the world's social inequality. When was this? The Pledge of Allegiance was written August 1892, for the 400th anniversary of Columbus's coming to the Americas. What is additionally interesting is that the "under God" within it was an addendum, not added to The Pledge of Allegiance until 1954. It is ironic that we hold dear the words in a pledge written by a socialist who would have had no problem with the concept of socialism in the United States, let alone the concept of the commons.

The commons are what we own and operate together. Common public services are managed by other citizens, either employees or elected representatives, of a city, state, or federal government. Through these democratically designed governmental organizations and our payment of taxes, we, the people actually *own* the commons. This also fails to fall under the umbrella of socialism. Since the term "socialism" has been demonized in our country by conservative manipulation, there is an urge to equate these two socio-economic systems when, in fact, they are different. Taxes are the price of living in a civilized society. Since the Iraq War, we have become acutely aware of the horrors of a devolving society. None of us desires the chaos, death, drama, and limitations we see in uncivilized countries. In a *Democratic Underground* blog by Scuba, "Seems There's a Lot of Folks Here Suddenly Worried About Tax Rates. Here's Some Advice...," a 102-point list quickly brings home the benefit of taxes and the unparalleled society they create. The list instructs readers what they should stop doing and using if they are in such opposition to taxes. A few examples from the list are:

- Do not call 911 when you get hurt.

- Do not drive on any paved road, highway, and interstate or over a bridge.

- Do not put your trash out for city garbage collectors.

- Do not drink clean water.

- Do not walk or ride on sidewalks.

- Do not watch weather reports and warnings provided by the National Weather Service.

- Do not use the internet that was develop by the military.

- Do not use public recreational facilities such as basketball and tennis courts.

- Do use the US Postal Service.

- Do not use any doctor licensed though the state.

Elinor Ostrom, a 2009 Nobel Prize winner in economic science, explains that the commons are really a "common pool of resources" that cannot exclude people. Public goods like knowledge can also be a common pool of resources. Clear examples of this are libraries and the internet. Because the internet must remain equal to us all, maintaining net neutrality is imperative to a democracy; we cannot allow it to be privatized by corporations.

Socialism is an economic system or social organization (political party) that advocates that the government, not the people, owns and controls major industries. It is the governmental entity itself, with all production of those industries being owned by the state. There is no private property in a socialistic society. When the term was first used, it was meant to describe non-coercive communities of people working non-competitively for the physical and spiritual wellbeing of society. This is not how the commons or democracy is organized.

Knowing more about the difference between the commons in a democracy and what socialism really is, we might one day be able to adopt President Franklin D. Roosevelt's Second Bill of Rights. What a different country we would have experienced if it had been adopted in 1944! The middle class would never have been abandoned. On the contrary, the Second Bill of Rights was a demonstration of highly valuing the middle class and government wanting to ensure its success. What an extraordinary country this would be for our middle class now and in the future if we could find the political will to enact that Second Bill of Rights today.

Back then the country had just suffered through the Great Depression. Desperate to improve life after that harsh reality, President Roosevelt believed the "political rights" contained in the Constitution and the Bill of Rights had "proved inadequate to assure us equality in the pursuit of happiness." Roosevelt asserted that the solution was to enact an "economic bill of rights." Looking back seventy years, we now see how accurate he was when it came to income inequality and the abandonment of the middle class, which is currently tearing our country apart. He delineated eight issues to be contained in the Second Bill of Rights:

1) Employment (a right to work)

2) Income to buy food, clothing, and leisure

3) Farmers having a fair right to income

4) Freedom from unfair competition and monopolies

5) Housing

6) Medicare

7) Social Security

8) Education

FDR believed that if all citizens were provided a minimal standard of living, it would guarantee American security. Based on our fairly successful Social Security and Medicare programs, we have learned that government really can manage programs of this nature without being socialist. Some call these giveaways, but what is really wrong with utilizing taxpayer money to help middle-class families, our country's valuable diamonds, instead of taxpayer money being utilized for the 1 percent to become even more wealthy and live more extravagantly?

To sum it up, in a democracy the commons is owned by *the people* through self-taxation and managed by elected representatives. Socialism is when the *State* owns the country's assets and economic production, not the people.

It is through Congress that the federal commons should be managed. However, we are realizing more and more that Congress is not doing its constitutional job, to "...form a more perfect union, establish justice, ensure domestic tranquility, provide for the common defense, promote the general welfare..." and so on. If it was ever the job of Congress to kill the middle class and enact steps on behalf of corporations and the wealthy, for the purposes of changing American democracy into an American oligarchy or corporatocracy, we could say they have done extremely well.

How well is it working? How hard is the Velvet Coup working to kill the middle class? Extraordinarily hard! No longer are middle class Americans in the majority. The Pew Research Center, a nonpartisan, non-advocacy public opinion think tank, in a report titled "The American Middle Class Is Losing Ground," stated that in the last forty-two years, the middle class represented a majority of the population. Now, with Reaganomics and austerity policies having become intensely successful, the middle class is shrinking – not only in numbers but financially as well. Our median wealth fell 28 percent from 2001 to 2013, robbing us of the political power we once had – unless, of course, more of us in the smaller and financially challenged middle class population take the time to stand up.

I just wanted to scream when, despite the Great Recession being several years behind us, I read that two-thirds of us would still struggle to come up with $1,000 for an unexpected expense. A May 2016 Associated Press-

NORC Center for Public Affairs Research article, "Poll: Two-thirds of U.S. Would Struggle To Cover $1,000 Crisis," reported:

> The more we learn about the balance sheets of Americans, it becomes quite alarming, said Caroline Ratcliffe, a senior fellow at the Urban Institute focusing on poverty and emergency savings issues. People are extremely vulnerable if they don't have savings. And it's a cost to taxpayers as well. Lack of savings can lead to homelessness, or other problems.

Actually, it may be even worse than the Associated Press reported, because in the same month, the May 2016 issue of *The Atlantic* contained an article titled "The Secret Shame of Middle-Class Americans." That article reported that the Federal Reserve Board conducted a survey. In that survey, the answer to one question was completely astounding. Neal Gabler, the American journalist and historian who wrote the article, explained how the survey respondents answered and shared his personal story:

> The Fed asked respondents how they would pay for a $400 emergency. The answer: *47 percent* of respondents said that either they would cover the expense by borrowing or selling something, or they would not be able to come up with the $400 at all. *Four hundred dollars!* Who knew? Well, *I* knew. I knew because I am in that 47 percent.

> I know what it is like to have to juggle creditors to make it through a week. I know what it is like to have to swallow my pride and constantly dun people to pay me so that I can pay others. I know what it is like to have liens slapped on me and to have my bank account levied by creditors. I know what it is like to be down to my last five dollars – literally – while I wait for a paycheck to arrive, and I know what it is like to subsist for days on a diet of eggs. I know what it is like to dread going to the mailbox, because there will always be new bills to pay but seldom a check with which to pay them. I know what it is like to have to tell my daughter that I didn't know if I would be able to pay for her wedding; it all depended on whether something good happened. And I know what it is like to have to borrow money from my adult daughters because my wife and I ran out of heating oil.

Neal Gabler's story and the two May 2016 reports is a barefaced sign that a majority of individuals and families never recovered from having to use their credit cards to maintain a standard of living and the housing mortgage theft perpetrated by Wall Street banksters. In fact, Social Security data shows that one out of every two people, half of Americans, lives in or very close to poverty. However, their predicament has been a boon to the payday lender industry.

Stand Up Activities

Below, for your consideration, are several suggested Stand Up Activities. For a further explanation of the Keep/Start/Stop organization tool, please see Chapter One. After reading this chapter, you may think of additional activities readers can implement. If you'd like to share your brilliant constructive, compelling and creative ideas, please do so at: www. facebook.com/americaabandoned.

KEEP:

1. Keep in mind that when PRIIF forces work to divide us (hate-talk radio, Dems versus GOP and vice versa, etc.) the infrastructure of the middle class – the social contract we have with one another. Bill Moyers, "People should be in the streets or in unions or in the voting booths, but are not because it is easier to adapt." Income inequality is outrageous but accepted by most people hurt by it." Don't adapt!

START:

1. Start to appreciate the integral role unions provide to a middle-class lifestyle. As unions have perished, so has that admirable lifestyle that the world used to envy and desire. Unions influenced salaries and benefits for all workers, not just their members. Germany requires employees to be on the corporation board of directors so that every point of view is represented in corporate operations. When Volkswagen opened a plant in Tennessee, the company wanted a United Auto Workers union to be organized; Tennessee's U.S. congressional Republican representatives did not.

2. Start informing yourself on middle-class issues and what can be done about them. Reading the Center for American Progress report, "The Middle-Class Squeeze," would be a good place to start.

3. Start contacting your representatives and ask for legislation to remove mandatory arbitration clauses from contracts. Contact the Consumer Finance Protection Bureau and ask to have our constitutional right to a jury restored.

STOP:

1. Stop equating the commons with socialism. The misconception of equality between the two only benefits the d-rich and privatizing forces.

One Marvelous Question

After reading this chapter, if you were going to do one thing marvelously well to move forward, what would that one thing be?

Is the middle class really a cache of diamonds?

CHAPTER ELEVEN

Families Abandoned

"We are healthy only to the extent that our ideas are humane."

Kurt Vonnegut

I think of a family as a diamond, although I may be over-romanticizing it a bit. I am an only child of two only children, and I have no siblings, no aunts or uncles, no nieces or nephews, no cousins, and no grandparents. As I mentioned at the outset of this book, my father was not present for most of my life, and my mother was emotionally damaged and agoraphobic. Thus, it is not surprising that I have always looked upon the functional and healthy families I have known with a certain amount of yearning.

Families are like diamonds because, just like precious gems, healthy ones are rare and beautiful things. I see each family member as a facet of that diamond, each contributing to its overall brilliance and value. Each member, regardless of age or gender, is an integral reflection of the family as a whole. Truly, I wish I could have created a family like a diamond.

As diamonds cannot be created without help from outside forces so, too, they cannot thrive without functioning communities within a healthy society where they are safe, able to learn and grow and raise children who will honor the same cycle for the next generation.

I fear we have become so conservative in our views that it is only *our* family that matters, not the other families in our communities or in society at large. Collectively, we have abandoned others. The self-absorbed, entitled, narcissistic point of view basically states that we only need to care about ourselves and our immediate family, not the kinfolk of others. This is often cloaked under the guise of *personal responsibility*. That is, if we are responsible for ourselves and our families, all will be well. Unfortunately and predictably, however, all is far from well.

This thought process does not take into consideration the historical economic advantages or disadvantages of a family (whether children are born into poverty or to the disgustingly rich), nor does it take into consideration the area of the country where the family may live (urban or rural). It does not consider the individual health of family members and if they are facing challenging physical or mental disabilities. It does not include the quality of schools or the tax basis that funds them. In short, it does not consider any variables other than reciting the platitude of that so-called personal responsibility. If you are poor, sick, or without a job, it must be entirely your fault. Only you are to blame, and no one else needs to be responsible for you. In other words, personal responsibility is our cover, our excuse for intentionally abandoning any responsibility toward other families in our society. This selfish mindset, spouting, "I am not responsible for you," also fails to work in a democracy. No man or family is an island.

George P. Lakoff, an American cognitive linguist, explained on the *State of Belief* August 22, 2015 podcast that there are two family structures: conservative (Strict Father) and progressive (Nurturing Parent).

In the Nurturing Parent family structure, both parents have equal authority. They raise their children to empathize with others; as parents, they show empathy toward their children and model empathy for others. They raise their children to take care of themselves and become independent, open thinkers. Progressive parents raise their children to assist others. Both parents function well socially and live fulfilling lives, and they teach their children to do the same. Children from a progressive family unit are more likely to question authority.

The Strict Father (or Mother, though it is usually Father) is an authoritarian. Children are taught not to question. The father knows what is right and wrong, and if a family member disagrees with him, punishment is forthcoming in the form of discipline or worse. The father's rules will be obeyed, or else. The conservative family structure, unlike equality in the progressive parental structure, contains a moral hierarchy: God over man, man over nature, adults over children, men over women, white over black, rich over poor, straight over gay, boy over girl, Western culture over all others, etc. These authoritarian ideas foster a man-is-superior mindset; therefore, women and children are viewed as inferior. It feeds selfishness and ego: "I can do whatever I want, and you do whatever I tell you." As mentioned, children from a conservative family unit are less likely to question authority and often become authoritarian followers, seeking the very authority figures that prevented them from becoming independent, free thinkers.

The most dramatic example of authoritarian followers needing a Strict Father leader was in September of 2015, when John Boehner suddenly resigned from his position as speaker of the House of Representatives. Republican congressmen, grown men suddenly bereft of a leader, were heard crying in the cloakroom.

I submit that it is the conservative Strict Father orthodoxy that is at the root of the abandonment of the family. Understanding this hierarchy leads to an understanding of how the authoritarian mentality teaches us to favor white families over black or other minority families, rich families over poor families, straight families over gay families, Western families over families of other cultures, which makes it much easier to bomb them, etc.

If the belief structure is that the only person who matters is the Strict Father, the authoritarian, the needs of women, children, other families or cultures are simply not considered. When this selfish mindset is translated into politics and policy, we see the family and its individual parts abandoned and neglected in an astonishing number of ways throughout the country.

Who is Abandoning Our Children?

"In the richest nation in the world, one in three kids live in poverty. Let that sink in." Christopher Ingraham, formerly of the Pew Research Center, made that statement in a *Washington Post* article titled, "Child Poverty in the U.S. Is Among the Worst in the Developed World." It related a statistic from a 2014 UNICEF report, declaring that the United States is near the "bottom of the pack of wealthy nations" in the area of child poverty. The only countries with child poverty rates worse than those in the United States are Mexico, Israel, Spain, Latvia, and Greece, in that order. America's child poverty is nearly as bad as Mexico's? Let that sink in. We understand what has happened in Greece, as they suffered a complete economic meltdown caused, in large part, by Goldman Sachs. That placed them in last place when it comes to wealthy nations. But what has happened to America? Simple: Our politicians are making policy choices that abandon children to fund the military industrial complex.

According to the *JAMA Pediatrics*, 25 percent of American children do not have enough food to eat. Let that sink in too.

Most still agree that breakfast is the most important meal of the day, but for millions of schoolchildren, one-quarter of them, in fact, lunch is. Why? Because it is the only meal they are certain about, since they will be fed in school. They may not get breakfast or dinner, but they can count on lunch. My head nearly exploded when I heard Paul Ryan (R-WI) tell a story his friend Eloise Anderson passed along. True or not, he recounted it at the 2014 CPAC Conference:

> A young boy from a poor family... Every day at school, he would get a free lunch from a government program. He told Eloise he didn't want a free lunch. He wanted his own lunch, one in a brown paper bag, just like the other kids. He wanted one, he said, because he knew a kid with a brown paper bag had someone who cared for him.

Paul Ryan took this to mean that Democrats do not understand that by offering children food at lunch, they were creating "empty souls." Kaboom!

When my son, who was identified with a mild form of dyslexia in second grade, was subsequently moved to another school for two years for a specialized program, he absolutely hated it, because he felt it made him different. If Paul Ryan's story is true, I believe it was misinterpreted to fit an ideology. The way it was taken was not actually what the child was saying.

In an article by Laura Clawsone, *Daily Kos* Contributing Editor, "Paul Ryan: Poor kids Should Go hungry so They Know They're Loved," she analyzed:

> Hey, maybe if we take that kid's free school lunch away, his parents will be able to scrounge up a brown paper bag to send him to school with every day. It'll be empty, like his stomach, but whatever. Brown paper bag equals love.

> What the left doesn't understand, apparently, is that this child should go hungry because it's been made clear to him that being poor means his parents somehow love him less. Trust Ryan to miss the pathos of a child having been taught this. And what about kids whose parents send them to school with lunch money, not brown paper bags, because both of their parents work and do not have time to be packing a lunch every day? Ryan's version of

parental love doesn't make room for them either. What else might he require for a family to qualify as loving – a mother who meets the kids at the door after school bearing freshly baked cookies?

Also, let's talk about that school lunch. There are strong PRIIF forces that do not even want impoverished school children to have a lunch at school, and they should not be dictated by government subsidy practices if they do get fed. Walter Einenkel, in an article titled, "How Do These Children's School Lunches from Around the World Compare to the United States?" provided a sample of what American children are offered in comparison to a few other countries:

- USA: fried popcorn chicken, mashed potatoes, peas, fruit cup, and chocolate cookie. (Anyone who has had a modicum of education in nutrition knows this menu is basically sugar and starch.)

- ITALY: Local fish on a bed of arugula, pasta with tomato sauce, caprese salad, baguette, and grapes

- BRAZIL: Pork with mixed vegetables, black beans and rice, salad, bread, and baked plantains.

- SOUTH KOREA: Fish soup, tofu over rice, kimchi, and fresh vegetables.

If America is an exceptional country, then we are exceptionally bad at feeding our children in school.

In 2013, in twenty-one states, the majority of children qualified for free or reduced-cost lunches. A startling 16.2 million children in this country are food insecure. This means they either do not know where their next meal will come from or they do not get enough food to be healthy and focused. Half of all Supplemental Nutrition Assistance Program (SNAP) recipients are children, and SNAP allows only $1.46 per meal. That cannot possibly provide all the nutritional requirements of a growing child. As No Kid Hungry website states, three out of four teachers say students regularly come to school hungry. When children eat school breakfast, they miss less school, get better grades, and are more likely to graduate from high school and 1 in 5 U.S. kids don't get the food they need. Thus, becoming well-rounded, quality citizens of their community and our society.

Our policymakers are acquainted with these facts, yet they still abandon our country's children and consistently try to deprive them of SNAP benefits and Head Start funding. It is ironic that the conservative ideology of personal responsibility does not consider its profound effect on children. By virtue of being dependent on adults for everything, a child cannot assume this personal responsibility. What about the elected policymakers' responsibility? Somehow, this conservative mindset of personal responsibility appears to only apply to others and not to them. What of *their* personal responsibility, as elected officials, to keep our children safe? Assuring safety, I believe, must include sixteen million children not going to bed hungry.

As shocking and heartbreaking as hungry children are, not having enough food is not the worst tragedy to beset American children. The number of children without a home to live in has surged in the past few years, to an all-time high. A state-by-state report titled "America's Youngest Outcasts," completed by the National Center on Family Homelessness, determined that one child in every thirty is homeless, in the richest country in the world. In other words, this country's policymakers have abandoned children to the streets, doubled-up housing, shelters, and motels. Yet another shocking revelation.

The director of the National Center on Family Homelessness and co-author of "America's Youngest Outcasts," Carmela DeCandia, observed that the federal government did make some progress in reducing homelessness among veterans and adults, but "the same level of attention and resources has not been targeted to help families and children." The states with the best scores were Minnesota, Nebraska, and Massachusetts; while Alabama, Mississippi, and California ranked among the worst. It seems odd that California would rank so poorly, but the cost of living and lack of affordable housing in the state, devoid of actionable leadership on the issue, easily explains the statistic. California is host to over half a million homeless children.

It is a safe assumption, as we consider these disturbing reports, that these issues, childhood hunger and homelessness, often describe the same child. Ms. DeCandia went on to say, "As a society, we're going to pay a high price in human and economic terms." Abandonment destroys. We are destroying millions of children's educational, emotional and social development, and that will affect them for the rest of their lives and our society for generations. What does that say about us?

Fright of the Forgotten Child

The most fragile and frightened children in our country are those of undocumented and/or deported parents. It is surprising that the federal government that deported 369,000 people from October 2012 to October 2013 did not track how many children were left behind, and this lack of interest continues to this day. Truly, the most frightened, helpless children in this country are those to whom we give no consideration. Our politicians' complete and cruel abandonment of these frightened little ones is further exacerbated by forced separation. Our immigration policy needs amending. Yet, the issues have been blown so out of proportion that the government is pressured to do more deporting and one of the unintended consequences are frightening children who are American and left behind for the opportunities our country provides.

We, as a country, routinely separate children from their parents. When we imprint abandonment into these little psyches, mental health issues such as depression and anxiety disorders inevitably take hold and eventually surface. These children experience flashbacks and severe nightmares, and some are even diagnosed with post-traumatic stress disorder (PTSD). Shame on us for destroying families by intentionally abandoning them because our politicians see them as disposable families! Shamefully, Iowa Representative Steve King describes of some of those parents who are desperately trying to get back to their children in a foul way:

> We could also electrify this wire [on the border] with the kind of current that would not kill somebody, but it would simply be a discouragement for them to be fooling around with it. We do that with livestock all the time.

> For every 1 who's a valedictorian, there're another 100 out there who weigh 130 pounds, and they've got calves the size of cantaloupes because they're hauling 75 pounds of marijuana across the desert.

Livestock? The first step in manipulating a mindset that there are *disposable* families is to dehumanize them.

Politics can frighten children too. The Southern Poverty Law Center, which tracks hate groups, issued a report titled, "The Trump Effect," which analyzed and discussed a Teaching Tolerance survey, ascertaining that presidential campaign rhetoric is having a very profound and negative effect on children and producing alarming levels of fear and anxiety in them.

The 2016 Republican campaign has exuded extreme Living-in-the-Red energies that ooze though our television sets and into society as a whole, heaping piles of worry and confusion upon our children, those of color specifically. The report stated, "Teachers have noted an increase in bullying, harassment, and intimidation of students whose races, religions, or nationalities have been the verbal target of candidates on the campaign trail."

Shame on these so-called adults, who are aspiring to hold high governmental offices. Scaring and victimizing children is totally unacceptable behavior for any so-called adult, let alone from those with ambitions to lead the country. What is especially alarming is that the children of the adults who support this bullying, harassment, and intimidation by their chosen politicians are also exemplifying this behavior for their children to see. As the song in the musical South Pacific says, "You have to be carefully taught."

Abandoning Childcare Responsibilities

How can any family become a diamond if they are struggling to work and find childcare? Families continue to be abandoned, by all levels of government, due to lack of funding. When it is financially difficult for cities to meet basic service needs such as filling potholes, there is no ability to provide leadership, coordination, or funding to assist middle- and lower-class families with childcare needs. To exacerbate the problem, the childcare workforce is highly underpaid. On average, childcare providers are paid $10.72 an hour, less than 97 percent of other occupations. This low value we place on caring for our children is a sad and prime example of the effects of the austerity theology applied to government. It hurts families as a whole and children as individuals. Nearly 10 million families in this country have one or more children under the age of 6, and fewer than 18 percent receive the financial assistance for which they qualify.

America has abandoned its childcare needs for generations. When I was a working mother, the best and safest childcare for my son was that offered by his elementary school. Unfortunately, there were far more children in need of the program than there were spaces available, so something akin to a lottery was held every year to determine which children could participate. A lottery! We won that lottery several times, so our son was able to walk quickly from his school classroom to the childcare room on the same campus, but we weren't the big winners one year. There were not many options, and the only place that had an opening required him to travel by bus to get there.

By the time that bus made several pickups at other schools and arrived at the care facility, his father was already there to pick him up. Thus, that year, our son was basically cared for by being toted around from school to school on a bus. We had resources, yet we faced this issue every year. This caused me unbelievable stress and worry, and I knew my son was not getting the attention and supervision he deserved as the wheels on that bus went 'round and round.' It begs the question: How does anyone deal with the situation when resources are finite? I cannot imagine how other families emotionally handle it. Abandoning our families and their children's childcare needs the way this country does is an abomination. Child Care Aware of America has factsheets available by state.

Invisible Citizens – The Homeless

I think most of us currently feel invisible to our country's politicians and power brokers, and we are just now waking up to the fact that we need to vote and be active in shaping America's future all year long, not merely during an election season. Still, there are Americans who truly are invisible people, those who were once part of a family but were abandoned to the elements, mental illness, drug and alcohol addiction, and/or poverty.

I remember watching an interview of someone who lived, I believe, in Denmark. He declared that if a homeless person existed there, they would feel they had failed as a society. The last point-in-time count of homeless individuals in the U.S. was in January of 2015, though more recent counts may be found by state. The result, on that one particular day, was that 564,708 people were living on our streets. If we were to measure our society with the same yardstick Denmark does, we could only see ourselves as miserable failures on a grand scale. Of that figure, 206,286 had living family members, and many were working full-time jobs but still could not afford a roof over their heads. More than 47,000 among the homeless population in the so-called Land of the Free are veterans who are not being respected at all, nor are they being provided the services they require and deserve after their faithful military service.

Several underfunded programs attempt to address the needs of our invisible American citizens. The National Alliance to End Homelessness, the National Coalition for the Homeless, and four organizations facing the veteran issue are among them: 1) Disabled American Veterans (DAV), 2) United States Veterans Initiative (U.S. VETS), 3) National Coalition for Homeless Veterans (NCHV), and 4) American Veterans (AMVETS).

However, Science Magazine relates a study that offers a fresh perspective and a new answer to assisting those who have been abandoned to the streets. In an article written by David Schultz, "A bit of cash can keep someone off the streets for 2 years or more," explains that the study, led by economist, James Sullivan, of the University of Notre Dame in South Bend, Indiana, found that giving a homeless person a single cash infusion of around $1,000 may, in fact, remove them from the streets, even permanently. Sullivan stated, "Although it might seem obvious that giving people money would keep them off the street, many anti-welfare critics have argued that such charity only prolongs the decline into homelessness... That appears not to be the case."

The exciting thought is that an infusion of one billion dollars might move *all* of our homeless population off the streets, with money to spare. Bill Gates. Are you listening? Congress? Anybody? When in America, perhaps we should do like the Danish do.

How the School to Prison Pipeline is Destroying Our Families

If you are poor or even middle class, it is easy to end up in jail. If you are rich, it is inconceivable that you will. We abandon families by putting so many of their members in prison. The consequence is to punish the innocent as well as the transgressor.

Statistics show that America incarcerates 1 person for every 100 people. We lock up more people in prison, per capita, than any other country, including China and other authoritarian- and dictator-led countries. What have we, the people become? We are a product, a commodity off of which to make a profit. Each of us has the potential to be a profit center to make stockholders rich. The War on Drugs, Three Strikes laws, and an economic hierarchy that disproportionally traps the poor and African-Americans (six times more than whites) has been a boon to business because our country has privatized many of its prisons. We have abandoned living, breathing, flesh-and-blood human beings to being treated like merchandise.

The greedy people who are currently marching toward privatizing our public school system have already been enormously successful in privatizing our country's prison system. The two major prison corporations, GEO Group and Correction Corp of America, from 1991 to 2012, publically traded 3 billion dollars ($300,000 million) and even pitched to their stockholders how wonderful it is that there is a high recidivism rate; this ensures that the profits will keep rolling in.

Since 1980, U.S. prison population has increased by 790 percent. Nearly two and a half million people are in prison, and one in thirty-one people (based on 2009 Pew Research Center data) are also controlled by the U.S. Dept. of Corrections via parole, probation, or other forms of incarceration such as immigration detention. Approximately half of all men and nearly 60 percent of women are in prison for drug-related crimes, a majority of them black. Even more shockingly, we know that whites use drugs at the same rate, but blacks are ten times more likely to be incarcerated for drug use and possession. So common and rampant is this issue that *Sesame Street* had to explain what *incarceration* meant to its little viewers, a sign of a devastating problem in this country.

Recently, the Department of Justice (DOJ) announced the end of its using private, for-profit prisons to incarcerate federal prisoners. The DOJ determined that private prisons are less safe and effective than those run by the government. In his *Talking Points* memo, David Dayen quoted Matt Nelson, the current managing director, from his article "The True Cost: Why the Private Prison Industry Is About so Much More than Prisons:"

> Delivering poor services at a premium price is part of the marketing strategy. They know that cutting costs, services and training for guards increases recidivism. They're familiar that if you have horrible conditions, people stay in the system longer. They know that the younger you incarcerate, it's more likely they will stay in the system. They keep customers coming back.

I am sure this is true of many former governmentally run programs that have been privatized. Maybe this will be the beginning of recapturing other programs that cost us more because of inserting the profit incentive. The DOJ's decision is big news and I hope it will begin to influence the state prison systems as well.

Shockingly, according to FBI estimates that one in three people in this country has a criminal record. When I served as chair of the Recreation and Tourism Department at San Jose State University, a deputy director for the California State Department of Parks told me they had to cancel a training academy for new park ranger hires because they did not find any candidates without a criminal record!

The criminal justice system is so ravenous that we now have a school-to-prison pipeline, a bitter journey that starts as young as 4 years old. The easiest way to explain this phenomenon is to tell a story, as related in an article by Fania E. Davis, Founding Director of Restorative Justice in Oakland, California, in her article, "Interrupting the School-to-Prison Pipeline Through Restorative Justice," shared a story about a little boy named Cameron:

> Cameron was first suspended at the age of 4. Here is how it happened: Every morning, when Cameron's mother dropped him off at school, she would hand him a bag of Skittles to quell the separation anxiety. One day, as Cameron entered the school building, the principal spied him with candy in hand. After a scolding, the principal reached down and grabbed the unopened bag of Skittles. Cameron's eyes were glued on the principal as he unlocked the door of his office, entered, and put the Skittles away in the bottom desk drawer before locking up and walking away.

> The toddler was bent on finding a way to get his Skittles back. Resourceful even at that age, he noticed that, though the office door was locked, there was an open window. The window was high up, but there was a chair nearby. Cameron pulled the chair over, got on it, and climbed through the window. He then walked over to the desk, opened the bottom drawer, and got his Skittles.

> The principal suspended the 4-year-old for 2 days – for theft.

> With that one act, at the age of 4, Cameron became entangled in a cycle often referred to as the school-to-prison pipeline. Lots of suspensions followed for Cameron, mostly for fighting and "defiance." In middle school, he and a friend tossed cartons of milk at one another in the cafeteria, for which he was arrested and served time for assault. By 16, he had about 150 suspensions, 4 expulsion hearings, and several arrests.

This pipeline has become prevalent all over America. Children, mostly minority, are harshly treated for some misconduct, and the hurt and stress on the family begins.

When researching this subject, I felt gut-punched by the stories I read about how some of our schools treat our children. In "The School Security America Doesn't Need," Chase Madar, a New York civil rights attorney, explains that as more police and school resource officers are placed and called onto school campuses, horrible things can happen:

> Just ask the three 9-year-old girls and an 8-year-old boy, who got into a fight at their Baltimore elementary school – then got *arrested* by real police. Or Salecia Johnson, age 6, cuffed and arrested for throwing a tantrum at her elementary school in Milledgeville, Georgia. Or Wilson Reyes, a 7-year-old at a Bronx, New York, elementary school who, last December 4, was *cuffed, hauled away, and interrogated* under suspicion of taking $5 from a classmate. (Another kid later confessed.)

The most painful experience was watching a video of a police officer handcuffing a 7-year-old child, tightly pulling his arms around a chair behind him, and hearing the little boy crying in desperation while the police officer just watched for four hours. The New York Police Department still does not understand what they did wrong and claim it was standard procedure for a juvenile arrest. I do not know what is more horrifying: that a 7-year-old is able to be arrested or that it is standard procedure.

Have we lost all perspective, so that we abandon empathic treatment of elementary school children? How can families feel secure when, on any random school day, their child may experience a life-altering trauma like this? Incidents like these brand a child, and so begins their fateful trip down the school-to-prison pipeline. This also does not teach children to respect authority. Could incidents like these be the moment a child becomes a cop-hater?

For countless adults and juveniles, family security is threatened or destroyed in the event of even a minor transgression such as marijuana possession. Our prisons are full of people who committed nonviolent acts or are innocent of any crime.

Governor Don Siegelman is an innocent man and an American political prisoner. Before he was governor of Alabama, he was attorney general and secretary of state. He had an exemplary career but was a successful Democrat in a basically Republican state. The whole story, notably quite lengthy, may be found at www.free-don.org. Needless to say, something is very wrong when 100 American attorney generals, including Republicans, write to advocate for Governor Siegelman's release, yet nothing happens. A former Attorney General for the State of New York said, "The Segelman trial could have been a chapter in a Kafka novel ... or in the former Soviet Union, but in the United States ... it's hard to believe."

Currently, a documentary, *Atticus v. the Architect*, is being filmed; hopefully, by the time this book is published, the film will be completed and Don Siegelman will be free (free-don.org). To help fund the documentary, a GoFundMe account was created, to which I was glad to contribute. A few weeks later, Governor Siegelman personally emailed, from prison, to thank all donors. I responded with a note of encouragement and told him we know the truth: that our criminal justice system abandoned him. I was surprised to receive a response from him:

Jill, so good to hear from you.

I am intrigued by the subject of your book, *Abandonment*.

Thank you for making the connection with me regarding the country. I could also add being abandoned by the Democratic Party, political associates, and elected officials. Both political parties and all elected officials should be concerned about what happened to me. Injustice is both blind and bipartisan.

You are on point to talk about how America's criminal justice system works to destroy families. While the BOP purports to have family in mind, they use keeping families apart as a means of punishment. By refusing to transfer an inmate closer to home, the FBOP punishes the spouse and children, causing relationships to pull apart and relationships to be forgotten and estranged between the infrequent visits.

An example: I am not narcissistic but using my situation. I am approximately 490 miles from Birmingham. It takes my family about eighteen hours to make a round trip. Visiting hours are only on Saturday and Sunday. So, to get here for a visit, leaving after work on Fridays at six p.m., they would arrive Saturday, about one thirty or two a.m., check in at a motel, and be at the Camp at eight thirty a.m. Sunday's visits always end early, so they can get home in time to get a good night's rest before going to work Monday.

I have been turned down three times for a closer-to-home transfer. The last time I was told not to reapply, even though Talladega is forty-five minutes from my home and Montgomery only an hour and a half.

It happens more often than not that inmates are refused a closer-to-home transfer.

You are on to something. Keep going!

All my best,
Don

Two days later, I learned that Governor Siegelman was put in solitary confinement for giving a telephone interview to a radio program, something he had done many times before throughout the years of his imprisonment. His family can no longer see him.

The reason I relate this story is to illustrate that by putting people in prison at an alarming rate and for the commitment of minimal offenses, we hurt and abandon the innocent, the family members. Governor's Siegelman's email makes it all too clear that keeping families apart is often intentional and fractures the family, the diamond. It is cruel to punish the innocent. As President Barak Obama once said about prisoners, "They are still Americans." Just as important, so are their families.

Stacking the Economic Deck Against Families

Families face numerous insecurities every day, in addition to those mentioned above. Some include: lack of paid family leave, unlivable minimum wage, payday lenders, Wall Street greed, billionaire entitlement, conservative economic values, lack of good employment opportunities, demonization of workers and their pensions, demonization of unions, and the war on women.

There is no guaranteed family leave for new parents in our country. However, *if* you work a certain number of hours, and *if* you work for a business with fifty or more employees, you are guaranteed twelve weeks of *unpaid* leave. How fortunate! Families can be home with their newborn child if they are rich enough to afford it. The problem? Not every family can afford to live with zero income for three months, particularly with a new little mouth to feed and a new little bottom to diaper. It would be comical if it were not so sad that this country abandons families at the very moment when they become a family. Among 185 countries, our country is 1 of only 3 that do not guarantee paid maternity leave, right alongside Oman and Papua New Guinea. As Adam Peck and Bryce Covert demonstrate in, "U.S. Paid Family Leave Versus The Rest Of The World, In 2 Disturbing Charts." How is America exceptional? Certainly not in supporting the success of a new family.

There are PRIIF forces that are not simply fighting an increase in the federal minimum wage but who want to abolish it altogether. Senator Tom Coburn (R-OK) speaks for those forces. He led a filibuster that quashed a Democratic attempt to raise the minimum wage, but he also wants to see the law itself abolished, contending that minimum wage hurts employment. Superficial thinking may support this belief, but in-depth studies show that raising the minimum wage boosts the overall economy and lifts millions out of poverty without hurting businesses. A higher federal minimum wage would also provide help to women and people of color, all of whom are members of families who would benefit. Importantly, 80 percent of Americans support raising the minimum wage, including two-thirds of Republicans, and they want their politicians to act.

Wall Street came a hair's breadth away from destroying the United States, and their greed still threatens our society, the setting in which the diamond is embedded. In the financial collapse of 2008, Wall Street *consumed* the savings of millions, forcing twenty-three million people out of their jobs and causing nearly ten million people to lose their health insurance *and* one million families to lose their homes. Robert Reich, former United States Secretary of Labor, states in his article, "Wall Street's Threat to the American Middle Class:" "A repeat performance is not unlikely." The word "consumed" is Robert Reich's, but the raw fact is Wall Street stole it all. It was the greatest theft in all of world history. No middle- or lower middle-class family was left untouched. Wall Street abandoned the very country that feeds their families and they would do it all again to become billionaires.

There is a yet-unnamed mental illness that seems to infect the brain when one realizes they have become a billionaire. The realization of having access to 100,000 million dollars triggers a *thought virus* that contaminates their thinking, spawning thoughts of power and grandeur that instantly turn people into conservatives. There are a few who are immune and do not become infected by this thought virus, but these are rare cases. Some examples include Nick Hanauer, Warren Buffet, Jeff Skoll, and Tom Steyer.

There are over 1,800 billionaires in the United States who are at risk for this thought virus, an epidemic of entitlement. Symptoms of the virus include a yearning to buy a politician or take over the country. The virus fosters demigod delusional thinking. This virus can be transmitted at birth, inherited, or may be contracted in relation to business or investment dealings. Privilege is toxic.

Stand Up Activities

Below, for your consideration, are several suggested Stand Up Activities. For a further explanation of the Keep/Start/Stop organization tool, please see Chapter One. After reading this chapter, you may think of additional activities readers can implement. If you'd like to share your brilliant constructive, compelling and creative ideas, please do so at: www.facebook.com/americaabandoned.

KEEP:

1. Keep in mind that families thrive when we honor our social contract with one another. Since the Velvet Coup began, politicians cannot find money for social programs, yet they always find funding for the Defense Department. Budgets are moral documents. Why is it immoral to fund social programs and moral to fund war? It makes no sense.

2. Keep fighting for a federal minimum wage. Nick Hanauer, as a guest on *Real Time* on June 3, 2016, stated that if the minimum wage had tracked with inflation, it would be $10.50 today; if it had tracked with productivity, it would be $22.00 an hour; and if it had tracked the wealth increase of the 1 percent, it would be $28.00 an hour.

START:

1. Start to reflect on your childhood. In what type of unit were you raised, the Nurturing Parent or the Strict Father? Understanding how you were raised will give you insight as to who you are and the choices you make today.

STOP:

1. Stop supporting politicians, organizations, or anyone who does not hold all our children in the highest regard and demonstrate that value through positive action.

One Marvelous Question

After reading this chapter, if you were going to do one thing marvelously well to move forward, what would that one thing be?

What leads us from darkness to light?

CHAPTER TWELVE

Public Education:
The Secret Abandonment

"I am patient with stupidity but not those who are proud of it."

Edith Sitwell

Thomas Jefferson, one of our founding fathers, the principal author of the Declaration of Independence and the founder of the first free university said, "Educate and inform the whole mass of the people... They are the only sure reliance for the preservation of our liberty." The privatization of our public school system is a violation of everything America's founding fathers believed and wanted for the new country they were creating. They never envisioned education becoming a profit center.

Samuel Adams, a leader of the American Revolution, said, "If virtue and knowledge are diffused among the people, they will never be enslaved. This will be their great security." The use of phrases like "mass of the people" and "diffused among the people" clearly informs us that they highly valued equal education for *all* Americans. Today, strong political, religious, industry and ideological (PRIIF) forces want to make a profit from the field of education and to be paid by public tax money while doing so. A profit motive inherently creates tension.

Collectively, we are abandoning public education. Nowhere else in the world does a public education system like ours exist, and it is how democracy can survive. It makes America different. Thomas Jefferson believed public education was essential to the preservation of a democracy. Horace Mann, an American politician and education champion, devoted his life to creating a nationwide public school system because he saw it as a means to equalize opportunity for all citizens. It took more than a century to build and just a few years to destroy. What was one of the ways this was done?

As mentioned in Chapter One, it was accomplished by the age-old manipulation method of demonization. PRIIF forces, seeing a large pot of public money that they wanted to get their hands on, developed a plan of attack on teachers, budgets, tenure, textbooks, and educational "methodologies," such as the scam known as the No Child Left Behind (NCLB) Act of 2001. All of these set the public school system up to fail so it would be weak enough to privatize. Of course, this was done with the help of a two-word, bumper sticker message: "education reform."

The NCLB was a test-based system that abandoned recognizing a child's unique multiple intelligences and created a new system that could only teach to the test. To make matters worse, it was never funded properly. School districts were put in the untenable position of meeting the NCLB criteria without the funding to accomplish it, a classic set-up-to-fail strategy; in other words, the public school system was drowned in a bathtub. Then, when the schools began to fail, PRIIF profiteers rode in with the private charter school concept, shouting the rallying cry that business is always better than government.

However, is there more going on in addition to making money? In an explosive series by Capital & Main, "Failing the Test: A New Series Examines Charter Schools," that examined charter schools, Kevin Wilner, Director of the National Education Policy Center at the University of Colorado at Boulder, explained, "They [philanthropists] like charters, in part because they decrease the publicness of public schools. They want a system much more based on market forces because they don't trust democracy." So the disgustingly rich do not like the *public* nature of *public* schools because they do not trust democracy? What the rich want to do is to tear down what is essential to democracy because they do not trust democracy. Are these people nuts? No. It is just that democracy gets in the way of an oligarchy.

The charter school concept has made such progress that now, for the first time in at least fifty-years, a majority of the students in public schools are from low-income families. Why? Because charter schools cherry-pick the students they want to enroll. Public schools are required to educate *all* children in the community, but private charter schools can pick the best-of-the-best and leave behind the special needs and lower-achieving students. John Oliver did an extensive analysis on his Last Week Tonight show, which may be seen on You Tube, regarding the devastating reality of the charter school experience.

In her article, "Five Devastating Facts About Charter Schools You Won't Hear from the 'National School Choice Week' Propaganda Campaign," Laurie Levy, M.Ed, related that there is no data to support that charter schools are superior to public schools and, as mentioned above, they can pick and choose their students. Children who are better resourced and have more family support do well in charter schools, but it is all about family income. There is no denying that family income and SAT scores are correlated. In addition, and as a myth-buster, public schools in many communities are doing fine. If fewer than 25 percent of the students are living in poverty, that school is likely to perform as well as any in the nation. Schools with fewer than 10 percent of students living in poverty outperform students in many countries. Valerie Strauss, of *The Washington Post* said:

> It bears mentioning that nations with high-performing school systems – whether Korea, Singapore, Finland, or Japan – have succeeded not by privatizing their schools or closing those with low scores but by strengthening the education profession. They also have less poverty than we do.

Now, American public school teachers have to deal with issues they have never faced before. In a January 16, 2015 *Washington Post* article, "Majority of U.S. Public School Students are in Poverty," we learn:

> "When they first come in my door in the morning, the first thing I do is an inventory of immediate needs: Did you eat? Are you playing? A part of my job is making them feel safe," said Sonya Romero-Smith, a veteran teacher at Lew Wallace elementary school in Albuquerque. Fourteen of her eighteen kindergartners are eligible for free lunches. She helps them clean up with bathroom wipes and toothbrushes, and she stocks a drawer with clean socks, underwear, pants, and shoes.

Kent McGuire, President of the Southern Education Foundation, stated in the same article:

> The fact is we've had growing inequality in the country for many years. It didn't happen overnight, but it's steadily been happening. Government used to be a source of leadership and innovation around issues of economic prosperity and upward mobility. Now we are a country disinclined to invest in our young people.

"Disinclined to invest in our young people"? In other words, our country has abandoned public education.

The abandonment of the public school system by PRIIF forces has become so heinous that in Chicago, many parents went on a hunger strike and led a march (albeit a slow one because they were so weak and tired) to try and save a high school from being closed. It was one of fifty-three public schools being closed by Mayor Rahm Emanual.

What has happened to us? In America, parents actually resort to starving themselves, surviving only on liquids, to try to get their children an education in their own neighborhood? Personally, I do not care if it is done in the name of tight budgets. There is no reason for budget issues. America is rich. This abandonment is the choice of our elected officials and the PRIIF forces that donate to those officials; they make the decision to build schools in Afghanistan and close them in America.

After thirty-four days, the parents ended their hunger strike. The Chicago Board of Education was forced to reopen the high school, but they voted to make it arts focused, with a technology component. The parents, knowing the community, wanted a global leadership and green technology school. In America, parents must resort to organizing a hunger strike, then still fail to get what they feel their children require?

Charter Schools v. Public Schools

There is a fight being waged to see where our property tax dollars will fall, in the pockets of our local communities or onto corporation ledger sheets for CEO and shareholder pockets.

Charter schools are public schools run independently of the public school system. They do not charge tuition because the public school system must give the private entity the money to support operations. The private group runs them under a charter, and they have more autonomy and are often exempt from certain state and local regulations.

Moving public money earmarked for serving the public into private pockets is the principal goal of the charter school movement. It is a privatization grab of public funds couched in terms, such as the ones billionaire Eli Broad uses to convince the Los Angeles Unified School District (LAUSD) to replace 50 percent of their public schools with charter schools through a program called Great Public Schools Now, a laughable moniker at best. Eli Broad owns $7 billion in wealth. He could fund his entire initiative himself, as it is estimated to cost half a billion dollars but instead, his initiative is focused on making the LAUSD pay for it. He says, "Such an effort will gather resources, help high-quality charters access facilities, develop a reliable pipeline of leadership and teaching talent, and replicate their success." He further stated, "If executed with fidelity, this plan will ensure that no Los Angeles student remains trapped in a low-performing school."

Let's analyze his statement:

- "...gather resources" means taking resources away from the public system to operate the charter schools/private enterprises.

- "...help high-quality charters access facilities" means private corporations will not pay for their facilities but be able to use publicly funded facilities for their private enterprise. All revenue and no capital expenditure is great for their bottom line. The Florida State Legislature already approved requiring their public school districts to share tens of millions of dollars in construction funds with rival charter schools.

- "...develop reliable pipeline of leadership in teaching talent" sounds good, but what does that really mean?

- "...replicate their success" means making more schools into business opportunities.

- "Students won't be trapped in a low-performing school" but that is the con. Is the public school really low performing, or is a charter school so much better that we allow our public money go into private pockets? In New York, the Village Academy Network, Inc. administrator is paid $500,000 a year. Wouldn't that go a long way in ensuring public school success every year? The New York Daily News ran an article listing numerous charter school executive salaries titled: "Top 16 NYC charter school executives earn more than Chancellor Dennis Walcott." These salaries are syphoning taxpayer money to fund.

Concurrently with billionaire Eli Broad's foisting his initiative onto LAUSD, The Center for Media and Democracy released data showing the rapid turnover of charter schools with a state-by-state list of closed charter schools. They are actually failing at a much higher rate than traditional public schools. Millions of federal dollars also went to groups planning to start a charter school that never opened. I have to wonder: Could that have been the point?

A Virginia company, K12 Inc., is now being audited by a bipartisan group of lawmakers It appears that the Wall Street-traded charter school company took tens of millions of public dollars but only graduated half of their high school students and that teachers were asked by the private, for-profit company to inflate attendance and enrollment records used to determine funding of the state's taxpayer dollars. It was a sweet deal for them until they get caught. In California, K12 Inc. received $310 million in state funding for its profitable but low-performing California Virtual Academies serving 15,000 students. In a settlement with the state, they are mandated to pay back $168.5 million for manipulating attendance records and overstating the progress records of their students. Some activities should not be privatized, and education is one of them.

The privatization con is to manipulate the message by saying public schools are bad, and charter schools are good. In triggering the most vulnerable parental psychological button, because parents naturally want the best for their children, this creates product demand for a questionable product. Toss in the message that teachers are bad, tenure is bad, and unions are bad, and the populace believes it then they are more than ready for a privatization takeover. In other words, parents are manipulated and prepped to abandon their public school system so profiteers can bleed public money into their own coffers.

Higher Education

America once had a tremendous public higher education system of community colleges and universities. I basically went to college in California for free. Now, the CalState system from which I graduated is talking about a 28 percent tuition increase, an increase that will lock even more students out of attending college than the already inflated tuition does. Student debt has become so onerous that parents are still paying off their college debt while trying to save for the college educations of their children. Shockingly, it has become a multi-generational issue.

College, once open to the middle class, is once again predicated on family income and resources, leaving behind bright and enthusiastic potential future leaders of our country. Inadequate opportunity leads to an inadequate country. College is an investment in our intellectual infrastructure. Until recently, both political parties agreed on the importance of mandating that all Americans have some access to higher education. Currently, higher education is being demonized. Colleges are called "indoctrination centers" or "liberal training grounds," and those with post-graduate degrees are labeled as "elites" and "snobs."

Why? Funding higher education has been a boon to the loan industry. President Obama's administration blocked a bankruptcy court from erasing a 65-year-old's student debt because it would jeopardize the loan program. Attorneys for the loan program said the senior citizen could easily go back to work or win the lottery! Businesses in this country can file for bankruptcy but those with student debt cannot. A *Ring of Fire* radio website article, "White House: Weapons Industry Gets Blank Check but Student Debt Relief Is Impossible," stated:

> Borrowers must prove that they face "certainty of hopelessness" and have a "total incapacity" to pay the loans back. In short, you have to be dead before the government considers you unable to pay the loans back. But, it will offer a multibillion-dollar bailout to Wall Street firms that cripple the economy.

Another boon to the industry is the Accrediting Council for Independent Colleges and Schools. They are supposed to be the private college accountability arm for hundreds of for-profit colleges to ensure quality in the profit college industry, but it is really a classic case of the wolf watching the henhouse. The formula repeated over and over by Republicans is to drown the government by not funding a governmental agency, such as the U.S. Education Department, then claim that business does best to watch itself and fund that private organization with taxpayer money. This cycle fosters corruption, and government is the only means we have to break that cycle.

Now, at least seventeen colleges certified by the Accrediting Council, such as the Corinthian College and the ITT Technical Institute chains, have had to close, face fraud allegations, or broke many other laws to bilk their students. As Senator Elizabeth Warren stated:

If accrediting agencies aren't willing to stand up against colleges that are breaking the law, colleges that are cheating their students, then I don't know what good they do, and I sure don't know why we would let them determine which colleges are eligible for federal dollars.

In the past three years, those colleges received more than $5.7 billion of hard-earned taxpayer money. Between handing our higher education system to the private loan industry and to private, for-profit colleges, trusting both to do the right thing by our youth, we abandoned higher education to the profiteers.

Stand Up Activities

Below, for your consideration, are several suggested Stand Up Activities. For a further explanation of the Keep/Start/Stop organization tool, please see Chapter One. After reading this chapter, you may think of additional activities readers can implement. If you'd like to share your brilliant constructive, compelling and creative ideas, please do so at: www.facebook.com/americaabandoned.

KEEP:

1. Keep standing with our founding fathers, such as Thomas Jefferson and Samuel Adams, who deeply believed democracy depended on an equal education for the masses. Not only is our public school system highly unequal because school districts are dependent on property taxes (your zip code should not matter), but the privatization of charter schools introduced a profit motive and caused even more educational inequality.

START:

1. Start reading Capital & Main's investigative report on charter schools. They explain who the winners and losers are, the charter school powerbrokers, and offer solutions. The five-report series may be found at Capital & Main: Investigating Power and Politics' website.

2. Start advocating for free or reasonable tuition.

STOP:

1. Stop the tuition boon to the loan industry. Contact your representatives and fight for bankruptcy laws to be put in place for tuition as they are for corporations. It makes no sense that business may files for bankruptcy to manage debt while students cannot. Fight for lower tuitions for higher institutions.

One Marvelous Question

After reading this chapter, if you were going to do *one* thing marvelously well to move forward, what would that one thing be?

Will everyone over 65 years of age need to win the lottery to survive in the future?

CHAPTER THIRTEEN

Social Security: The Coming Theft

*"If you don't understand what happened behind you,
then you won't understand what's going on around you."*

James Baldwin

The Social Security Act of 1935 and the program it created have been hated by very powerful conservative forces since its inception. Those haters who want it abandoned or, better yet, privatized, have been demonizing it for eighty years. They call it socialism, a Ponzi scheme, going bankrupt, and claim that the young will never benefit. They say it is an entitlement that adds to the deficit and so on, but none of it is true.

The haters also call Social Security a tax. They are half-right, but they ignore the other half of the truth because it does not serve their purposes. As David Kay Johnson, an American investigative journalist and a specialist in economics and tax issues who also won the 2001 Pulitzer Prize, wrote for the Forward in the book *Social Security Works:*

> Social Security is a form of national insurance, its premiums paid with a dedicated tax on what the law calls *compensation for services.* This includes wages, including bonuses, salaries and stock option profits, up to the annual salary cap of $117,000 in 2014. Compensation above that level is not taxed and is not counted in calculating benefits.

Social Security has been a success story like no other in this country. It is a national insurance program and not – as some would have you think – socialism. The government does not *own* it and does not receive profits from it. The federal government holds the *people's* premium insurance money (taxes) in *trust* for when it may be needed in the future. We buy car insurance, fire, and property insurance in case we need it in the future, and no one whines about those programs. We buy that insurance because we know that if our homes burn down, we will need help to rebuild and continue to live. Social Security insurance is there for when our bodies burn down, either from old age or a disability. It will allow us to live, and orphans and widows are literally tossed in for safekeeping.

An overwhelming majority, 89 percent, of the people believe Social Security is "more important now that ever." Another 84 percent say they do not mind paying Social Security taxes because it "provides security and stability to millions." Further, 75 percent of the people think the program should be *expanded,* not reduced. When do we ever see the American public agree like this? Also, 50 percent say Social Security will be their main source of income, if not the only source, when they are elderly. If it is so successful and enormously appreciated, why are there those who want to abandon or privatize it? The answer is because they want to get their grubby little hands on all that money. The *trust* is a huge pot of money, and they cannot stand seeing it sit in government *trust* coffers when they could play with it in the stock market.

Could the program be tweaked? Of course it could. Is it "insolvent" or any of those other fear-based manipulations we hear as mentioned above? Absolutely not.

The Progressive Change Institute implemented "The Big Ideas Project" and received over a million votes on 2,616 ideas from the public (https:// thinkbig.us). From those, they created the Top 20 list. What was number one on that list? It was all about Social Security. The report stated:

> Now is the time to expand Social Security – not cut it. Social Security benefits simply haven't kept up with the rising costs that seniors face – for medicine, food, and housing. We're facing a retirement crisis where seniors can't rely on pensions and other parts of the social contract. We need to increase benefits to make sure they reflect the true costs seniors face. Expanding Social Security is the best way to ensure all Americans have the economic security they need to retire with dignity.

Third on the Top 20 list of "Big Ideas" was also about Social Security. The report stated:

> Tax equality. This means that 100 percent of everyone's income is taxed for Social Security, not just middle class people (scrap the cap). It means that no matter the source of your income, it

is all treated the same for tax purposes (no more calling a salary "carried interest" to change the tax rate on it, no more taxing dividends and capital gains at a different rate).

Their findings fall in direct alignment with the data. People want Social Security to remain the way it is, managed by the government and not abandoned and privatized, so they are willing to pay more into the insurance program through taxes. Moreover, 81 percent of the working public said they cannot wait until 70 years of age to retire, which is what Republicans and Wall Street want. In *Social Security Works*, the authors wrote:

> Out of sight from most Americans, powerful, organized, and determined moneyed interests have waged a more than three-decade-long, billionaire-funded campaign to dismantle Social Security, brick by brick. That campaign has enjoyed some success. And it is still with us.

Billionaire Peter G. Peterson is the one we really need to worry about. He has made it his life's work to destroy Social Security. He held a position in Richard Nixon's cabinet, one of the country's most corrupt presidencies, and was CEO of Lehman Brothers. He has also written many articles on Social Security promoting falsities, some dating as far back as 1982, projecting a crash in the program that has yet to happen, even after thirty-four years. Still, his outspoken assumptions and accusations do foster doubt. He also created The Peterson Foundation, the purpose of which is to promote the product of doubt.

If they write lies often enough, publish disinformation strategically, and have a billion dollars to spend to propagate doubt (they even made a movie!) they may still win an argument to a problem that does not actually exist. There are other disgustingly rich, of course, who want to create a cultural environment where we will willingly abandon the Social Security program, such as Charles Koch, who founded and funds the Cato Institute and the Heritage Foundation. The least-known and the most powerful when it comes to destroying Social Security is Pete Peterson, so keep an eye on him.

In 2012, *The Los Angeles Times* printed an article titled "Unmasking the Most Influential Billionaire in U.S. Politics." Who were they unmasking? Peter G. Peterson, and here is an excerpt:

Who's the most influential billionaire business figure in national politics?

If you answered one of the Koch brothers [Charles or David] or George Soros, you're wearing your partisan blinders. The former are known for their devotion to conservative causes, the latter to liberal. In either case, you're wrong.

The most influential billionaire in America is Peter G. Peterson. The son of Greek immigrants, Peterson, 86, served as Commerce secretary under President Nixon, then became chairman and chief executive of Lehman Bros. Subsequently, he made his big money as cofounder of the Wall Street private equity firm Blackstone Group.

Peterson doesn't attract venom from the left like the Koch family or bile from the right like Soros. In Washington, he's treated with sedulous respect as a serious thinker about public policy willing to support earnest public discussion with cold cash. His money backs a large number of think tanks across the political spectrum; he has started a news outlet churning out articles about fiscal matters and is funding a high school curriculum aimed, according to its creators at Columbia University, at "teaching kids about the national debt."

Peterson's views are subtly infiltrating the Washington debate – which is why Americans should start getting worried about him.

In addition to billionaires, there is a Libertarian tribe consisting of right-wing Republicans and the Tea Party, to watch, and many of them are in Congress. The Republicans like to label Social Security an *entitlement,* and they have gone to great efforts to demonize that word as well, in an all-out bastardization of it. If we had fire insurance and our house burned down, we would feel *entitled* to the coverage of our insurance policy because we made regular premium payments to receive it if we ever had cause to need it. However, their demonization of the whole idea of any entitlement makes people think of it as a freebie, a giveaway, and a handout. They aim to manipulate us into thinking someone else, someone less deserving, is stealing our tax money, in a classic us-versus-them manipulation. Social Security is an insurance premium payout, not a handout.

This Libertarian tribe also foists the concept of austerity onto the country, claiming it will be better for the country. It really is a means to take money from the middle class to give to the rich. No one can *grow* a country by spending *less*. It is absurd on the face of it, yet this economic theory took over Europe and then America. Senior Political Writer for *Daily Kos*, Joan McCarter, wrote an article titled, *"Social Security Already Hit by the Austerity Squeeze,"* in which she said:

> The loudest battles over Social Security are about potential benefit cuts like the recently vanquished "chained CPI" proposal. But another, less noticed fight has been going on for years. It's aimed at undermining Social Security through systematic budget cutting by Congress of the operating budget of the SSA, the agency charged with providing customer service to the public.

> The SSA has received less than its budget request in fourteen of the past sixteen years. In fiscal 2012, for example, SSA operated with 88 percent of the amount requested ($11.4 billion).

> "It's part of a raging fight by conservatives to get rid of the government's footprint wherever possible," says Nancy Altman, co-director of Strengthen Social Security, an advocacy group.

I think it is extremely important to realize what life was like before the Social Security Act was passed in 1935. On the Disability History Museum website is an article by Dr. David Wagner, "Poor Relief and Almshouse." It begins by painting this picture:

> For an amazingly long 300 years prior to the passage of the Social Security Act of 1935, the only aid available to people who were poor, elderly, disabled, widowed, orphaned, or otherwise in need came from local authorities who administered the "Poor Laws," laws which came to the United States with English settlers in the 1620s. Whether you were a once-prosperous man who was hurt in an accident or a poor woman who had an illegitimate child, you needed to go to your town or city's overseers of the poor, who would judge whether you were "deserving" or "worthy" enough to secure some minimal aid. They also examined whether you were a person deemed "settled" in the particular town or city. Overseers of the poor were local officials, like selectman or freeholders, who usually knew little or nothing of poverty but came from the middle

or even upper classes. Some no doubt were compassionate, some not so much.

It is the "some not so much" phrase that strikes terror in the heart. Can you imagine someone like Peter G. Peterson, a fervent foe of Social Security, or any other billionaire being an overseer of the poor? Another symptom of the virus we discussed is that most billionaires lose their compassion, humility, and empathy, which is what is exactly needed when assisting those less fortunate or those who did not win the sperm lottery.

In <u>Social Security Works</u>, Nancy J. Altman and Eric R. Kingson write:

> Thanks to all these forces (billionaires, conservative think tanks, right-wing foundations, doubt-spinners), political and media elites have lost an understanding of the conceptual underpinnings that have led to Social Security's popularity, and have been convinced to see Social Security as a problem rather than the solution that it is.

The coming theft of our popular Social Security program will not be a frontal attack, which is what George W. Bush tried to do in attempting to privatize it; the attack will come from cutting its budget. Right now, the Republican-held congress is cutting millions of dollars from the Social Security budget so the program is forced to reduce hours, furlough employees and even close offices. In this way, we will think the Social Security management is incompetent, not that the budget has been syphoned.

What is one of the ways America *is* exceptional? Our unique Social Security program. We cannot abandon it by listening to falsehoods spread by only those who would benefit from it being dismantled. Where would all that money currently held in trust go? The d-rich and Wall Street are breathlessly waiting, with their computer-enhanced, nano-second hedge funds ready to pluck it.

Social Security was designed to thank Americans who spend their lives making America exceptional, repaying them with the freedom to grow old with dignity.

Stand Up Activities

Below, for your consideration, are several suggested Stand Up Activities. For a further explanation of the Keep/Start/Stop organization tool, please see Chapter One. After reading this chapter, you may think of additional activities readers can implement. If you'd like to share your brilliant constructive, compelling and creative ideas, please do so at: www. facebook.com/americaabandoned.

KEEP:

1. Keep in mind that Social Security is not insolvent, as the d-rich want you to believe. Social Security has a moral purpose. Do you think those who demonize it have a moral purpose in wanting to win control over the program?

START:

1. Start reading on the subject. Find information and find out how you can save its operational budget at: http://www. socialsecurityworks.org. Their book, Social Security Works!, contains a chapter that refutes every charge against the program and details actions for making the program stronger.

2. Start joining organization such as the Pension Rights center at: www.pensionrights.org.

STOP:

1. Stop believing billionaire propaganda and realize what their true agenda is entirely profit motivated.

One Marvelous Question

After reading this chapter, if you were going to do *one* thing marvelously well to move forward, what would that one thing be?

Does the Second Amendment really mean what we think it means?

CHAPTER FOURTEEN

Personal Freedom or Guns? Finding Balance

"Belief is the death of intelligence. As soon as one believes a doctrine of any sort or assumes certitude, one stops thinking about that aspect of existence."

Robert Anton Wilson

We have abandoned our country to guns. We have abandoned our children, our elementary schools, our colleges, our shopping malls, our movie theaters, our places of worship, and even our places where we celebrate and have fun. More dramatically, we have abandoned our *everyday personal freedom* to guns. Not one of us knows if we will come home safely from that shopping mall or movie theater. We may be walking down a random street when someone with a semiautomatic decides to take his hate and pain out on the innocent. Ironically, our daily freedom to live our lives has been stolen by an organization, the National Rifle Association (NRA), and businesses such as gun manufactures who are populated with people who speak vehemently about personal freedom. Freedom for whom?

It is shamefully clear that personal freedom in this country is only for gun owners, businesses that make a profit from selling guns, and the NRA. Deplorably, personal freedom is not available to the rest of us.

It was tragically ironic. I was writing this very chapter when the largest mass assignation in the history of America occurred in Orlando, Florida, as people were dancing and having fun. Forty-nine people were slaughtered, fifty-three people were seriously injured, and countless individuals will be scarred for life, thanks to an attack by only one man in a matter of minutes, a few hundred seconds and their families are ruined for life. This all due to us, collectively, abandoning our country to guns and the NRA in a way that makes it extremely easy to kill a whole lot of people quickly. We have literally abandoned everyone and everywhere to weapons of war.

On January 14, 1990, retired Supreme Court Chief Justice Warren Burger wrote an article titled "The Right to Bear Arms" for *Parade Magazine*, in which he stated:

> The gun lobby's interpretation of the Second Amendment is one of the greatest pieces of fraud; I repeat the word fraud, on the American people by special interest groups that I have ever seen in my lifetime. The real purpose of the Second Amendment was to ensure that state armies—the militia—would be maintained for the defense of the State. The very language of the Second Amendment refutes any argument that it was intended to guarantee every citizen an unfettered right to any kind of weapon he or she desires.

We truly must take a step back in time to gain a true understanding of where we are now. What did our forefathers know as guns? They could not possibly have envisioned the weapons of today, high-powered, fast-shooting, super-powerful devices that would have seemed like silly science-fiction notions to them. As Chief Justice Burger highlighted, our forefathers never intended for an armed citizenry to keep the government in check; rather, it was about *not* allowing a standing army that can, in fact, have the capability to take over the government, as was recently attempted in Turkey. In their view, the people would be armed to protect themselves *and* the government from foreign and domestic threats. A document penned in 1789 by James Madison clearly stated that the right to bear arms "shall not be infringed" because a "well-regulated militia" was the "best security for a free country."

When it comes to gun regulations, we have lost our way. Actually, we have been pushed, bullied, and manipulated. The efforts of gun supporters have been so successful that many gun owners become totally irrational when the topic is raised. On one hand, they claim to be supporting State rights, yet on the other, when any state attempts to implement any kind of gun rules whatsoever, they respond vehemently and bitterly, as is currently happening in the State of California. Rather than a constitutional issue, it has become a political and cultural issue. We must ask ourselves who is truly benefiting by making gun ownership a political and cultural issue?

The answer is simple: The gun manufacturers do, and the NRA keeps raking in profits for their elite livelihood. The head of the NRA, Wayne LaPierre, earns a million dollars a year. In his article, "The NRA's Profit Soars as Deaths from Gun Massacres Mount," Brett Arends, a columnist for *MarketWatch*, stated, "As the rest of America mourns yet another murderous gun spree on campus, a review of financial filing shows just how far the mammoth gun organization has been able to cash in, big time on the fallout of Sandy Hook in December 2012." The more irrational the NRA and gun manufacturers can cause gun owners' faulty reasoning, the more guns are sold.

Colonel Lawrence Wilkerson, Chief of Staff to Secretary of State Colin Powell and a lifelong Republican, said, in reference to the Orlando shooting, on *Real Time* on June 17, 2016, "Incontrovertibly, we need some kind of control on the weapons in this country... We do not need large-capacity magazine, semiautomatic weapons in the hands of anybody in the country accept other than, possibly, law enforcement. Period."

Stephen Kerr, Warriors Basketball Coach, said after the Orlando assassinations:

> I just have to get this off my chest. Let's have some checks. It's easier to get a gun than it is [to get] a driver's license, and it's insane... As somebody who has had a family member shot and killed, it just devastates me every time I read about this stuff, like what happened in Orlando, and then it's even more devastating to see the government just cowing to the NRA and going to this totally outdated Bill of Rights, right to bear arms. You know, if you want to own a musket, fine, but come on.

Stephen Kerr's father was murdered when he was 19 years old.

There are 357 million guns in circulation, more in this country than our population of 323 million people. Let that sink in. The number of guns in this country is twenty-five times higher, per capita, than it is in twenty-two developed countries; war-torn Yemen holds a distant second place. There is nothing like it anywhere else in the world. In Japan, someone is more likely to be hit by lightning than be killed by a gun. America experiences a mass shooting, defined as four or more people, every day. Guns are not protecting us. They are killing us, and it is a horrifying public crisis.

What is additionally horrifying and astounding is that even though the American Medical Association has wisely and accurately deemed gun violence a "public health crisis," the federal government is banned from taking any action on the issue. This is due to a Republican Congress. In

1997, they passed an amendment on an operations bill that barred the Center for Disease Control (CDC) from implementing any research that will "advocate or promote gun control." The amendment allowed for research on injuries and deaths caused by firearms, but the Republican Congress cut the funding, a common technique used by Congress so they will appear to be supporting a program while they do not support it in reality. The public rarely follows what happens with the budget. As a result, Congress gets the best of both worlds: positive press for allegedly supporting research and pacifying the NRA by not truly funding it.

After the most recent, high-profile, mass assassinations:

- Newtown, Connecticut: twenty-six first-graders and two adults butchered in their classroom.

- Aurora, Colorado: twelve people gunned down and fifty-eight injured in a movie theater.

- San Bernardino, California: fourteen county employees killed and twenty injured at a holiday party.

- Orlando, Florida: forty-nine people mowed down and fifty-three injured in a nightclub.

The Democrats are finally showing a spine and a long-lost ray of leadership. As Egberto Willies, a political activist, author, and blogger, said in his article, "When We Break the Gun Lobby, We Win on All Fronts," "Many likely believed the Democrats would do what they normally do: hide on security issues or not counterpunch when engaged too forcefully."

Political cartoonist, Rob Rogers, drew a single pane cartoon of a news anchor reading a breaking news story, "We interrupt our coverage of the terror attack in Nice, France ... which interrupted our coverage of the massacre in Dallas ... which interrupted our coverage of the shootings in Baton Rouge and Minnesota ... which interrupted our coverage of ..." America is an embarrassment. The rest of the world is puzzled by our illogical and emotional mismanagement of guns in our society. Even a few countries are issuing travel warnings to their citizens who want to come here on vacation.

On June 14, 2016, Chris Murphy (D-CT) led a fifteen-hour filibuster, talking specifically about gun violence. Of course it was nothing like the

"Green Eggs and Ham" filibuster speech delivered by Ted Cruz in his bid to shut down the government, but from June 22 to June 23, 2016, for twenty-five hours, the Democrats showed they had had enough after gun legislation, supported by over 90 percent of the American people, was voted down by the House Republicans. A Pundifact article, "Laura Ingraham Wrongly Says Claim that 90% Support for Gun Background Checks Has Been Debunked," clearly debunks a debunker.

In response, the House Democrats held an impromptu sit-in on the House floor, Occupy Congress. The Democrats are the minority party and, constitutionally, have no other leverage besides civil disobedience. There was no other means to demonstrate that, on this issue, they are Sustaining Politicians, life-affirming ones ready to represent their constituents.

House Majority Leader Paul Ryan responded by calling the sit-in "a stunt, a television ploy, and a fundraising plan," then ordered that the CSPAN cameras to be turned off; the House leader manages the cameras! He also cut off the microphones; so much for transparency and democracy. His typical bullying tactics were those of a Syphoning NRA-affirming political operation. The Republicans receive hundreds of thousands of dollars each year from the NRA. They cannot bite the hand that feeds them.

The House Republican tribe mentality is so powerful that no member may break ranks. Somehow, what the NRA wants has become equated to being a good conservative: If you hate the president and government, you also stand with the NRA and need their stamp of approval. In response to the sit-in, the Republicans passed bills with no discussion and literally left Congress in the middle of the night for their July 4 summer break.

Who governs the NRA? The membership recently elected some of the most reprehensible people in our country. As a Daily Beast article, "Ted Nugent and the Gang: Meet the Batsh*t Crazies of the NRAs Board," explains the top vote getter was Ollie North, who sold weapons to Iran but did not go to prison for his treason because of a technicality. The next highest voted was Ted Nugent, who admittedly pooped on himself and did not clean himself for eight days just so he could avoid the draft. The NRA is no longer a mainstream organization, as they would like us to think. It is a tribe. The majority of its members would ordinarily stand on principle regarding selling weapons to Iran or be against the unpatriotic – if not plain vile – act of dodging the draft to avoid serving in the military. Shockingly, the membership voted individuals like these to their governing board. Each of us, when we learn a politician supports the NRA, should ask why they stand with an organization that elects soulless crazies.

It is a common meme, perpetuated by the NRA to their zealot following, that if any gun safety legislation is passed at all, every gun they own will be seized, leaving them with nothing with which to protect themselves. Nothing gets this very frightened group of people, mostly men, more worked up. Rational gun legislation does not involve snatching everyone's gun away. That is a lie believed by zombies.

Responsible gun owners understand a weapon's power and do not use firearms to enhance their ego or enflame fear. They lock up their guns and teach their children respect for the weapon and its purpose to kill. Owning a firearm is not an all-or-nothing game. A fair line can be drawn between those who want to own a gun and those who want to live free of being shot.

Death by guns is leveled by gangs, desperately sad people who commit suicide, comprising two-thirds of all gun deaths, and those who want to look like big shots at public rallies or at Starbucks. More tragically than anything previously mentioned are toddlers playing with something dangerous, something they cannot possibly safely manage or understand. These few examples are shocking:

- A Chicago father was afraid of gang retaliation and put a gun in some pajamas on top of the refrigerator. He crazily showed his 6-year-old where it was. When the parents were not home, the child used the gun to shoot his brother while playing cops and robbers, shattering that diamond forever.

- A 2-year-old in South Carolina found a gun in the back seat of the car he was riding in and accidently shot his grandmother, who was sitting in the passenger seat, shattering that diamond forever.

- In Florida, a grandfather is dead after his 6-year-old grandson accidentally pulled the trigger of his uncle's unattended rifle during a barbecue at the family's home, shattering that diamond forever.

- A 4-year-old was fatally shot while holding his parents' gun, found in his parents' bedroom in Merrillville, Indiana, shattering that diamond forever.

- A 2-year-old accidentally shot and killed his mother at a northern Idaho Walmart when he reached into her purse and her concealed gun fired, shattering that diamond forever.

The shattering goes on and on. In fact, as of this writing, it has happened forty-three times. In 2015, toddlers have shot someone weekly, according to a Washington Post article, "People Are Getting Shot by Toddlers on a Weekly Basis This Year." In addition, Elizabeth Warren proclaimed in a You Tube video that it is time to make a choice about what is killing our children.

There is no fixing stupid. The NRA's position that the only way to stop a bad guy with a gun is a good guy with a gun is boneheaded. How do you stop *bad* toddlers from using a gun? Arm *good* toddlers? This bad-good concept is ridiculous on its face and infantile at its core. Now, the NRA is encouraging gun owners to store guns in their children's bedrooms as highlighted in a Think Progress article, "NRA Tells Parents To Keep Guns in Kids' Rooms for Safety." What possibly could go wrong? The NRA had passed from selling fear to selling insanity. Who benefits from this fear and insanity? The gun manufactures, and children's bedrooms are their newest marketing opportunity.

The NRA has abandoned safety and personal freedom for the masses for profits to gun manufacturers, gun shops owners, and themselves. "What's Wrong with America Shown in This One Tweet,' from The Daily Kos, explains that nothing more readily demonstrates the perversion of gun sales in this country than a tweet of a picture of a smiling gun saleswoman happily saying: "Always a rush after a big shooting." The sickening fact is that she is right: Guns sales always go up after a mass murder.

There is a powerful faction in our country who think their guns will be taken away, and they believe anything the NRA and gun manufactures want them to believe. As Jeffery Toobin, Staff Writer for *The New Yorker* said in his article, "So You Think You Know the Second Amendment?" "the reinterpretation of the Second Amendment was an elaborate and brilliantly executed political operation, inside and outside government."

Because of this brilliant plan, gun zealots believe it is their constitutional right, bestowed by our forefathers, for individuals to bear arms. In fact, there was no right to *individually* possess a gun until a 2008 the *District of Columbia v. Heller* case was decided by the Republican majority-held

Supreme Court. The NRA had their "activist" judges (to use a GOP term) on the high court, and those judges used their positions of power to validate an NRA political operation and sales tool for the gun industry. Chief Justice Warren E. Burger, Fifteenth Chief Justice of the Supreme Court from 1969 to 1986, called the idea of individuals having an unfettered right, as was the NRA's propaganda, "a fraud on the America Public."

What did our forefathers, in fact, intend when the Second Amendment was written? This question is answered in Politico Magazine article, "How the NRA Rewrote the Second Amendment." They actually had two intentions. They were concerned about standing armies and the potential of an army overthrowing the government in a military coup. They believed a "well-regulated militia" was the answer to that issue. Also, the militias were known in the South as Slave Patrols. The Slave Patrols protected the Southern economy and perpetuated slavery by finding runaway slaves and returning them to their owners. The Second Amendment, disgracefully, was written to protect the use of Slave Patrols. Thom Hartmann's blog, "We Need To Throw Out the Second Amendment," expands on this point.

Alan Grayson (D-FL), said, "You can't know what is in people's heads or their hearts, but you can know what's in their hands." Those hands are killing our American families, our diamonds, eighty-eight times a day from coast to coast, including seven incidents of children and teens every day, in addition to the mass shootings. At the same time, others joyfully profit from those deaths. These profiteers have abandoned their souls.

In a year, over 32,000 men, women and children are killed with guns. That is more fatalities than ten 9/11s. Remember how we reacted when Ebola entered our country? We were so afraid of the disease spreading, yet only one death occurred. We have a disease all right, an epidemic, in fact, and it is a zombie-like, NRA-contrived obsession with guns.

Stand Up Activities

Below, for your consideration, are several suggested Stand Up Activities. For a further explanation of the Keep/Start/Stop organization tool, please see Chapter One. After reading this chapter, you may think of additional activities readers can implement. If you'd like to share your brilliant constructive, compelling and creative ideas, please do so at: www.facebook.com/americaabandoned.

KEEP:

1. Keep June 2 reserved on your calendar every year to wear orange in honor of those who die daily from gun violence.

2. Keep in mind that the U.S. Supreme Court did not grant unlimited rights to own guns. Read the *Big Think* article titled, "The Supreme Court Ruling on the 2nd Amendment Did NOT Grant an Unlimited Right to Own Guns."

3. Keep in mind when you hear NRA propaganda such as, "guns don't kill people; only people kill people," that guns were designed as a weapon to kill, not to be used as a political weapon to pit one American against another. Only the NRA does that for their profit making agenda.

4. Keep in mind that the personal liberty of the majority of the American people has been stolen by a minority and that is counter to protecting the general welfare and of democracy.

5. Keep in mind that words and rhetoric matter and those who speak violently and foster Living in the Red energies around the use and ownership of guns is not acting in the best interest of a civil society. Look for the agenda behind the words.

6. Keep in mind as Congress repeatedly votes down commonsense gun violence legislation that the NRA is a powerful lobby and we need to "blow up the phones" of the Congressional switchboard to counteract their power. As Gabby Giffords, a former Arizona House Representative and gunshot survivor, said of US Senators who voted against common sense gun legislation: "The senators who voted no will say a lot of things about the votes they cast, and perhaps they might even say they were afraid (of the NRA). But make no mistake, their fear was nothing compared to what far too many victims of gun violence have faced. Theirs was a decision of political calculations."

START:

1. Start watching *Frontline* investigative reports on guns. *Frontline* is one of the last trustworthy investigative sources that do not promote an opinion. There are several more documentaries on their website, but start with these five:

    - Gunned Down: The Power of the NRA
    - The Evolution of Wayne LaPierre
    - How Loaded is the Gun Lobby?
    - NRA Insiders on the Politics of Guns
    - How the Gun-Rights Lobby Won After Newtown

2. Start considering the idea of treating guns as we do automobiles. Before we are allowed to drive, we are required to obtain a license so we have a uniform standard of knowledge to ensure a level of safety on the public highways. The license and the automobile are registered with the State, and those registrations are renewed on a regular basis. Insurance is also required to protect the public, and there is a penalty for those who do not purchase a policy but still drive. Why can we not treat guns the same as automobiles?

3. Start to ask those who stand with the NRA why they support people, like those who have been elected to their board of directors? Make politicians and neighbors accountable.

4. Start advocating, to your elected representatives, that federal agencies should be authorized to study the effects of gun violence. Currently, Congress refuses to acknowledge the American Medical Association position that gun violence *is* a public health epidemic.

5. Start advocating for the ban of high-capacity magazines and bullet buttons that make it easy for shooters to quickly reload, thus maximizing their ability to kill as many people as possible.

STOP:

1. Stop gun violence by joining organizations who fight to regain our personal freedom so we may have liberty to live our daily lives free from the fear of being shot, such as: Everytown for Gun Safety: The Movement to End Gun Violence (everytown.org), The Brady Campaign (bradycampaign.org), The Coalition to Stop Gun Violence (csgv.org), and Americans for Responsible Solutions (americansforresponsiblesolutions.org).

One Marvelous Question

After reading this chapter, if you were going to do *one* thing marvelously well to move forward, what would that one thing be?

As a society and as a people, can we be it anymore? Can we be bold?

CHAPTER FIFTEEN

Be Bold, America

"Only when we are brave enough to explore the darkness will we discover the infinite power of our light."

Brene Brown

I am waiting for boldness. What a joy it would be to see us jump out of the boiling water to save ourselves. It would be a bold undertaking. The question is, can we do it?

America is not very interesting anymore. We have abandoned boldness. In decades past, our country thrived on bold, exciting ideas and adventures that brought us together, from time to time, as one country.

For example, in 1958, the National Aeronautics and Space Administration (NASA) was created under President Eisenhower's administration. For nearly fifty years, NASA thrilled and captivated the country, adults and children alike, with the X-15 Rocket Plane, Project Mercury, Project Gemini, Project Apollo, Skylab, Apollo-Soyuz Test Project, the International Space Station and the Space Shuttle Program. These bold governmental programs brought us together as one America.

The space shuttle program alone engaged in 135 missions and ended with the landing of the *Atlantis* on July 21, 2011. The program spanned 30 years, and over 300 astronauts risked their lives to venture into space. We all lived vicariously through their flights, and numerous technological inventions resulted that benefited all of society, such as the GPS we now use every day in our cars and smartphones.

However, being a governmentally funded program and with the corporate privatization and anti-government (anti-we, the people) belief system taking hold, NASA had to be privatized. We cannot have the people venturing into space. There must be a buck made off of it.

Now, our captivation with astronauts and space travel is basically over. It was a thrilling adventure for generations and inspired millions of children. We are no longer brought together by our TV screens as one America to see what our country will do next in space. NASA is a shadow if its former grand self. The idea of bringing people together on bold, real adventures into space has been abandoned. We used to actually want to see the final frontier and galaxies far, far away, but now we have *Star Trek* and *Star Wars* instead.

We also had a unique, nationwide car culture. We invented the automobile. Automobile manufacturers were intensely interested in new designs, aerodynamics, color, and chrome (actually a detailing accent on vehicles long before it was a common internet browser.) The designs were stunning. One bold design that made us all laugh together as one nation was the Ford Edsel. A gorgeous vehicular specimen we all dreamt of owning—or at least I did—was the Corvette Stingray. Muscle cars were defining cultural icons of the 1950s, brightly painted and full of power and personality. Cars started conversations and offered a sense of community among enthusiasts. Clubs were formed for Mustangs, Corvettes, and GTOs, but the economic downturn the Velvet Coup caused has left the middle-class without the funds to save for a favorite car. Robert Samuelson, a *Washington Post* reporter, penned the article "Is the Car Culture Crashing?" In that article, he claimed that, due to economic factors, "The car culture may be dying or, at any rate, slumping into prolonged era of eclipse." The automobile culture that once brought us together has slammed its brakes; like so many other great parts of our history, it is now abandoned.

We no longer have an interesting, bold, or exciting society. It has been chipped away by mediocre thinking, lackluster politicians, austerity economics, zealot ideology, and, worst of all, the greed of the disgustingly rich, who apparently want all the money in this country for themselves. We are a rich country. We could do bold and exciting things again, but the money is tied up by just a handful of people and corporations who have no loyalty, conscience, or a desire to see this country to be bold again. That would mean they would have to let go of some money and pay higher taxes. We look to private corporations now for boldness. Where will the next new idea come from? Ideas like the iPhone or Tesla? We no longer think of ourselves as a people and culture, as being and doing bold things together. Could the America of today come together as a nation, as we did to end World War II?

Can we be bold to wrest control of our democracy back from the oligarchs? It would require many more of us to activate our citizenship though our daily activities, our vote, and our character. Chris Hedges said, "Those of us who care about recovering agency within our country, overthrowing the corporate coup d'etat that has taken place ... we are going to have to step outside that system." Until that *outside system* formulates, we must vote and be unrelenting in expressing our voice (to work outside the system, you may be interested in joining Our Revolution).

To wrest control from the oligarchs, it would require many more of us to Live in the Black and make constructive, compelling choices for ourselves and for our country, as well as choices that bring us together as a society, rejecting the efforts of political, religious, industry and ideological forces (PRIIF) that pull us apart for their own agendas. It would require many of us to be bold and actually change our minds, to let go of an ideology or leave a tribe. It would require us to punch holes in our enveloping certainty. Do we have it in us?

It would take many more of us to fight for campaign finance reform so the people would once again possess the power to influence our political representatives. At this point in time, the people have no impact on Congress: none, zero, *nada.* Congress members only work for those who gives them the most money. It will require boldness to reverse the Citizens United Supreme Court decision that opened the wide and inviting floodgates of dark money, domestic and foreign, which is used to buy politicians, sway initiatives, and to fool us into thinking their moneyed interests are also what is best for us. It will take great boldness to challenge mega-corporates and their phalanx of lawyers to change the law that bestowed personhood upon corporation, making their rights equal to those of real human beings. Can we do it?

Can we learn from the past? There has been a long-term and intentional takeover of America by the Velvet Coup. It will require boldness to reverse the decades of legislation that has torn down our democracy, such as reversing the decision to give a financial construct, money, free speech rights. There is a euphemism that money talks, but now it *legally* talks. Whoever has more money has more speech. Are we able to realize that the Libertarian belief system is a clever, political framework for selfishness? Libertarianism is not democracy. Do we possess the boldness it will take to reinstitute the republic our founding fathers hoped and suffered for? The Fourth Estate is dead. Corporate media has been bought by oligarchs.

Just a few years ago, there were fifty-two news media outlets. Now, there are only five. Jeff Bezos of Amazon owns *The Washington Post*. Rupert Murdock, of News Corp owns just about everything else and, in some case, all the media sources in one city. There is no such thing as the "liberal media;" that is a zombie lie. There is only one interest represented by the media: corporate interest, because our media outlets are owned and operated by corporations that have entirely different agendas than we do. We want news, but they want money. We watch television for the shows, but they think shows are filler, because it is ads that bring in the money. That is why the network is in business. Do we have the boldness required to stand up to our legislators and media lobbyists and demand that newsrooms are once again protected from the demand for profit? News died when making a buck became more important than an educated public. Do we have the boldness to bring back the firewall between making a profit and making the news?

Can the middle class return? It will require many of us to be bold and make decisions and elect politicians who understand that a vibrant middle class makes a vibrant country. Can we be bold enough to enact something like FDR's Second Bill of Rights, ones relevant for our times? We are not a bold country now because we do not currently have a bold middle class. Our country's exceptionalism was based on the unique and bold idea of a middle class and the constructs that supported it such as public education, Social Security, and nurtured families. Nowhere on Earth had there been such a population that could build a safe, honorable life for themselves and each other, and we called it the American Dream. Can we be bold and build the dream again?

We must show just how bold we can be to confront the NRA. There may be nothing more difficult than facing a bully with so much money and so many guns, but that is what the NRA has become. I once read a letter to the editor that said, "Gun advocates tell us, 'Guns don't kill people. People kill people.' So does that mean that in order to stop killing, we must eliminate all the people?" Of course not! That would be silly. What we need to do is eliminate the power of the NRA over our politicians and the minds of our most fearful neighbors and friends. Can our neighbors and friends be bold and let go of an ideology whose only purpose is to make money for the gun manufactures?

Are we, as individuals and collectively, bold enough to no longer be a fearful people? Fear is a product to sell us a bill of goods. Guns manufacturers are the obvious beneficiaries of fear, but fear, in and of itself, is a product.

Irresponsible hate rhetoric is a product of fear that has made millions for numerous radio and TV talk show hosts. An entire news network was built on the product of fear, and media outlets, in general, consistently use fear to boost ratings. If it bleeds, it leads! The media creates conflict where none exists, just for the ratings. Our society is riddled with those who sell fear for personal and political gain.

The answer to these questions is yes! But how do we do it when we feel so beaten down? We get up, dust ourselves off, and get going. We roll up our sleeves, work hard, and refuse to give up. There is nothing tricky about it. We must only make it a priority and work to bridge the knowing-doing gap. We now understand we have lost something of great value and we want it back. There have been attempts at boldness, such as the Occupy Movement and Bernie Sanders's political movement. We know what it looks like when we see it. We know in our hearts that it is genuine and authentic when it happens. Each of us must make a promise to ourselves to be one of the facets in our democracy that will pick a cause, take a stand, and recapture our democracy from the manipulative powers that have taken it from us. It took decades to lose, but it does not have to take decades to rebuild, as long as we reengage as citizens of the most unique and wonderful of countries.

We, the people must decide what makes up the heart and soul of our country. Answers will be found in addressing questions such as these:

- Will we have a country for the billionaires or a country for the rest of us?

- Will we allow the Velvet Coup to be completed by placing a billionaire in the highest and most powerful office in the world?

- Will we throw our birthright away, or will we decide that voting is a requirement of truehearted citizenship?

- Will we each get up, dust ourselves off, and get active? Will we make the change we must to save ourselves by running for office, writing letters, placing phone calls, become a citizen activist, and realize that powerlessness is not an option?

- Will we be a Sustaining Citizen in all our walks of life or – and more importantly – if we realize we have succumbed to being a

Syphoning Citizen, will we personally make the shift from the unsustainable to the sustainable?

- Will we elect serious people to Congress, people who understand that the stakes for our country and planet are higher than those of a political ideology? Will we vote for people who put the middle class first, rather than the billionaire class?

- Will we recapture our public education system from the profiteers and treat the system and its teachers with respect and commensurate funding to ensure our children's success?

- Will we make one simple change to the Social Security insurance program and raise the annual salary cap from $117,000 to $250,000, to keep it robust for years to come?

- Will we have the courage and political will to stand up to the bullies with guns?

- Will we be bold?

One Marvelous Question

After reading this chapter, if you were going to do *one*, **bold** thing marvelously well, what would that one, **bold** thing be?

"Everything will be all right in the end, and if isn't all right, then it's not yet the end."

Sonny Kapoor, The Best Exotic Marigold Hotel

RESOURCES

Chapter One:

1. Martin Gilens and Benjamin I. Page. "Testing Theories of American Politics: Elites, Interest Groups, and Average Citizens." American Political Science Association, 2014. Reprinted with the permission of Cambridge University Press.

2. Jon Ronson, *The Psychopath Test*. Picador, Riverhead Books, 2011.

3. Chase Peterson-Withorn. "2015 Forbes 400: Full List of America's Richest People." Forbes.com, Sept. 2015.

4. "Libertarianism." Wikipedia.com, CCX-BY-SA, http://creativecommons.org/licenses/by-sa/3.0/.

5. Michael Hilzik. "Unmasking the Most Influential Billionaire in U.S. Politics." *Los Angeles Times*, 2012. Reprinted with permission.

6. Mark Calvey. "He Said What?! The 5 Most Outrageous Things Said Last Night at the S.F." Commonwealth Club, *San Francisco Business Times*, Feb. 2014.

7. Joel Christie. "Multi-billionaire who gave a lecture about American's 'needing to have less things and live a smaller existence' owns a staggering FIVE mansions... including the nation's most expensive home." Daily Mail, Jan 24, 2015.

8. Mark Calvey, "He said what?! The 5 most outrageous things Tom Perkins said last night at S.F. Commonwealth Club." San Francisco Business Times, Feb 14, 2014.

9. Russell Sage Foundation. "The 1% Are Different." Ecointerest.com, May 30, 2014.

10. Paul Buchheit. "How 14 People Made More Money Than the Entire Food Stamp Budget for 50,000,000 People." Truth Out BuzzFlash.com, Oct. 6, 2014.

11. Joel Kotkin. "Today's Tech Oligarchs Are Worse than the Robber Barons." *The Daily Beast*, Aug 11, 2016.

12. Oxfam America. "An Economy for the 1%." Jan 17, 2016. Printed with permission.

13. "Antilia (building)," Wikipedia.com, CCX-BY-SA, http://creativecommons.org/licenses/by-sa/3.0/

14. Michael Winship. "The Kochs Are Ghostwriting America's Story." Moyers & Company, Feb. 9, 2016.

15. Don Terry. "Bringing Back Birch." Southern Poverty Law Center, Mar. 1, 2013.

16. Sam Pizzigati. "America's Greediest: The 2013 Top Ten," *Too Much: A Commentary on Excess and Inequality*, Dec. 16, 2013.

17. Thom Hartmann, "Time to Rein in the Robber Barons Again." Jul 14, 2016.

18. Graeme Wearden. "Oxfam: 85 Richest People as Wealthy as Poorest Half of the World." *The Guardian*, Jan. 20, 2014.

Chapter Two:

1. Nick Hauauer. "The Pitchforks Are Coming ... For Us Plutocrats," Jul-Aug, 2014.

2. Nicholas Confessore, Sarah Cohen, and Karen Yourish, "The Families Funding the 2016 Election." The New York Times, Oct. 10, 2015.

3. Open letter. "We Are New York's Millionaires, and We Say: Raise Our Taxes," The Guardian, Mar. 12, 2016.

4. Chrystia Freeland. Plutocrats: The Rise of the New Global Super-Rich and the Fall of Everyone Else. Penguin Random House, 2012.

5. Eliza Collins. "David Duke: Voting Against Trump is 'Treason to Your Heritage.'" Politico, Feb. 25, 2016.

Chapter Three:

1. Henry Wallace. "The Danger of American Fascism." New Deal Network, Democracy Reborn, New York, 1944.

2. Sidney Blumenthal. *The Rise of the Counter-Establishment.* Union Square Press, 1986.

3. Jacob S. Hacker and Paul Pierson. "The Powell Memo: A Call-to-Arms for Corporations." Moyers & Company, Sept. 14, 2014.

4. People for the American Way. "ALEC: The Voice of Corporate Special Interests in State Legislatures." In Focus, Right Wing Watch, 2012.

5. Lisa Graves. "ALEC Is a Corporate Lobby Masquerading as a Charity." *Truth Out*, Nov. 1, 2013.

6. Corporate Accountability Project. "It's No Accident that Coors Is the *Right* Beer for America," http://www.corporations.org/coors/article.html.

7. Sarah Posner. "Secret Society: Just Who Is the Council for National Policy, and Why Isn't It Paying Taxes?" *Alternet*, Feb. 28, 2005.

8. Mehrun Etebari. "Trickle-Down Economics: Four Reasons Why It Just Doesn't Work." United for a Fair Economy, July 17, 2003.

9. Donald Cohen. "The History of Privatization: How an Ideological and Political Attack on Government Became a Corporate Grab for Gold." *The Hidden History of the Privatization of Everything Series: Talking Points Memo.*

10. Thom Hartmann. "What the Reagan Revolution Brought Us." Blog, Jul. 11, 2013.

11. Connie Cass. "Poll Reveals Americans Don't Trust Each Other Anymore." *USA Today*, Feb. 30, 2013.

12. Steve Rendall. "The Fairness Doctrine: How We Lost It and Why We Need It Back." *Fair & Accuracy in Reporting*, Jan. 1, 2005. Reprinted with permission.

Chapter Four:

1. Public Citizen. "NAFTA's 20-Year Legacy and the Fate of the Trans-Pacific Partnership." *Trade Watch*, Feb. 2014.

2. Clinton Alexander. "Beef and Pork Country-of-Origin Labeling Laws: WTO Favors Canada, Mexico Over U.S." *The New American*, Dec. 14, 2014.

3. David Rose. "Murdoch's Media Monopoly." *Filmmaker Magazine*, Dec. 5, 2012.

4. Gene Kimmelman, Mark Cooper, and Magda Herra. "Failure of Competition Under the 1996 Telecommunications Act." *Federal Communications Law Journal*: Vol. 58: Iss. 3, Article 9, 2006.

5. Adam Johnson *"Washington Post Ran 16 Negative Stories on Bernie Sanders in 16 Hours." Fair & Accuracy in Reporting*, Mar. 8, 2016.

6. Sheryl Gay Stolberg. "Pugnacious Builder of the Business Lobby." *New York Times*, June 1, 2013.

7. Alyssa Katz. *The Influence Machine*. Penguin Random House. 2015.

8. David Brodwin. "The Chamber's Secrets." *U.S. News & World Report*, Oct. 22, 2015.

9. Joseph G. Peschek. *The Politics of Empire: War, Terror and Hegemony*. Taylor & Francis, 2006.

10. The Center for Media and Democracy. "Project for the New American Century."

11. Sourcewatch, Mar 13, 2003.

12. Naomi Klein. "The Bailout: Bush's Final Pillage." Naomi Klein website, Oct 29, 2008.

13. Paul Waldman. "Nearly All the GOP Candidates Bow Down to Grover Norquist." *The Washington Post*, Aug. 13, 2015.

14. Citizen Trade Campaign. "Campaign, Central American Free Trade Agreement (CAFTA)." http://www.citizenstrade.org.

15. Lee Drutman. "How Corporate Lobbyists Conquered American Democracy." *The Atlantic*, Apr. 20, 2015.

16. NumberOf.net. "Number of Lobbyists per Congressman." www.numberof.net, Jun 12, 2010.

17. Public Citizen. "Trans-Pacific Partnership (TPP): Expanded Corporate Power, Lower Wages, Unsafe Food Imports." www.citizen.org. Jun 2016.

Chapter Five:

1. Sam Fulwood III. "Race and Beyond: Why Young, Minority, and Low-Income Citizens Don't Vote." Center for American Progress, Nov. 6, 2014.

2. Sean McElwee. "One Big Reason for Voter Turnout Decline and Income Inequality: Smaller Unions." *The American Prospect*, Jan. 30, 2015.

3. Thom Hartman. *What Would Jefferson Do? A Return to Democracy*. Three Rivers Press, 2004.

4. Amanda Taub. "American Authoritarianism: The Political Science Theory that Explains Trump Rally Violence." Vox. com, Vox Media, Mar. 14, 2016.

5. Bill Moyers. "Voting Is Important: Here's Why." Moyers & Company, Oct. 31, 2008.

Chapter Six:

1. Tommy Lopez. "Shelby County: One Year Later." Brennan Center for Justice, June 24, 2014.

2. Wendy R. Weiser. "Voter Suppression: How Bad? (Pretty Bad)." *The American Prospect*, Oct. 1, 2014.

3. "What Happens To Democracy After You Gut the Voting Rights Act, in One Map," Think Progress, Apr. 12, 2016.

4. Ethan Magoc. "Flurry of Voter ID Laws Tied to Conservative Group ALEC." *NBC News Investigations*, Aug. 21, 2012.

5. The Center for Media and Democracy. "Voter ID Act." ALEC Exposed, 2009.

6. "If You Think Voter ID Is About Voter Fraud, This Republican Congressman Has News for You." Think Progress, Apr. 6, 2016.

7. Karin Kamp, "Unbelievable GOP Statement on Voter Suppression." Moyers & Company, Oct. 24, 2014.

8. Catherine Rampell. "Where Are All the Young Voters?" *The Washington Post*, Jul. 23, 2015.

9. Ari Berman. *Give Us The Ballot: The Modern Struggle for Voting Rights in America.* Macmillan Publishers, 2015.

10. LaFeminista. "Breaking: New Scary Chart Released!!!" Daily Kos, Oct 25, 2014.

Chapter Seven:

1. Lawrence Norden and Christopher Famighetti. "America's Voting Machines at Risk," The Brennan Center for Justice at New York University School of Law, 2015.

2. Beth Clarkson. "How Trustworthy Are Electronic Voting Systems in the U.S.?" American Statistical Association, June 5, 2015.

3. Victoria Collier. "How to Rig an Election: The G.O.P. Aims To Paint the Country Red." *Harper's Magazine*, Nov. 2012. Reproduced by special permission.

4. Bob Fitrakis. "Diebold, Electronic Voting, and the Vast Right-Wing Conspiracy." Free Press, Feb. 24, 2004.

Chapter Eight:

1. Matt Krantz. "Maximum Wage! How much CEOs Earn an Hour." *USA Today Money*, Apr. 6, 2015.

2. "Broken at the Top," Oxfam America Media Briefing, Apr. 14, 2016.

3. Ian Millhiser. "The Future of the Democratic Party Will Be Decided by the Supreme Court." Think Progress, Oct. 19, 2015.

4. Adam Liptak. "Justices Offer Receptive Ear to Business Interests." *The New York Times*, Dec. 18, 2010.

5. Erwin Chemerinsky. "Justice for Big Business." *The New York Times*, July 2, 2013.

6. Thom Hartmann. "The Supreme Court Doesn't Give a Rat's Patootie About You and Me." Blog, Feb. 24, 2015.

Chapter Nine:

1. David McCandless. "Left Right Infographic," *Information Is Beautiful*, ItsBeenReal.co.uk.

2. Jack Block and Jeanne H. Block. "Nursery School Personality and Political Orientation Two Decades Later." *Journal of Research in Personality*, 2005.

3. Thomas L. Friedman. "Nursery School Personality and Political Orientation Two Decades Later." *The New York Times*, Jun 7, 2016.

4. Paul Krugman. "Trillion-Dollar Fraudsters," *The New York Times*, Mar 20, 2015.

5. Ari Rabin-Havt. *Lies Incorporated*. Penguin Random House, Apr. 19, 2016.

6. Mel Gilles. "The Politics of Victimization." *The Daily Kos* (Mathew Gross), Nov. 8, 2004.

7. Thomas Frank. *Listen Liberal: What Ever Happened to the Party of the People?* Metropolitan Books, 2016.

8. Katrina vanden Heuvel. "Clinton May Take the Nomination, but Sanders Has Won the Debate." *The Washington Post*, June 7, 2016.

9. Bill Barrow. "Why do Republicans say the sky is falling?" *Associated Press*, Jul 19, 2016.

Chapter Ten:

1. "50 Years Of Shrinking Union Membership, In One Map," NPR, *Planet Money*, Feb. 23, 2015.

2. Harold Meyerson. "How To Raise Americans' Wages." *The American Prospect*, Mar. 18, 2014.

3. Katherine V.W. Stone and Alexander J.S. Colvin. "The Arbitration Epidemic

4. Mandatory Arbitration Deprives Workers and Consumers of Their Rights." Economic Policy Institute, Dec. 7, 2015.

5. Jennifer Erickson, Editor. "The Middle-Class Squeeze: A Picture of Stagnant Incomes, Rising Costs, and What We Can Do to Strengthen America's Middle Class." Center for American Progress, Sep. 24, 2014.

6. Scuba. "Seems There's a Lot of Folks Here Suddenly Worried About Tax Rates. Here's Some Advice..." *Democratic Underground*, Apr. 27, 2016.

7. "The American Middle Class Is Losing Ground: No Longer the Majority and Falling Behind Financially." Pew Research Center, Dec. 9, 2015.

8. Ken Sweet and Emily Swanson. "Poll: Two-thirds of U.S.

Would Struggle To Cover $1,000 Crisis," Associated Press, May 19, 2016.

9. Neal Gabler. "The Secret Shame of Middle-Class Americans." *The Atlantic*, May 2016.

Chapter Eleven:

1. Christopher Ingraham. "Child Poverty in the U.S. Is Among the Worst in the Developed World." *The Washington Post*, Oct. 29, 2014.

2. Laura Clawsone. "Paul Ryan: Poor kids Should Go hungry so They Know They're Loved," Daily Kos, Mar 6, 2014.

3. Walter Einenkal. "How Do These Children's School Lunches from Around the World Compare to the United States?" *The Daily Kos*, Feb. 9, 2015.

4. Ellen L. Bassuk, Carmela J. DeCandia, Corey Anne Beach, and Fred Berman. "America's Youngest Outcasts: A Report Card on Child Homelessness." American Institutes for Research, Nov. 2014.

5. "Child Care in America: 2016 State Fact Sheets." Child Care Aware of America, http://usa.childcareaware.org/.

6. David Shultz. "A bit of cash can keep someone off the streets for 2 years or more." Science, Aug 11, 2016.

7. David Dayen. "The True Cost: Why the Private Prison Industry Is About so Much More than Prisons." *The Hidden History of the Privatization of Everything Series: Talking Points Memo.*

8. Fania E. Davis. "Interrupting the School-to-Prison Pipeline Through Restorative Justice." *Huffington Post*, Oct. 5, 2015.

9. Adam Peck and Bryce Covert. "U.S. Paid Family Leave Versus the Rest of the World, in 2 Disturbing Charts." Think Progress, July 30, 2014.

10. Robert Reich. "Wall Street's Threat to the American Middle Class." robertreich.org, Jan. 26, 2015.

Chapter Twelve:

1. Bill Raden. "Failing the Test: A New Series Examines Charter Schools." *Capital & Main Investigating Power and Politics*, May 31, 2016.

2. Laurie Levy. "Five Devastating Facts About Charter Schools You Won't Hear from the 'National School Choice Week' Propaganda Campaign." Alternet, Jan 27, 2015.

3. Lyndsey Layton "Majority of U.S. Public School Students Are in Poverty." *The Washington Post*, Jan. 16, 2015.

4. Rachel Monahan. "Top 16 NYC Charter School Executives Earn More than Chancellor Dennis Walcott." *New York Daily News*, Oct. 27, 2013.

5. "White House: Weapons Industry Gets Blank Check but Student Debt Relief Is Impossible." *Ring of Fire*, Oct. 22, 2015.

6. Bill Raden. "Failing the Test: A New Series Examines Charter Schools." Capital & Main, May 31, 2016.

Chapter Thirteen:

1. "Big Ideas Project." Progressive Change Institute, https://thinkbig.us, Dec. 2014.

2. Michael Hilzik. "Unmasking the Most Influential Billionaire in U.S. Politics." *Los Angeles Times*, 2012. Reprinted with permission.

3. Joan McCarter. "Social Security Already Hit by the Austerity Squeeze." *The Daily Kos*, Mar. 21, 2014.

4. David Wagner. "Poor Relief and Almshouse." Disability History Museum, http://www.disabilitymuseum.org/dhm/edu/essay.html?id=60.

Chapter Fourteen:

1. Helen E. Veit, Editor, et al. "The Origins of the American Constitution, A Documentary History (extracted)." The Johns Hopkins University Press, 1991.

2. Brett Arends. "The NRA's Profit Soars as Deaths from Gun Massacres Mount." *Market Watch*, Oct. 2, 2015.

3. Lauren Carroll. "Laura Ingraham Wrongly Says Claim that 90% Support for Gun Background Checks Has Been Debunked," Pundifact, Jan. 5, 2016.

4. Cliff Schecter. "Ted Nugent and the Gang: Meet the Batsh*t Crazies of the NRAs Board." *The Daily Beast*, May 24, 2016.

5. Christopher Ingraham. "People Are Getting Shot by Toddlers on a Weekly Basis This Year." *The Washington Post*, Oct. 14, 2015.

6. "NRA Tells Parents To Keep Guns in Kids' Rooms for Safety." Think Progress, May 31, 2016.

7. SemDem. "What's Wrong with America Shown in This One Tweet." *The Daily Kos*, Oct. 4, 2015.

8. Jeffery Toobin. "So You think You know the Second Amendment?" *The New Yorker*, Dec. 17, 2012.

9. Michael Waldman. "How the NRA Rewrote the Second Amendment." *Politico Magazine*, May 19, 2014.

10. Thom Hartmann. "We Need To Throw Out the Second Amendment." Blog, June 20, 2016.

11. David Ropeik. "The Supreme Court Ruling on the 2nd Amendment Did NOT Grant an Unlimited Right to Own Guns." Big Think, 2015.

ABOUT THE AUTHOR
Jill Cody

As a natural-born teacher and champion for activism, Jill's 31-year career in public service, was imbued with a life-long passion for knowledge and a will to inspire change in politics, the environment, higher education and organizational development.

Jill was personally trained and authorized by vice president Al Gore to share his astonishing *"An Inconvenient Truth"* presentation with schools and community groups across Silicon Valley. This revelatory information caused Jill to realize America's abandonment, not only of the planet, but in many other important aspects of society. *America Abandoned ~ The Secret Velvet Coup That Cost Us Our Democracy*, explores the myriad ways abandonment is unknowingly permeating the lives of the American public and what "We, the People" can do to reverse this course.

Jill was honored to assist in leading and facilitating national and international strategic planning meetings on Information Literacy in Washington D.C., Prague and Egypt, building teams from around the world to bring Information Literacy skills to their country.

Jill earned a master's degree in public administration from San Jose State University's Political Science Department and was named distinguished alumna in the College of Applied Arts and Sciences. Jill is proud to serve on the university's Emeritus and Retired Faculty Association Executive Board.

Jill lives with her husband, Jerry, and their two dogs, Sassy and Scooter.

CLIMATE ABANDONED

Uncovering the Real Reasons for the Climate Crisis

There has been a massive cover up of catastrophic proportion.

In 1966, a fossil fuel senior scientist and the National Academy of Sciences published a report with shocking results: The buildup rate of carbon dioxide (CO_2) in the atmosphere almost directly corresponded with the rate of production of carbon dioxide by human consumption of fossil fuels.

In 1977, the same senior scientist warned Exxon that fossil fuel emissions could threaten our planet and Exxon confirmed the scientific discoveries with their own internal research. Despite these consistent results, by the 1980s, Exxon Mobil executives had made a conscience, horrific decision to abandon civilization for the sake of their bottom line.

With great gusto and a multimillion-dollar funding scheme behind them, the fossil fuel industry, in collaboration with the Republican Party, added another product to sell to the fuel-hungry public: in addition to oil, coal and gas ... they would sell the product of doubt about climate change. Unfortunately, it became one of their hottest sellers, and the public ate it up.

Climate Abandoned reveals the *real* reasons why the public is divided about the reality of the climate crisis, and why the fossil fuel industry and their servile politicians continue to abandon the human species despite the facts and pressures from the rest of the world. In addition, this eye-popping book will relate little known, current effects of climate change on all humanity. Will baseball's favorite wooden bat become extinct?

Read *Climate Abandoned* coming in fall of 2017, and find out.